Lecture Notes in Computer Science　　9421

Commenced Publication in 1973
Founding and Former Series Editors:
Gerhard Goos, Juris Hartmanis, and Jan van Leeuwen

More information about this series at http://www.springer.com/series/7408

Thomas Hildebrandt · António Ravara
Jan Martijn van der Werf · Matthias Weidlich (Eds.)

Web Services, Formal Methods, and Behavioral Types

11th International Workshop, WS-FM 2014
Eindhoven, The Netherlands, September 11–12, 2014
and 12th International Workshop, WS-FM/BEAT 2015
Madrid, Spain, September 4–5, 2015
Revised Selected Papers

 Springer

Editors

Thomas Hildebrandt
IT University of Copenhagen
Copenhagen
Denmark

António Ravara
Universidade NOVA de Lisboa
Caparica
Portugal

Jan Martijn van der Werf
Universiteit Utrecht
Utrecht
The Netherlands

Matthias Weidlich
Humboldt-Universität zu Berlin
Berlin
Germany

ISSN 0302-9743   ISSN 1611-3349 (electronic)
Lecture Notes in Computer Science
ISBN 978-3-319-33611-4   ISBN 978-3-319-33612-1 (eBook)
DOI 10.1007/978-3-319-33612-1

Library of Congress Control Number: 2016936989

LNCS Sublibrary: SL2 – Programming and Software Engineering

Printed on acid-free paper

This Springer imprint is published by Springer Nature
The registered company is Springer International Publishing AG Switzerland

Preface

Large software systems are becoming more and more distributed, collaborative, and communication-centered systems. Services in terms of functional and autonomous building blocks and the interactions between them have been established as fundamental concepts to design, implement, and deploy complex systems. Yet, independent of platforms and programming languages, formal methods play a key role in research on complex, service-based systems. They can help us to define unambiguous semantics for the languages that underpin existing infrastructures, facilitate consistency checking of interactions, empower dynamic discovery, and drive the analysis of security and performance properties of applications.

This volume contains the joint proceedings of two initiatives that have been devoted to the formal foundations of complex systems: the WS-FM:FASOCC 2014 and WS-FM/BEAT 2015 workshops.

The 11th International Workshop on Web Services and Formal Methods: Formal Aspects of Service-Oriented and Cloud Computing (WS-FM:FASOCC 2014) brought together researchers working on service-oriented computing, cloud computing, and formal methods in order to catalyze fruitful collaboration. It was part of the WS-FM workshop series that has a strong tradition of attracting submissions on formal approaches to enterprise systems modelling in general, and business process modelling in particular. Previous editions of the WS-FM workshop series took place in Pisa (2004), Versailles (2005), Vienna (2006), Brisbane (2007), Milan (2008), Bologna (2009), Hoboken (2010), Clermont-Ferrand (2011), Tallinn (2012), and Beijing (2013). WS-FM:FASOCC 2014 was planned to be held in Haifa, Israel, co-located with the 12th International Conference on Business Process Management (BPM 2014). However, the continuous uncertainty regarding the situation in southern Israel and Gaza led to a relocation of BPM 2014 and WS-FM:FASOCC 2014, so that the workshop took place September 11–12, 2014, in Eindhoven, The Netherlands.

In 2015, the WS-FM workshop and the International Workshop on Behavioural Types (BEAT) joined forces, resulting in the International Symposium on Web Services, Formal Methods and Behavioural Types (WS-FM/BEAT 2015). Both, WS-FM and BEAT, target the same research setting, i.e., large-scale behavioral software systems. The aim of this joint workshop event was to bring together researchers and practitioners in all aspects of behavioral software systems and their applications, in order to share results, consolidate the community, and discover opportunities for new collaborations and future directions. Previous editions of the BEAT workshop series took place in Lisbon (2011), Rome (2012 and 2014), and Madrid (2013). The first joint edition of the WS-FM and BEAT workshop series, WS-FM/BEAT 2015, took place September 4–5, 2015, in Madrid, Spain. It was part of the "MADRID MEET 2015 Meeting", which comprised a one-week scientific event with conferences and workshops in the areas of formal and quantitative analysis of systems, performance engineering, computer safety, and industrial critical applications. The program of the second day of the symposium was shared with that of the 14th International Workshop on Foundations of Coordination Languages and Self-Adaptive Systems (FOCLASA).

The WS-FM:FASOCC 2014 program included keynotes by Giuseppe De Giacomo from the Sapienza Università di Roma, Italy, and Fabrizio Montesi from the University of Southern Denmark, and two sessions with research paper presentations. The WS-FM:FASOCC 2014 workshop attracted a total of 10 submissions, which were each reviewed by at least three members of the Program Committee. Eventually, the committee decided to accept four papers. Further, two of the best papers of the closely related 6th Central European Workshop on Services and Their Composition (ZEUS 2015) were invited to submit extended and revised versions for inclusion in the proceedings. After a review process with the WS-FM:FASOCC 2014 Program Committee, one of these papers was accepted.

The WS-FM/BEAT 2015 program featured keynotes by Cosimo Laneve from the Università di Bologna, Italy, and Javier Esparza from the Technische Universität München, Germany, and four sessions with research paper presentations (including four presentations selected from the submissions to WS-FM/BEAT). The WS-FM/BEAT 2015 workshop attracted a total of six submissions, which were each reviewed by at least three members of the Program Committee. Eventually, the committee decided to accept three papers to include in this volume.

We wish to thank the WS-FM:FASOCC 2014 and WS-FM/BEAT 2015 Program Committees and the external reviewers for their accurate and timely reviewing and acknowledge the support of EasyChair for managing the review process. Finally, we are grateful to the local organization teams of WS-FM:FASOCC 2014 in Haifa (Pnina Soffer, Nilly Schnapp, and others) and Eindhoven (Wil van der Aalst, Ine van der Ligt, and others) and of WS-FM/BEAT 2015 in Madrid (David de Frutos and others). They all did an excellent job in the preparation of the workshops — thanks a lot!

December 2015

Thomas Hildebrandt
Matthias Weidlich
António Ravara
Jan Martijn van der Werf

Organization

WS-FM:FASOCC 2014 Program Co-chairs

Thomas Hildebrandt   IT University of Copenhagen, Denmark
Matthias Weidlich   Imperial College London, UK

WS-FM:FASOCC 2014 Program Committee

Farhad Arbab	CWI and Leiden University, The Netherlands
Ahmed Awad	Cairo University, Egypt
Massimo Bartoletti	Università degli Studi di Cagliari, Italy
Laura Bocchi	Imperial College London, UK
Mario Bravetti	University of Bologna, Italy
Roberto Bruni	Università di Pisa, Italy
Marco Carbone	IT University of Copenhagen, Denmark
Erik De Vink	Technische Universiteit Eindhoven, The Netherlands
Marlon Dumas	University of Tartu, Estonia
Schahram Dustdar	TU Wien, Austria
Dirk Fahland	Technische Universiteit Eindhoven, The Netherlands
José Luiz Fiadeiro	Royal Holloway, University of London, UK
Roberto Guanciale	Università degli Studi di Pisa, Italy
Sylvain Hallé	Université du Québec à Chicoutimi, Canada
Ivan Lanese	University of Bologna/Inria, Italy/France
Niels Lohmann	Universität Rostock, Germany
Marco Montali	Free University of Bozen-Bolzano, Italy
Chun Ouyang	Queensland University of Technology, Australia
Artem Polyvyanyy	Queensland University of Technology, Australia
Alexandra Poulovassilis	Birkbeck College, University of London, UK
Rosario Pugliese	Università degli Studi di Firenze, Italy
António Ravara	Universidade Nova de Lisboa, Portugal
Tijs Slaats	IT University of Copenhagen, Denmark
Jianwen Su	University of California at Santa Barbara, USA
Maurice H. Ter Beek	ISTI-CNR Pisa, Italy
Hugo Torres Vieira	Universidade de Lisboa, Portugal
Emilio Tuosto	University of Leicester, UK
Wil van der Aalst	Technische Universiteit Eindhoven, The Netherlands
Lijie Wen	Tsinghua University, China
Martin Wirsing	Ludwig-Maximilians-Universität München, Germany
Karsten Wolf	Universität Rostock, Germany
Nobuko Yoshida	Imperial College London, UK
Gianluigi Zavattaro	University of Bologna, Italy

WS-FM:FASOCC 2014 Additional Reviewers

Søren Debois
Alexander Knapp
Julien Lange

WS-FM/BEAT 2015 Program Co-chairs

Antonio Ravara	Universidade Nova de Lisboa, Portugal
Jan Martijn van der Werf	Utrecht University, The Netherlands

WS-FM/BEAT 2015 Program Committee

Robin Bergenthum	FernUni Hagen, Germany
Laura Bocchi	University of Kent, UK
Sara Capecchi	Università degli Studi di Torino, Italy
Marlon Dumas	University of Tartu, Estonia
Adrian Francalanza	University of Malta, Malta
Thomas Hildebrandt	IT University of Copenhagen, Denmark
Jeroen Keiren	Open University, The Netherlands
Natallia Kokash	Leiden Institute of Advanced Computer Science, The Netherlands
Hernán Melgratti	Universidad de Buenos Aires, Argentina
Dimitris Mostrous	University of Lisbon, Portugal
Jovanka Pantovic	University of Novi Sad, Serbia
Artem Polyvyanyy	Queensland University of Technology, Australia
Natalia Sidorova	Eindhoven University of Technology, The Netherlands

WS-FM/BEAT 2015 Additional Reviewers

Natallia Kokash
Rumyana Neykova

WS-FM Steering Committee

Mario Bravetti	University of Bologna, Italy
Marlon Dumas	University of Tartu, Estonia
José Luiz Fiadeiro	Royal Holloway, University of London, UK
Wil van der Aalst	Technische Universiteit Eindhoven, The Netherlands
Gianluigi Zavattaro	University of Bologna, Italy

Abstracts of Invited Talks

Verification of Data-Aware Processes

Giuseppe De Giacomo

Sapienza Università di Roma, Rome, Italy
degiacomo@dis.uniromal.it

Keynote Abstract

Information systems are based on two pillars: data, which constitute the information asset of the organization, and business processes, which constitute its modus operandi. Traditionally these two aspects are considered, conceptualized, and formalized more or less in isolation. Such form of separation of concerns has been considered quite fruitful and it led to significant advances in both data and process management fields. However it has recently been questioned by the so called artifact-centric approach that advocates a holistic view of data and processes as a unity. In this talk, we will look at recent progresses in the analysis of processes that live side-by-side with data, both as first-class citizens. These systems are inherently infinite state and pose serious challenges to traditional verification techniques such as model checking.

Kickstarting Choreographic Programming

Fabrizio Montesi[✉]

University of Southern Denmark, Odense, Denmark
fmontesi@imada.sdu.dk

Abstract. We present an overview of some recent efforts aimed at the development of *Choreographic Programming*, a programming paradigm for the production of concurrent software that is guaranteed to be correct by construction from global descriptions of communication behaviour.

Static Analysis of Unbounded Networks with Behavioral Types

Cosimo Laneve

Department of Computer Science and Engineering,
University of Bologna – INRIA Focus, Bologna, Italy
cosimo.laneve@unibo.it

Keynote Abstract

The analysis of concurrent programs with infinite state models is extremely difficult due to the inability of statically reasoning about unbounded structures. As an example, consider those adaptive systems that, in order to reply to peaks of requests, create networks with arbitrary numbers of servers. In such systems, server interaction becomes complex and is hard to predict or to detect during testing. Additionally, even when possible, it can be tricky to reproduce bugs and find their causes. It turns out that, in these cases, the current analysers either return imprecise answers or do not scale.

This invited talk presents an analysis technique that have been used to verify properties such as deadlock freedom [5, 6], upper bounds of resource usages [3], and upper bounds of the computational cost [4] of programs that do not have a finite model. The proof technique is modular and consists of two parts: a type (inference) system that associates a *behavioural type* to a program and an *algorithm for analysing the behavioural types*.

Behavioural types are simple terms that feature recursion and resource creation – therefore their underlying model is infinite state – and express features of the programs that are relevant to the property one wants to analyze. For example, in case of deadlock analysis, behavioural types highlight resource dependencies; in case of resource analysis, they highlight resource usages; in case of computational cost analysis, they highlight the cost in time of instructions.

The behavioural type system typically performs standard abstractions, such as computing aliases and effects of updates, and its correctness is expressed in a standard way by means of a *subject reduction theorem*. In this setting, the subject-reduction states that: if (*i*) a program P is typable in an environment Γ with behavioural type $\mathbb{b}$ and (*ii*) P reduces to P' then there exists an environment Γ' that types P' with behavioural type $\mathbb{b}'$. It is worth to notice that the types $\mathbb{b}$ and $\mathbb{b}'$ are *different* because, in contrast to standard types, they change during the computation. Nevertheless, these changes are regulated by a relation, called *later-stage relation*, which specifies the correctness of the behavioural type analyzer (see below).

The analysis of behavioural types is performed either by ad-hoc algorithms – this is the case of deadlock analysis [5, 6] – or by automatic off-the-shelf solvers, whenever they are available – this is the case of resource and computational analysis [3, 4].

No matter what property is, analyzer's correctness is demonstrated by verifying that the analysis of behavioural types in the later stage relation, which include those types related by the subject-reduction theorem, always return identical values. That is, if one type has a deadlock (respectively, consumes at most n resources) then the other one in later-stage relation has a deadlock as well (respectively, consumes at most n resources as well).

Our techniques have been prototyped by taking a concurrent object-oriented language as reference language. The prototypes for deadlock analysis and resource analysis are available at [1, 2], respectively, while the prototype for computational cost analysis is under development.

A relevant advantage of the analysis technique presented in the talk derives from modularity. Because of modularity, the technique may be applied to several languages by simply changing the type system and support several behavioural type analysis algorithms.

References

1. Garcia, A., Giachino, E., Laneve, C., Lienhardt, M.: The deadlock framework for ABS (2014). df4abs.nws.cs.unibo.it
2. Garcia, A., Laneve, C.: Static analyzer of resource usage upper bounds (2015). sra.cs.unibo.it
3. Garcia, A., Laneve, C. Lienhardt, M.: Static analysis of cloud elasticity. In: Proceedings of PPDP 2015, pp. 125–136. ACM (2015)
4. Giachino, E., Johnsen, E. B., Laneve, C., Pun, K. I.: Time complexity of concurrent programs. In: Braga, C., Ölveczky, P.C. (eds.) FACS 2015. LNCS, vol. 9539, pp. 199–216. Springer, Berlin (2016)
5. Giachino, E., Kobayashi, N., Laneve, C.: Deadlock analysis of unbounded process networks. In: Baldan,. P., Gorla, D. (eds.) CONCUR 2014, vol. 8704, pp. 63–77. Springer, Berlin (2014)
6. Giachino, E., Laneve, C., Lienhardt, M.: A framework for deadlock detection in core ABS. Software and Systems Modeling, pp. 1–36 (2015)

A Petri-Net-like Model for Multiplayer Distributed Negotiations

Javier Esparza

Fakultät für Informatik, Technische Universität München, Germany
esparza@tum.de

Keynote Abstract

Many modern distributed systems consist of components whose behavior is only partially known. Typical examples include multi-agent systems, business processes, or protocols for conducting elections and auctions. An interaction between these components can be abstractly described as a negotiation in which several parties (the components involved in the negotiation) nondeterministically agree on an outcome, which results in a transformation of the internal states of the parties. In this talk we introduce *negotiations*, a formal model of concurrency close to Petri nets, with multiparty negotiation as primitive.

Negotiations can be ill designed: the parties can reach a deadlock or a livelock (a state from which the termination cannot successfully terminate anymore). In a *sound* negotiation this is not possible: from every reachable marking the final marking of the distributed negotiation can always be reached. A sound distributed negotiation has an equivalent one-step negotiation, called a *summary*. Loosely speaking, an external observer that only sees the initial and final states of the parties cannot distinguish a negotiation from its summary.

In the first part of the talk we study two problems: deciding whether a given negotiation is sound, and computing the summary of a given sound negotiation. We introduce *deterministic* negotiations, in which each participant can always be engaged in at most one next atomic negotiation. We show that, while both problems are untractable for arbitrary negotiations, there are efficient algorithms for the deterministic case. More precisely, we provide a complete set of *reduction rules* for deterministic negotiations. The rules reduce the negotiation to its summary iff the negotiation is sound. Further, the summary is computed after a polynomial number of rule applications.

In the second part of the talk we introduce *negotiation programs*, a global structured modelling language for negotiations, and show that it has the same expressive power as sound and deterministic negotiations: every program can be implemented by an equivalent sound and deterministic negotiation, and every sound and deterministic negotiation is modelled by an equivalent program. Here, a program and a negotiation are equivalent if they have the same Mazurkiewicz traces and thus the same concurrent runs.

The talk is based on joint work with Jörg Desel, published in [1–4].

References

1. Esparza, J., Desel, J.: On negotiation as concurrency primitive. In: D'Argenio, P.R., Melgratti, H.C. (eds.) CONCUR. LNCS, vol. 8052, pp. 440–454. Springer, Berlin (2013). Extended version in CoRR abs/1307.2145
2. Esparza, J., Desel, J.: On negotiation as concurrency primitive II: deterministic cyclic negotiations. In: Muscholl, A. (ed.) FoSSaCS. LNCS, vol. 8412, pp. 258–273. Springer, Berlin (2014). Extended version in CoRR abs/1403.4958
3. Esparza, J., Desel, J.: Negotiation programs. In: Devillers, R.R., Valmari, A. (eds.) PETRI NETS 2015. LNCS, vol. 9115, pp. 157–178. Springer, Berlin (2015)
4. Desel, J., Esparza, J.: Negotiations and Petri nets. In: Moldt, D., Rölke, H., Störrle, H. (eds.) Proceedings of the International Workshop on Petri Nets and Software Engineering. PNSE 2015, vol. 1372, pp. 41–57. CEUR Workshop Proceedings, CEUR-WS.org (2015)

Contents

Invited Talk

Kickstarting Choreographic Programming

Fabrizio Montesi$^{(\boxtimes)}$

University of Southern Denmark, Odense, Denmark
fmontesi@imada.sdu.dk

Abstract. We present an overview of some recent efforts aimed at the development of *Choreographic Programming*, a programming paradigm for the production of concurrent software that is guaranteed to be correct by construction from global descriptions of communication behaviour.

1 Introduction

Programming communications among the endpoints in a concurrent system is challenging, because it is notoriously difficult to predict how nontrivial programs executed simultaneously may interact [19]. To mitigate this issue, *choreographies* can be used to give precise specifications of communication behaviour [1,28].

A choreography specifies the expected communications among endpoints from a global viewpoint, in contrast with the standard methodology of giving a separate specification for each endpoint that defines its Input/Output (I/O) actions. As an example, consider the following choreographic specification (whose syntax is derived from the "Alice and Bob" notation from [23]):

$$\text{Alice} \rightarrow \text{Bob} : book; \quad \text{Bob} \rightarrow \text{Alice} : money$$

The choreography above describes the behaviour of two endpoints, Alice and Bob. First, Alice sends to Bob a *book*; then, Bob replies to Alice with some *money* as payment. The motivation for using a choreography as specification is that it is always "correct by design", since it explicitly describes the intended communications in a system. In other words, a choreography can be seen as a formalisation of the communication flow intended by the system designer.

A choreography can be compiled to the local specifications of the I/O actions that each endpoint should perform [10,18,27], as depicted below:

$$\boxed{\begin{array}{c}\text{Choreography Spec.}\\ \textit{(correct by design)}\end{array}} \quad \xrightarrow{\ EPP\ } \quad \boxed{\begin{array}{c}\text{Endpoint Spec.}\\ \textit{(correct by construction)}\end{array}}$$

In the methodology above, an Endpoint Projection (EPP) procedure is used to generate the specifications for each endpoint starting from a global choreographic specification. The endpoint specifications are therefore correct by construction, because they are computed from a correct-by-design choreography. A major consequent benefit is that such endpoint specifications are also deadlock-free,

© Springer International Publishing Switzerland 2016
T. Hildebrandt et al. (Eds.): WS-FM 2014/WS-FM 2015, LNCS 9421, pp. 3–10, 2016.
DOI: 10.1007/978-3-319-33612-1_1

because I/O actions cannot be defined separately in choreographies and are therefore always paired correctly in the result of EPP.

In this paper, we give an overview of some recent results by the author and collaborators aimed at applying the choreography-based methodology as a fully-fledged programming paradigm, rather than as a specification method. In this paradigm, called *Choreographic Programming*, choreographies are concrete programs and EPP is a compiler targeting executable distributed code:

Choreography Program	$\xrightarrow{\text{EPP (compiler)}}$	Executable Endpoint Programs
(correct by design)		*(correct by construction)*

Ideally, this methodology will allow developers to program systems from a global viewpoint, which is less error-prone than writing endpoint programs directly, and then to obtain executable code that is correct by construction.

To kickstart the development of choreographic programming, we are interested in finding suitable language models (Sect. 2) and their implementation (Sect. 3). We discuss them in the remainder of the paper, following the syntax from [20].

2   Language Models

In [11] we present the Choreography Calculus (CC), a language model for choreographic programming that follows the correct-by-construction methodology discussed in Sect. 1 and provides an interpretation of concurrent behaviour in choreographies. The key first-class elements of CC are *processes* and *sessions*, respectively representing endpoints that execute concurrently and the conversations among them. The basic statement of choreographic programs, ranged over by C, is a communication:

$$\mathsf{p}.e \rightarrow \mathsf{q}.x : k; C$$

which reads "process p sends the value of expression e to process q, which receives it on variable x, over session k; then, the system executes the continuation choreography C". We comment the model by giving the following toy example on a replicated journaling file system.

Example 1 (Replicated Journaling File System, write operation). We define a choreography, denoted C_{jfs}, in which a client c uses a session k to send some data to be written in a journaling file system replicated on two storage nodes.

$$C_{\mathsf{jfs}} \quad \overset{\text{def}}{=} \quad
\begin{array}{ll}
1. & \mathsf{c}.data \rightarrow \mathsf{j}_1.data_1 : k; \\
2. & \mathsf{c}.data \rightarrow \mathsf{j}_2.data_2 : k; \\
3. & \mathsf{j}_1.\mathsf{blocks}(data_1) \rightarrow \mathsf{s}_1.blocks_1 : k'; \\
4. & \mathsf{j}_2.\mathsf{blocks}(data_2) \rightarrow \mathsf{s}_2.blocks_2 : k'; \\
5. & \mathsf{j}_1 \rightarrow \mathsf{c} : k; \\
6. & \mathsf{j}_2 \rightarrow \mathsf{c} : k
\end{array}$$

In the choreography C_{jfs}, the client c uses session k to send the *data* to be written to two processes, j_1 and j_2, which we assume log the operation in their respective journals upon reception (Lines 1–2). The two journal processes then use another session, k', to forward the data to be written to their respective processes handling the actual data storage, s_1 and s_2 (Lines 3–4). Finally, at the same time, processes j_1 and j_2 send an empty message on session k to the client, in order to inform it that the operation has been completed (Lines 5–6).

Concurrency. Process identifiers (c, j_1, j_2, s_1 and s_2 in our example) are key to formalising concurrent behaviour in CC. Observe Lines 3–4: since processes run in parallel, the communication between j_2 and s_2 in Line 4 could be completed before the communication between j_1 and s_1 in Line 3. In CC, the semantics of the sequential operator is thus relaxed by a syntactic *swapping congruence relation* $\simeq_C$, which allows two statements to be swapped if they do not share any processes. For example, the choreography C_{jfs} would be equivalent to a choreography C'_{jfs}, denoted $C_{\text{jfs}} \simeq_C C'_{\text{jfs}}$, where in C'_{jfs} Lines 3 and 4 are exchanged. In [20], the relation $\simeq_C$ is validated by showing that it corresponds to the typical interleaving semantics of the parallel operator found in process calculi.

Sessions and Typing. The communications in Lines 1–2, 5–6 and the communications in Lines 3–4 are included in different sessions, respectively k and k'. Each session represents a logically-separate conversation, as in other session-based calculi (e.g., [4,15]), and is strongly typed in CC with a typing discipline that checks for adherence to protocols expressed as multiparty session types [16]. We give an example of how protocols are mapped to choreographies in Sect. 3.

Endpoint Projection. CC comes with an EPP that compiles choreographies to distributed implementations in terms of the π-calculus [11]. The generated code follows that of the originating choreography, according to a small-step operational semantics. As a corollary, the produced code is also deadlock-free: senders and receivers are always ready to communicate when they have to, as I/O actions cannot be mismatched in choreographies.

Modularity. In [22], we extend CC to support the implementation and reuse of external libraries/services (modular development), using a notion of external participants in sessions. For example, we can split the choreography C_{jfs} in two modules, a client choreography C_{cli} and a server choreography C_{srv}:

$$
C_{\text{cli}} \overset{\text{def}}{=}
\begin{array}{l}
1.\ \text{c}.data \to \text{J1} : k; \\
2.\ \text{c}.data \to \text{J2} : k; \\
3.\ \text{J1} \to \text{c} : k; \\
4.\ \text{J1} \to \text{c} : k
\end{array}
\qquad
C_{\text{srv}} \overset{\text{def}}{=}
\begin{array}{l}
1.\ \text{c} \to j_1.data_1 : k; \\
2.\ \text{c} \to j_2.data_2 : k; \\
3.\ j_1.\text{blocks}(data_1) \to s_1.blocks_1 : k'; \\
4.\ j_2.\text{blocks}(data_2) \to s_2.blocks_2 : k'; \\
5.\ j_1 \to \text{c} : k; \\
6.\ j_2 \to \text{c} : k
\end{array}
$$

The choreographies above refer to each other using references to external processes, e.g., J1 in C_{cli} is a reference to process j_1 in C_{srv}. Separate choreography modules can be compiled and deployed separately, with the guarantee that their generated implementations will interact with each other as expected.

Extraction. In [12], we present a proofs-as-programs Curry-Howard correspondence between Internal Compositional Choreographies (ICC, a simplification of CC) and a generalisation of Linear Logic [14], inspired by [8]. ICC is a first step in defining a canonical model for choreographies and formalising logical reasoning on choreographic programs. In such correspondence, EPP is formalised as a transformation between logically-equivalent proofs, one corresponding to a choreography program and the other corresponding to a π-calculus term. The transformation is invertible, yielding a procedure for automatically extracting the choreography that a π-calculus term typed with linear logic is following.

3   Implementation

The Choreography Calculus (CC), along with related work on models for choreography languages [10,18,27], offers insight on how choreographic programming can be formally understood as a self-standing paradigm. To practically evaluate choreographic programming, we developed the Chor programming language[1], an open source prototype implementation of CC [20].

In Chor, the correct-by-construction methodology of choreographic programming is proposed as a concrete software development process, depicted in Fig. 1. Choreographies are written using an Integrated Development Environment (IDE), which visualises on-the-fly errors regarding syntax and protocol verification, as in the screenshot in Fig. 2. Then, a choreography can be projected to executable code via an implementation of EPP that follows the ideas of CC. In this case, the target language is Jolie[2] [21]. Once the compiler has generated the Jolie programs for the endpoints described in the choreography, the developer can customise their deployments. This is done using the Jolie primitives for integrating with standard communication protocols and technologies, which do not alter the behaviour of the code generated by the Chor compiler. The resulting code can finally be executed using the Jolie interpreter.

In Chor, the syntax from CC is extended with operation names for communications (as in Web Services [2]) and data manipulation primitives. As an example, we show an extended implementation of the scenario from Example 1.

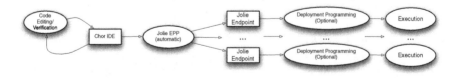

Fig. 1. Chor, development methodology (from [11]).

---

[1] http://www.chor-lang.org/.
[2] http://www.jolie-lang.org/.

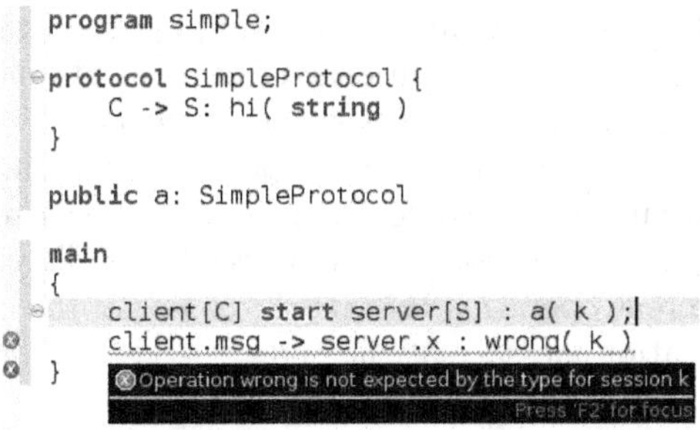

```
program simple;

protocol SimpleProtocol {
    C -> S: hi( string )
}

public a: SimpleProtocol

main
{
    client[C] start server[S] : a( k );|
    client.msg -> server.x : wrong( k )
}
```
Operation wrong is not expected by the type for session k
Press 'F2' for focus

Fig. 2. Chor, example of error reporting (from [20]).

```
1   protocol Write {
2     C -> J1: { write(string);
3                    C -> J2: write(string);
4                    J1 -> C: ok(void);
5                    J2 -> C: ok(void),
6                writeAsync(string);
7                    C -> J2: writeAsync(string)
8     }
9   }
10
11  protocol Store { J1 -> S1: write(string);
12                    J2 -> S2: write(string)  }
13
14  define computeBlocks(j1, j2) { /* ... */ }
15
16  define write(c, j1, j2, s1, s2)
17  (k[ Write:c[C], j1[J1], j2[J2] ],
18   k2[ Store:j1[J1], j2[J2], s1[S1], s2[S2] ]) {
19    if (sync)@c {
20      c.data -> j1.data : write(k);
21      c.data -> j2.data : write(k);
22      computeBlocks( j1, j2 );
23      j1.blocks -> s1.blocks : write( k2 );
24      j2.blocks -> s2.blocks : write( k2 );
25      j1 -> c : ok( k );
26      j2 -> c : ok( k )
27    } else {
28      c.data -> j1.data : writeAsync( k );
29      c.data -> j2.data : writeAsync( k );
30      computeBlocks( j1, j2 );
31      j1.data -> s1.data : write( k2 );
32      j2.data -> s2.data : write( k2 )
33    }
34  }
```

We briefly comment the program above, referring the reader to [20] for a more complete description of Chor. Procedure `write` implements the behaviour of the processes from Example 2. The sessions `k` and `k2` (k and k' in Example 2) are typed by the protocols `Write` and `Store` respectively. In Line 19, the client `c` checks its internal variable `sync` to determine whether the write operation should be synchronous or not. In the first case we proceed as in Example 2. Otherwise, process `c` uses a different operation `writeAsync` to notify the others that it does not expect a confirmation message at the end.

4   Related Work

The idea of using choreography-like descriptions for communication behaviour has been used for a long time, for example in software engineering [17], security [5,7,9], and specification languages for business processes [1,28].

The development of the formal models that we described in Sect. 2 was made possible by many other previous works on languages for expressing communication behaviour. The notion of session in CC is a variation of that presented in [4] for a process calculus. The theory of modular choreographies was inspired by the article [3], where types for I/O actions are mixed with types for global communications, and by Multiparty Session Types [16], from which we took the type language to interface compatible choreographies. Interestingly, combining multiparty session types with choreographies yields a type inference technique and a deadlock-freedom analysis that do not require additional machinery as in other works in the context of processes [4]. The criteria for a correct Endpoint Projection (EPP) procedure was investigated in many settings, e.g., in [6,10,18,27].

The Chor language and its compiler have already been used as basis for implementing other projects. For example, AIOCJ [26] is a choreographic language supporting the update of executable code at runtime, equipped with a formal calculus that ensure deadlock-freedom [25]. Choreographies have also been applied for the design of communication protocols. In particular, Scribble is a specification language for protocols written from a global viewpoint [29], which can be used to generate correct-by-construction runtime monitors (see, e.g., [24]).

5   Conclusions and Future Work

We presented some recent efforts aimed at kickstarting the development of choreographic programming as a fully-fledged programming paradigm. While the paradigm holds potential, there is still a lot of work to be done before reaching a productive real-world programming framework. We describe below some possible research directions, some of which are planned for in the current research project behind Chor, the CRC project[3].

Integration. A key factor for the adoption of choreographic programming will be interoperability with existing software. Chor can be extended with local computation primitives that would interact with libraries written in other programming languages, e.g., Java or Scala, similarly to how it is done in Jolie [21].

---

[3] http://www.chor-lang.org/.

Classification. Just like there are many different language models for different aspects of concurrent programming, e.g., code mobility and multicast, it should be possible to similarly extend choreography models. This suggests a potential benefit in having systematic classifications of choreography languages, to observe the effect that such extensions have on expressiveness and see how far the correct-by-construction methodology can be applied.

Exceptions. Introducing exception handling in choreography program raises the issue of coordinating many participants in a global escape (as in [13]), and whether a suitable strategy can always be found, statically or at runtime.

Formal Implementation. The EPP procedure in CC is based on π-calculus channels, but its implementation in Chor uses data (protocol headers) to route messages instead, as in many other enterprise frameworks [2]. To the best of the author's knowledge, realising π-calculus channels using data-based message routing has still to be formally investigated, and the implementation of Chor could provide an initial stepping stone in such a study.

Acknowledgements. The author was supported by the Danish Council for Independent Research project *Choreographies for Reliable and efficient Communication software* (CRC), grant No. DFF–4005-00304, and by the EU COST Action IC1201 *Behavioural Types for Reliable Large-Scale Software Systems* (BETTY).

References

1. Business Process Model and Notation. http://www.omg.org/spec/BPMN/2.0/
2. WS-BPEL OASIS Web Services Business Process Execution Language. http://docs.oasis-open.org/wsbpel/2.0/wsbpel-specification-draft.html
3. Baltazar, P., Caires, L., Vasconcelos, V.T., Vieira, H.T.: A type system for flexible role assignment in multiparty communicating systems. In: Palamidessi, C., Ryan, M.D. (eds.) TGC 2012. LNCS, vol. 8191, pp. 82–96. Springer, Heidelberg (2013)
4. Bettini, L., Coppo, M., D'Antoni, L., De Luca, M., Dezani-Ciancaglini, M., Yoshida, N.: Global progress in dynamically interleaved multiparty sessions. In: van Breugel, F., Chechik, M. (eds.) CONCUR 2008. LNCS, vol. 5201, pp. 418–433. Springer, Heidelberg (2008)
5. Bhargavan, K., Corin, R., Deniélou, P.-M., Fournet, C., Leifer, J.J.: Cryptographic protocol synthesis and verification for multiparty sessions. In: CSF, pp. 124–140. IEEE Computer Society (2009)
6. Bravetti, M., Zavattaro, G.: Towards a unifying theory for choreography conformance and contract compliance. In: Lumpe, M., Vanderperren, W. (eds.) SC 2007. LNCS, vol. 4829, pp. 34–50. Springer, Heidelberg (2007)
7. Briais, S., Nestmann, U.: A formal semantics for protocol narrations. Theor. Comput. Sci. **389**(3), 484–511 (2007)
8. Caires, L., Pfenning, F.: Session types as intuitionistic linear propositions. In: Gastin, P., Laroussinie, F. (eds.) CONCUR 2010. LNCS, vol. 6269, pp. 222–236. Springer, Heidelberg (2010)
9. Caleiro, C., Viganò, L., Basin, D.A.: On the semantics of Alice&Bob specifications of security protocols. Theor. Comput. Sci. **367**(1–2), 88–122 (2006)

10. Carbone, M., Honda, K., Yoshida, N.: Structured communication-centered programming for web services. ACM Trans. Program. Lang. Syst. **34**(2), 8 (2012)
11. Carbone, M., Montesi, F.: Deadlock-freedom-by-design: multiparty asynchronous global programming. In: POPL, pp. 263–274 (2013)
12. Carbone, M., Montesi, F., Schürmann, C.: Choreographies, logically. In: Baldan, P., Gorla, D. (eds.) CONCUR 2014. LNCS, vol. 8704, pp. 47–62. Springer, Heidelberg (2014)
13. Carbone, M., Yoshida, N., Honda, K.: Asynchronous session types: exceptions and multiparty interactions. In: Bernardo, M., Padovani, L., Zavattaro, G. (eds.) SFM 2009. LNCS, vol. 5569, pp. 187–212. Springer, Heidelberg (2009)
14. Girard, J.-Y.: Linear logic. Theor. Comput. Sci. **50**, 1–102 (1987)
15. Honda, K., Vasconcelos, V.T., Kubo, M.: Language primitives and type discipline for structured communication-based programming. In: Hankin, C. (ed.) ESOP 1998. LNCS, vol. 1381, pp. 122–138. Springer, Heidelberg (1998)
16. Honda, K., Yoshida, N., Carbone, M.: Multiparty asynchronous session types. In: Proceedings of the POPL, vol. 43, no. 1, pp. 273–284. ACM (2008)
17. International Telecommunication Union: Recommendation Z.120: message sequence chart (1996)
18. Lanese, I., Guidi, C., Montesi, F., Zavattaro, G.: Bridging the gap between interaction- and process-oriented choreographies. In: Proceedings of SEFM, pp. 323–332. IEEE (2008)
19. Lu, S., Park, S., Seo, E., Zhou, Y.: Learning from mistakes: a comprehensive study on real world concurrency bug characteristics. ACM SIGARCH Comput. Archit. News **36**(1), 329–339 (2008)
20. Montesi, F.: Choreographic programming. Ph.D. thesis, IT University of Copenhagen (2013). http://fabriziomontesi.com/files/m13_phdthesis.pdf
21. Montesi, F., Guidi, C., Zavattaro, G.: Service-oriented programming with Jolie. In: Web Services Foundations, pp. 81–107 (2014)
22. Montesi, F., Yoshida, N.: Compositional choreographies. In: D'Argenio, P.R., Melgratti, H. (eds.) CONCUR 2013 – Concurrency Theory. LNCS, vol. 8052, pp. 425–439. Springer, Heidelberg (2013)
23. Needham, R.M., Schroeder, M.D.: Using encryption for authentication in large networks of computers. Commun. ACM **21**(12), 993–999 (1978)
24. Neykova, R., Yoshida, N., Hu, R.: SPY: local verification of global protocols. In: Legay, A., Bensalem, S. (eds.) RV 2013. LNCS, vol. 8174, pp. 358–363. Springer, Heidelberg (2013)
25. Preda, M.D., Gabbrielli, M., Giallorenzo, S., Lanese, I., Mauro, J.: Deadlock freedom by construction for distributed adaptive applications. CoRR, abs/1407.0970 (2014)
26. Dalla Preda, M., Giallorenzo, S., Lanese, I., Mauro, J., Gabbrielli, M.: AIOCJ: a choreographic framework for safe adaptive distributed applications. In: Combemale, B., Pearce, D.J., Barais, O., Vinju, J.J. (eds.) SLE 2014. LNCS, vol. 8706, pp. 161–170. springer, Heidelberg (2014)
27. Qiu, Z., Zhao, X., Cai, C., Yang, H.: Towards the theoretical foundation of choreography. In: WWW, pp. 973–982, United States. IEEE Computer Society Press (2007)
28. W3C WS-CDL Working Group: Web services choreography description language version 1.0. (2004). http://www.w3.org/TR/2004/WD-ws-cdl-10-20040427/
29. Yoshida, N., Hu, R., Neykova, R., Ng, N.: The scribble protocol language. In: Abadi, M., Lluch Lafuente, A. (eds.) TGC 2013. LNCS, vol. 8358, pp. 22–41. Springer, Heidelberg (2014)

Expressiveness of Behavioral Models

On the Suitability of Generalized Behavioral Profiles for Process Model Comparison

Abel Armas-Cervantes[1]([⊠]), Marlon Dumas[1], Luciano García-Bañuelos[1], and Artem Polyvyanyy[2]

[1] Institute of Computer Science, University of Tartu, Tartu, Estonia
{abel.armas,marlon.dumas,luciano.garcia}@ut.ee
[2] Queensland University of Technology, Brisbane, Australia
artem.polyvyanyy@qut.edu.au

Abstract. Given two process models, the problem of behavioral comparison is that of determining if these models are behaviorally equivalent (e.g., by trace equivalence) and, if not, identifying how can the differences be presented in a compact manner? Behavioral profiles have been proposed as a convenient abstraction for this problem. A behavioral profile is a matrix, where each cell encodes a behavioral relation between a pair of tasks (e.g., causality or conflict). Thus, the problem of behavioral comparison can be reduced to matrix comparison. It has been observed that while behavioral profiles can be efficiently computed, they are not accurate insofar as behaviorally different process models may map to the same behavioral profile. This paper investigates the question of how accurate existing behavioral profiles are. The paper shows that behavioral profiles are fully behavior preserving for the class of acyclic unlabeled nets with respect to configuration equivalence. However, for the general class of acyclic nets, existing behavioral profiles are exponentially inaccurate, meaning that two acyclic nets with the same behavioral profile may differ in an exponential number of configurations.

1 Introduction

Pairwise process model comparison is a basic primitive in the context of management of process model collections. Such comparison can be made from a lexical, syntactical and/or behavioral perspective. This paper deals with the latter. In this context, behavioral profiles [1] have been proposed as an abstract representation of process models for the purpose of comparison. A behavioral profile of a process model can be seen as a complete graph over the set of tasks of the model, where edges are annotated by types of behavioral relations. Alternatively, a behavioral profile is a matrix where rows and columns represent tasks and each cell is labeled by a behavioral relation between a pair of tasks.

Thus, the problem of behavioral comparison of process models can be mapped to that of comparing two matrices. This provides a convenient basis for computing behavioral similarity between pairs of process models [2].

© Springer International Publishing Switzerland 2016
T. Hildebrandt et al. (Eds.): WS-FM 2014/WS-FM 2015, LNCS 9421, pp. 13–28, 2016.
DOI: 10.1007/978-3-319-33612-1_2

Figure 1 depicts a process model represented as a Petri net system and alongside its behavioral profile.[1] In the matrix representation, the strict order relation ($\mapsto$) denotes causal precedence between a pair of tasks in all the computations of the model. Exclusive order relation (+) denotes that a pair of tasks never occurs in the same computation. Finally, interleaving ($\|$) represents the absence of order in the execution of a pair of tasks.

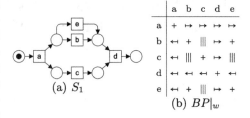

(a) S_1

(b) $BP|_w$

	a	b	c	d	e
a	+	$\mapsto$	$\mapsto$	$\mapsto$	$\mapsto$
b	$\mapsfrom$	+	$\|$	$\mapsto$	+
c	$\mapsfrom$	$\|$	+	$\mapsto$	$\|$
d	$\mapsfrom$	$\mapsfrom$	$\mapsfrom$	+	$\mapsfrom$
e	$\mapsfrom$	+	$\|$	$\mapsto$	+

Fig. 1. Net system and its behavioral profile

In the context of behavioral comparison of process models, the adoption of a notion of behavioral equivalence is crucial since it establishes the ground rules for the comparison. Unfortunately, since the introduction of the concept of behavioral profiles [1], the authors pointed out that this representation does not correspond to any of the well-known notions of behavioral equivalence, i.e., two behaviorally different models (e.g., by trace equivalence), may have the same matrix representation. Interestingly, different families of binary relations have been proposed as extensions of [1]; causal behavioral profile [3] and the relations of the 4C spectrum [4] are cases in point. However, none of them has been shown to preserve any well-known notion of equivalence.

In this paper, we analyze three different behavioral profiles and study their suitability for the representation of the behavior of a process model. All the considered behavioral profiles use $O(|\Lambda|^2)$ space to capture behavior.[2] In the light of the above, the contributions we make in this paper are as follows:

 (i) we give an execution semantics to the behavioral profiles proposed in [1],
 (ii) we show that, for a restricted family of (unlabeled) Petri net systems, behavioral profiles can ensure configuration equivalence [5], and
(iii) we show that, even for the family of acyclic labeled Petri net systems, the three considered behavioral profiles cannot provide an accurate representation of behavior.

The rest of the paper is structured as follows. Section 2 introduces basic concepts of Petri nets, workflow nets, flow nets and flow event structures. Section 3 develops the contributions (i) and (ii) listed above, whereas the contribution (iii) is presented in Sect. 4. Finally, Sect. 5 concludes the paper.

2 Background

This section introduces the necessary concepts used in further sections. Firstly, we recall basic definitions of Petri nets and present two families of nets: workflow and

---

[1] The behavioral profile in Fig. 1 is computed using the relations in [1].

[2] In the rest of the paper, we will say that the size of the behavioral profile of a process model is $O(|\Lambda|^2)$, where Λ is the set of tasks of the model.

flow nets. Then, we review basic definitions of flow event structures and introduce the adopted notion of behavioral equivalence, configuration equivalence.

2.1 Petri Nets

Definition 1 ((Labeled) Petri Net, Net System). *A Petri net, or a net, is a tuple (P, T, F), where P is a set of* places, *T is a set of* transitions, *such that $P \cap T = \emptyset$ and $P \cup T \neq \emptyset$, and $F \subseteq (P \times T) \cup (T \times P)$ is the* flow relation. *A* labeled *net is a tuple $(P, T, F, \Lambda, \lambda)$, where (P, T, F) is a net, Λ is a set of* labels, *and $\lambda : T \to \Lambda \cup \{\tau\}$ is a function that maps transitions to labels, where τ is a special label, $\tau \notin \Lambda$. If $\lambda(t) = \tau$, where $t \in T$, then t is said to be* silent; *otherwise t is* observable. *A* marking *of a net (P, T, F) is a function $M : P \to \mathbb{N}_0$ that maps places to natural numbers (viz.,* tokens*). A Petri net* system, *or a net system, is a pair (N, M), where $N = (P, T, F)$ is a Petri net and M is a marking of N.*

Places and transitions are conjointly referred to as *nodes*. We write $\bullet y = \{x \in P \cup T \mid (x, y) \in F\}$ and $y \bullet = \{z \in P \cup T \mid (y, z) \in F\}$ to denote the *preset* and *postset* of the node $y \in P \cup T$, respectively. Similarly, for a set of nodes $X \subseteq P \cup T$, $\bullet X = \bigcup \{\bullet x \mid x \in X\}$ and $X \bullet = \bigcup \{x \bullet \mid x \in X\}$.

One approach to define the execution semantics of a net system is in terms of markings. A marking M of a net $N = (P, T, F)$ *enables* a transition $t \in T$, denoted as $M[t\rangle$, iff $\forall p \in \bullet t : M(p) > 0$. Moreover, an occurrence of t, such that $M[t\rangle$, leads to a fresh marking M' of N, denoted as $M \xrightarrow{t} M'$, where $M'(p) = M(p) - 1$ if $p \in \bullet t \setminus t \bullet$, $M'(p) = M(p) + 1$ if $p \in t \bullet \setminus \bullet t$, and $M'(p) = M(p)$ otherwise.

Definition 2 (Firing Sequence, Execution). *Let $S = (N, M_0)$, $N = (P, T, F)$, be a Petri net system.*

- *A sequence of transitions $\sigma = t_1 \dots t_n$ in N, where $n \in \mathbb{N}_0$, is a* firing sequence *in S iff σ is empty or it holds that $M_0 \xrightarrow{t_1} M_1 \xrightarrow{t_2} M_2 \dots \xrightarrow{t_n} M_n$. In the latter case, we say that σ* leads *from M_0 to M_n.*
- *A marking M is* reachable *in S iff $M = M_0$ or there exist a firing sequence σ that leads from M_0 to M. The notation $M' \in [N, M\rangle$ represents that M' is reachable in (N, M).*
- *A marking M of N is* terminal *iff there exist no transition enabled at M.*
- *A firing sequence σ that leads from M_0 to M, where M is terminal, is called an* execution. *By $\Theta(S)$, we denote the set of all executions of S.*

A marking M of a net $N = (P, T, F)$ is *n-safe* iff for every place $p \in P$ it holds that $M(p) \leq n$, $n \in \mathbb{N}_0$. A net system S is said to be *n-safe* if all its reachable markings are *n-safe*. We restrict the subsequent discussions to *1-safe* net systems. Note that one can identify a *1-safe* marking M of a net (P, T, F) as the set of places $\{p \in P \mid M(p) = 1\}$.

Workflow nets [6] are a class of nets with a dedicated source and sink place, such that every transition is on a path from the source to the sink place.

Definition 3 (WF-Net, WF-System). *A Petri net $N = (P, T, F)$ is a work-flow net, or a WF-net, iff N has a dedicated source place $i \in P$, with $\bullet i = \varnothing$, N has a dedicated sink place $o \in P$, with $o\bullet = \varnothing$, and the short-circuit net $N^* = (P, T \cup \{t^*\}, F \cup \{(o, t^*), (t^*, i)\})$ of N is strongly connected, $t^* \notin T$. A WF-net system is a net system (N, M), where N is a WF-net with the source place i and $M = \{i\}$.*

Soundness [7] is the commonly adopted criterion of correctness for WF-net systems. For example, a sound WF-net system guarantees that every execution ends with one token in the sink place and no tokens elsewhere.

Definition 4 (Liveness, Boundedness, Soundness). *Let $S = (N, M)$, $N = (P, T, F)$, be a Petri net system.*

- *S is live iff for every reachable marking $M' \in [N, M\rangle$ and for every transition $t \in T$ there exist a marking $M'' \in [N, M'\rangle$ such that $M''[t\rangle$.*
- *S is bounded iff there exist a number $n \in \mathbb{N}_0$ such that S is n-safe.*

A WF-net system (N, M) is sound iff the net system (N^*, M), where N^* is the short-circuit net of N, is live and bounded.

Flow nets form another family of Petri nets [8]. This type of nets is semantically acyclic, meaning that in any firing sequence, a place cannot be marked more than once. Thus, all the transitions in a firing sequence are distinct. In the context of flow nets, the notion of causal dependency between transitions is defined w.r.t. places. A transition t_j causally depends on a transition t_i iff $\exists p \in t_i \bullet \cap \bullet t_j$, such that whenever both transitions occur in a firing sequence, then t_i is the only transition that puts a token in p; p is said to be a *strong postcondition* of t_i. Finally, a flow net is defined as follows.

Definition 5 (Flow Net, Flow Net System). *A net system $S = (N, M)$, $N = (P, T, F)$, is a flow net system and N is a flow net iff for every firing sequence $\sigma = t_1 t_2 \ldots t_n$ in S and for every $i, j \in \mathbb{N}$, s.t. $1 \leq i < j \leq n$, it holds that:*

- *a place $p \in P$ is in a preset of at most one transition of σ, i.e., $\bullet t_i \cap \bullet t_j = \varnothing$, and*
- *if $t_i \bullet \cap \bullet t_j \neq \varnothing$ then $\exists p \in t_i \bullet \cap \bullet t_j$, s.t., p is a strong postcondition of t_i.*

An alternative way to define the execution semantics of a net system is using the notion of a configuration. The main difference between firing sequences and configurations is that the former capture the interleaving semantics, whereas the latter describe the partial order semantics (aka true concurrency). In the case of flow nets, firing sequences and configurations are in the close relation, which is due to the next definition.

Definition 6 (Flow Net Configuration). *A configuration of a flow net system $S = (N, M)$, $N = (P, T, F)$, is a subset $C \subseteq T$ of transitions of N such that there exist a firing sequence σ in S that consists of the transitions in C, i.e.,*

$$\sigma = t_1 t_2 \ldots t_n \quad and \quad C = \{t_1, t_2, \ldots, t_n\}$$

The set of all configurations of S is denoted by $Conf(S)$.

Set inclusion ($\subseteq$) defines an order over configurations. We say that a configuration C *evolves into* a configuration C' if $C \subseteq C'$.

The discussions throughout the paper consider Petri nets in the intersection of two families: sound WF-nets and flow nets (shorthanded as WF-flow nets, see Fig. 2). More specifically, the focus of this work is on WF-nets that are acyclic, sound and have the properties of flow nets (Definition 5).

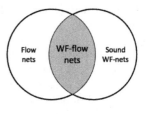

Fig. 2. WF-flow nets

2.2   Flow Event Structures

Flow Event Structures [8] (FES) is a well-known model of concurrency. It describes the behavior of a net system by means of events (occurrences of actions) and two binary behavioral relations, namely *flow* and *conflict*.

Definition 7 ((Labeled) Flow Event Structure). *A flow event structure (FES) is a tuple* $\mathbb{F} = (E, \#, \prec)$, *where*

- *E is a set of events,*
- *$\# \subseteq E \times E$ is the* conflict *relation, which is symmetric, and*
- *$\prec \subseteq E \times E$ is the* flow *relation, which is irreflexive.*

A labeled FES is a tuple $\mathbb{F} = (E, \#, \prec, \Lambda, \lambda)$, *where* $(E, \#, \prec)$ *is a FES,* Λ *is a set of labels, and* $\lambda : E \to \Lambda \cup \{\tau\}$ *is a function that maps events to labels. Again, if* $\lambda(e) = \tau$, *where* $e \in E$, *then* e *is said to be* silent; *otherwise* e *is* observable.

Intuitively, the flow relation represents possible immediate precedence, meaning that if two events e and e' are in the flow relation, i.e., $e \prec e'$, then event e can potentially occur before e'. The conflict relation represents mutual exclusion. Two events e and e' in the conflict relation, i.e., $e\#e'$, cannot occur together in the same execution. The conflict relation is reflexive and then self-conflicting events are allowed. Even though self-conflicting events never occur in any configuration, in general, they cannot be removed from a FES without affecting the set of configurations [8].

Similar to flow nets, the behavior of FESs can be given in terms of configurations, and it is defined as follows.

Definition 8 (FES Configuration). *A configuration of a FES* $\mathbb{F} = (E, \#, \prec)$ *is a subset* $C \subseteq E$ *of events of* $\mathbb{F}$ *s.t.:*

- *C is conflict free, i.e.,* $\forall\, e, e' \in C : \neg(e\#e')$,
- *C has no flow cycles, i.e., the transitive closure of* $\prec$ *between the events in* C *($\prec^*_C$) is a partial order, and*
- *for all events* $e' \in C$ *and* $e \notin C$ *such that* $e \prec e'$ *it holds that there exist an event* $e'' \in C$ *such that* $e\#e''$ *and* $e'' \prec e'$.

The set of all configurations of $\mathbb{F}$ *is denoted by* $Conf(\mathbb{F})$.

An alternative formulation of configurations is done using proving sequences.

Definition 9 (Proving Sequence). *A* proving sequence *in a FES* $\mathbb{F} = (E, \#, <)$ *is a (finite or infinite) sequence* $\sigma = e_1 \ldots e_n \ldots$ *of distinct non-conflicting events, s.t.* $\forall i \forall e \in E : e < e_i \Rightarrow (\exists j < i : e \# e_j \wedge e_j < e_i)$.
      A subset of events $C \subseteq E$ *is* a configuration *of a FES* $\mathbb{F} = (E, \#, <)$, *s.t.* $C = \{e_1, \ldots, e_n\}$, *if and only if* C *is conflict free and for every event* $e_k \in C$, $k \leq n$ *it holds that* $e_1 \ldots e_k$ *is a proving sequence in* $\mathbb{F}$, *cf.* [8].

In [8], Boudol shows that FES corresponds to the family of flow nets, i.e., it is always possible to compute a FES for a given flow net system, where configurations of FES are derived from firing sequences in the system. Interestingly, for a sound WF-flow net, it is possible to establish a bijection between its transitions and events in the corresponding FES representation.[3]

The next definition suggests how to construct a FES from a flow net system. Different from [8], we do not consider self-conflicting events, thus there is a bijection between the transitions in the net and the events in the FES. Hence, we use T to represent both, events and transitions, indistinctively.

Definition 10 (FES of a Flow Net). *Let* $S = (N, M)$, $N = (P, T, F)$, *be a flow net system. The FES of* S *is the tuple* $\mathbb{F} = (T, \#, <)$, *where for every two transitions* $t \in T$ *and* $t' \in T$ *it holds that:*

- $t \# t' \Leftrightarrow_{def} \forall C \in Conf(S) : \{t, t'\} \nsubseteq C$, *and*
- $t < t' \Leftrightarrow_{def} \neg(t \# t') \wedge t \bullet \cap \bullet t' \neq \varnothing$.

2.3   Configuration Equivalence

The equivalence notion adopted in this work is configuration equivalence, a well-known notion of equivalence in the spectrum of true concurrency [5].[4] Note that this notion is stronger than trace equivalence. As showed before, the behavior of a flow net system or a FES can be described, in partial order semantics, by means of configurations. Intuitively, a pair of structures (in our context, either flow event structures or flow net systems) are configuration equivalent if (1) there is a bijection between elements (events or transitions), and (2) the structures represent, essentially, the same set of configurations. Below, we provide a definition of the configuration equivalence for flow net systems, but it can be straightforwardly adapted to FESs.

Definition 11 (Configuration Equivalence $\approx_{conf}$). *Let* $S = (N, M_0)$ *and* $S' = (N', M_0')$ *be two flow net systems, where* $N = (P, T, F)$ *and* $N' = (P', T', F')$, *and let* $\gamma : T \to T'$ *be a bijective function between the transitions of the nets. Let* $S :: \sim_{conf} S'$ *denote that for any configuration* C *in* S *there is a corresponding configuration* C' *in* S' *consisting of the images of* C. *I.e.,* $\forall C \in Conf(S) \exists C' \in Conf(S') : C' = \{\gamma(t) \mid t \in C\}$.
      The pair of net systems S, S' *are* configuration equivalent, *denoted* $S \approx_{conf} S'$, *iff* $S :: \sim_{conf} S'$ *and* $S' :: \sim_{conf} S$.

---

[3] Additional self-conflicting events can be required in a FES when, in the context of WF-nets, a net system does not meet the property of liveness. We refer the reader to [8] for more details about the introduction of self-conflicting events.

[4] The authors of [5] use *pomset-trace equivalence*. A pomset is basically a set of configurations augmented with the order induced by set inclusion. Since we are not interested in such order, we keep the equivalence at the level of configurations.

3 Behavioral Profiles of Acyclic Unlabeled WF-flow Nets

This section proposes an execution semantics for the behavioral profiles defined in [1], hereinafter referred to as *classic behavioral profiles* and denoted as $BP|_w$. We show that, for the case of acyclic unlabeled WF-flow nets, classic behavioral profiles are behavior preserving under configuration equivalence. The section is organized as follows, Subsect. 3.1 presents a generalized notion of behavioral profiles. Subsection 3.2 presents a behavioral profile $BP|_{fes}$ derived from flow event structures. Then, in Subsect. 3.3, a transformation from $BP|_w$ into $BP|_{fes}$ is proposed and it is shown that $BP|_w$ is behaviorally preserving for acyclic unlabeled WF-flow nets. Finally, Subsect. 3.4 discusses about the suitability of the $BP|_w$ for the behavioral comparison of processes.

3.1 Generalized Behavioral Profiles

Behavioral profiles can be seen as a framework that is concretely defined according to a set of behavioral relations. Roughly speaking, a behavioral profile $BP|_R$ of a process model is a complete graph over the set of tasks' labels, which uses a set of relations R as edge labels. This general notion of behavioral profiles results useful for uniformly analyze the different formalisms considered in this paper.

A behavioral profiles is said *behavior preserving*, if a pair of net systems that are behavior-equivalent (under certain notion of quivalence) have isomorphic behavioral profiles (denoted as $\equiv_{iso}$); and vice-versa. The intuition above is captured in the following definition.

Definition 12 (Behavior-Preserving $BP|_R$). *Let $\mathcal{N}$ be a class of nets and $\approx$ be an equivalence relation on $\mathcal{N}$. A behavioral profile $BP|_R$ is behavior-preserving on $\mathcal{N}$, if for any $N, N' \in \mathcal{N}$ with net systems $S = (N, M_0), S' = (N', M_0')$ and behavioral profiles $BP|_R(S)$ and $BP|_R(S')$, respectively, the following holds:*

$$S \approx S' \Leftrightarrow BP|_R(S) \equiv_{iso} BP|_R(S').$$

3.2 Behavioral Profiles and FES

The correspondence between FESs and flow nets investigated by Boudol [8] shows that given a flow net, it is possible to construct a FES, such that the firing sequences in the net are configurations in the FES; and vice-versa.

The following proposition restates the results proved in [8] for flow nets. Although, we refer concretely to the set of all WF-flow nets and represent by $\mathcal{N}$.

Proposition 1 (Proposition 3.4 in [8]). *Let $S = (N, M_0)$ be a WF-flow net system, with a net $N = (P, T, F) \in \mathcal{N}$, and let $\mathbb{F}$ be its corresponding FES (see Definition 10), we have that $Conf(S) = Conf(\mathbb{F})$. More precisely, a sequence $t_1 \dots t_n$ is firable in S if and only if it is a proving sequence in $\mathbb{F}$.*

Thus, a result from Proposition 1 is that a pair of configuration equivalent WF-flow nets have, similarly, configuration equivalent FESs.

Corollary 1. *Let N, N' be nets in $\mathcal{N}$. Moreover, let $\mathbb{F}$ and $\mathbb{F}'$ be the FESs of S and S', respectively. Then, it holds that:*

$$S \approx_{conf} S' \Leftrightarrow \mathbb{F} \approx_{conf} \mathbb{F}'$$

A type of behavioral profiles for WF-flow nets can be defined using FESs when there is a bijection between the transitions in the net and the events in event structure. Thus, let us refer to the behavioral profile of a net system S given by the FES as $BP|_{fes}(S)$. In this case, the tasks in $BP|_{fes}(S)$ are the events in the FES, and the set of binary relations are flow and conflict. Finally, one can notice that it is possible to define a behavioral profile $BP|_{fes}$ that contains all the behavior of a net system S, such that any conclusion (w.r.t. behavior) derived from $BP|_{fes}$ holds in S.

The following proposition shows that every place in a WF-flow net is, in fact, a strong postcondition of a transition w.r.t. a firing sequence.

Proposition 2. *Let $S = (N, M_0)$ be a WF-flow net system, with a net $N = (P, T, F)$, and let $\sigma = t_1\ t_2 \ldots t_n \in \Theta(S)$ be an execution of S. Then, a place $p \in t_j\bullet$ is a strong postcondition of a transition t_j, where $1 \le j \le n$.*

Proof. In this case, it is shown that the property holds for an execution σ, but then it also holds for any firing sequence, which elements are part of σ.

Note that if p is the source place then it cannot be a postcondition of any transition, since $\bullet p = \varnothing$. Conversely, consider the case when p is not the source place, thus $\bullet p \ne \varnothing$. Then, let us show that there is a unique t_j, where $1 \le j \le n$, such that $p \in t_j\bullet$. Suppose that there is another transition t_k, where $1 \le k \le n$, such that $k \ne j \wedge p \in t_k\bullet$. The place p cannot be the sink place, because if t_j and t_k fire, then p would have two tokens, but it contradicts the fact that the net is 1-safe. Thus, it means that p was marked in two different occasions and, since the net is 1-safe, it was necessary to consume one of the tokens before the other was set. Hence, p was the preset of two different transitions in σ. Nevertheless, it violates the condition 1 in Definition 5. Therefore, if $p \in t_j\bullet$ then p is a strong postcondition of t_j. $\qquad\square$

The proposition above, however, implies that every place between a pair of transitions in a WF-flow net defines a flow relation. As a result, the behavioral profiles $BP|_{fes}$, w.r.t. Definition 10, are not behavior preserving (see Definition 12). For instance, a net system can have implicit places that would define unnecessary flow relations between the events in the FES. Nevertheless, we believe that by providing a more elaborated definition for constructing a FES of a net system, one can find a behavior preserving $BP|_{fes}$. Although, the last is left for future work, since Definition 10 is enough for the scope of this paper.

3.3   An Execution Semantics for the Classic Behavioral Profiles

In this subsection, we focus on the classic behavioral profiles $(BP|_w)$. This type of behavioral profiles uses three behavior relations, namely *strict order* ($\mapsto$), *exclusive order* ($+$) and *interleaving* ($\|$). The following definition formalizes the behavior relations comprising any $BP|_w$, along with its computation.

Definition 13 ($BP|_w$, see [1]). *Let $S = (N, M)$ be a net system, with $N = (P, T, F)$. A pair of transitions $t, t' \in T$ is in one of the following relations:*

- Strict order relation, *denoted by $t \mapsto t'$, if for every firing sequence $\sigma \in \Theta(S)$, with $\sigma = t_1 \, t_2 \dots t_n$ such that $t_i = t$ and $t_j = t'$, it holds $1 \leq i < j \leq n$.*
- Exclusive order relation, *denoted by $t + t'$, if for every firing sequence $\sigma \in \Theta(S)$: $\sigma = t_1 \, t_2 \dots t_n$ there are no t_i, t_j, where $1 \leq i, j \leq n$, s.t. $i \neq j$, $t_i = t$ and $t_j = t'$.*
- Interleaving relation, *denoted by $t \;|||\; t'$, if $\neg(t \mapsto t')$, $\neg(t' \mapsto t)$ and $\neg(t + t')$.*

For technical reasons, we also define the direct strict order. *Transitions t and t' are in direct strict order, denoted by $t \twoheadrightarrow t'$, iff*

$$t_i \mapsto t_j \;\wedge\; t_i \bullet \cap \bullet t_j \neq \oslash$$

The set $BP|_w(S) = \{\mapsto, +, |||\}$ is the classic behavioral profile *of S.*

The following definition formalizes the transformation from $BP|_w$ to $BP|_{fes}$.

Definition 14 ($BP|_w^{fes}$). *Let $BP|_w(S) = \{\mapsto, +, |||\}$ be a classic behavioral profile of a WF-flow net system $S = (N, M)$, with $N = (P, T, F)$. Let $+'$ be the exclusive order relation without the self-exclusive order relations, i.e., $+' = +\backslash\{(t, t) \mid t \in T\}$. Then $BP|_{fes}$ of $BP|_w(S)$ is defined as $BP|_w^{fes}(S) = \{\twoheadrightarrow, +'\}$.*

The definition presented above gives $BP|_w$ an execution semantics on FES through $BP|_w^{fes}$. Thus, given a $BP|_w$ and the $\twoheadrightarrow$ relation, one can derive the configurations of the corresponding net by reusing the notion of configuration of FES over $BP|_w^{fes}$. The following proposition shows that the $BP|_w^{fes}(S)$ computed from $BP|_w(S)$ is isomorphic to $BP|_{fes}(S)$, i.e., $BP|_w^{fes}(S)$ captures the same relations as $BP|_{fes}(S)$ and so $BP|_w^{fes}(S)$ captures all the behavior of S. Note that for the reminder of this section, we focus on unlabeled WF-flow nets, which will be denoted as $\mathcal{N}_{\overline{\lambda}}$.

Proposition 3. *Let $S = (N, M)$ be a net system, where $N = (P, T, F) \in \mathcal{N}_{\overline{\lambda}}$ is an unlabeled WF-flow net, and $BP|_w(S) = \{\mapsto, +, |||\}$ be the classic behavioral profile of S. Thus, $BP|_w^{fes}(S) = \{\twoheadrightarrow, +\}$ is isomorphic to $BP|_{fes}(S) = \{<, \#\}$, in specific, for any two transitions $x, y \in T$ 1. $x+y \Leftrightarrow x\#y$, and 2. $x \twoheadrightarrow y \Leftrightarrow x < y$.*

Proof. Given that the nets are unlabeled, then for any transition in T there is a task in $BP|_{fes}$ and in $BP|_w$ (and so in $BP|_w^{fes}$). Therefore, let us consider the same set of elements T throughout the different structures.

1. $x + y \Leftrightarrow x\#y$. It is easy to check that the definition of exclusive ordering relation $(+)$ in $BP|_w$ and conflict $(\#)$ in $BP|_{fes}$ is the same. So, the conflict in the FES coincides with the exclusive order relation in $BP|_w$.

2. $x \twoheadrightarrow y \Leftrightarrow x \prec y$. ($\Rightarrow$) Consider a pair of transitions $x, y \in T : x \twoheadrightarrow y$. By Definition 13, $\exists \sigma = t_1 \, t_2 \ldots, t_n : x = t_i, y = t_j \land i < j$. Additionally, since the causal relation is direct, then there is at least a place $p \in x \bullet \cap \bullet y$. Thus, by Definition 10, $x \prec y$ in $BP|_{fes}(S)$.

($\Leftarrow$) Suppose $x \prec y$ in $BP|_{fes}(S)$, and $\neg(x \twoheadrightarrow y)$ in $BP|_w^{fes}(S)$. By Definition 10, since $x \prec y$ then $x \bullet \cap \bullet y \neq \oslash$ and $\neg(x \# y)$. Let $p \in x \bullet \cap \bullet y$ be a strong postcondition of x. The first thing to notice is that $\neg(x+y)$, since $\neg(x \# y)$ – see previous case. Thus, there exist a firing sequence $\sigma = t_1 \, t_2 \ldots, t_n : x = t_i, y = t_j$, where $1 \leq i < j \leq n$. Hence, the only case where $\neg(x \mapsto y)$ can hold is if there exist an execution $\sigma' \in \Theta(S)$, s.t., $\sigma' = t_1', t_2', \ldots, t_n'$ and $\exists t_i' = x, t_j' = y : 1 \leq j < i \leq n$, in which case it would hold $x \parallel\!\parallel y$. Given that y occurred in σ' and $p \in \bullet y$, then p had a token prior the firing of y, and as p is a strong postcondition of x, then x occurred before y (by Proposition 2), but then σ' has two occurrences of x because $t_i' = x, t_j' = y : 1 \leq j < i \leq n$. The last contradicts the fact that N is a flow net because, by Definition 5(1), the places in the present of x cannot be marked more than once by the transitions in σ'. Thus, if $x \prec y$ then $x \twoheadrightarrow y$. □

In what follows, $BP|_w$ is shown to be behavior preserving for the $\mathcal{N}_{\overline{\lambda}}$.

Proposition 4. *Consider a pair of nets $N = (P, T, F)$ and $N' = (P', T', F')$ in $\mathcal{N}_{\overline{\lambda}}$, such that there is a bijection between the transitions $\gamma : T \to T'$, and let $S = (N, M_0)$ and $S' = (N', M_0')$ be net systems with initial markings M_0 and M_0'. Thus, the following holds:*

$$BP|_w(S) \equiv_{iso} BP|_w(S') \Leftrightarrow S \approx_{conf} S'.$$

Proof. ($\Rightarrow$) Firstly, let us show that if $BP|_w(S) \equiv_{iso} BP|_w(S')$ then $S \approx_{conf} S'$.

Suppose that $BP|_w(S) \equiv_{iso} BP|_w(S')$, but $\neg(S \approx_{conf} S')$. By Corollary 1, we have $\neg(BP|_w^{fes}(S) \approx_{conf} BP|_w^{fes}(S'))$ since $\neg(S \approx_{conf} S')$.

Assume a configuration $C \subseteq T$ in $BP|_w^{fes}(S)$ and its mapping $C' = \{\gamma(t') \mid t' \in C\}$ in S', such that C' is not a configuration in $BP|_w^{fes}(S')$. By Definition 8, the configuration C (i) is conflict free, (ii) for all $e' \in C$ and $e \notin C$, s.t., $e \prec e'$ there exist an $e'' \in C$ s.t. $e \# e'' \prec e'$, and (iii) has no flow cycles. Therefore, we must consider the following cases:

(i) Conflict freeness. Since C is a configuration in $BP|_w^{fes}(S)$, then for any $e, e' \in C$ it holds $\neg(e \# e')$ and, in consequence, $\neg(e + e')$ in $BP|_w(S)$ by Proposition 3(1). Then, by the assumption on the isomorphism of the $BP|_w$'s, $\exists e_1, e_1' \in C' : \gamma(e) = e_1 \land \gamma(e') = e_1'$, such that $\neg(e_1 + e_1')$ and thus $\neg(e_1 \# e_1')$. So, C' is also conflict free iff C is conflict free, and every pair of $e_1, e_1' \in C'$ is either in $\parallel\!\parallel$ or $\mapsto$ ordering relations.

(ii) For any $e_1'' \in C'$ and $e_1 \notin C'$, s.t., $e_1 \prec e_1''$, there exist an $e_1' \in C' : e_1 \# e_1' \prec e_1''$. Suppose that there is an event $e_1 \notin C'$, such that $\exists e_1'' \in C' : e_1 \prec e_1''$ and $\forall e_1' \in C' : \neg(e_1 \# e_1')$. Given that $e_1 \prec e_1''$, then $e_1 \mapsto e_1''$ (more specifically, $e_1 \twoheadrightarrow e_1''$), and since $\neg(e_1 \# e_1')$ then $\neg(e_1 + e_1')$ for any $e_1' \in C'$, by Proposition 3. Hence, by the isomorphism of BP_w's, then $\exists e \notin C, e'' \in C : \gamma(e) = e_1 \land \gamma(e'') = e_1'' \land e \mapsto e''$ and for any $e' \in C$

it holds $\neg(e + e')$. However, the last contradicts the fact that C is a configuration in $BP|_w^{fes}(S)$, because e would necessarily be in C. Henceforth, condition 2 also holds for C'.

(iii) Free of flow cycles. The only case remaining, so that C' is not a configuration in $BP|_w^{fes}(S')$, is when C' contains cycles, i.e., $<_{C'}^*$ is not a partial order. This case simply cannot happen because WF-flow nets are acyclic and any firing sequence contains at most one occurrence of each activity.

Therefore, if C is a configuration in $BP|_w^{fes}(S)$, then C' must also be a configuration in $BP|_w^{fes}(S')$.

($\Leftarrow$) The opposite case, $S \approx_{conf} S' \Rightarrow BP|_w(S) \equiv_{iso} BP|_w(S')$, follows directly from the construction of the $BP|_w$, see Definition 13.   □

Armed with the above, one can easily see that $BP|_w$ is behavior-preserving for the class of $\mathcal{N}_{\overline{\lambda}}$. This fact is captured in the following Corollary.

Corollary 2. *The behavioral profiles $BP|_w$ is behavior-preserving for the class $\mathcal{N}_{\overline{\lambda}}$, w.r.t. configurations equivalence $\approx_{conf}$.*

The above results also holds for the different extensions of the classic behavioral profiles that have strict and exclusive order relations, e.g., causal behavioral profile [3] and behavioral profiles based on the relations of the 4C spectrum [4].

3.4   On the Interpretation of Behavioral Differences Using $BP|_w$

The process model comparison aims not just at determining if a pair of process models are (behaviorally) equivalent, but also at explaining the existing differences between the process models. This section analyzes the suitability of the classic behavioral profiles when used to interpret encountered differences between a pair of behavioral profiles.

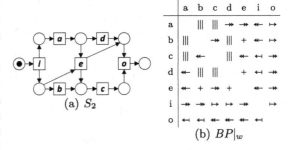

(a) S_2

	a	b	c	d	e	i	o
a		|||	|||	⇢	⇢	⇠	↦
b	|||		⇢	|||	+	⇠	↦
c	|||	⇠		|||	⇠	⇠	⇢
d	⇠	|||	|||		+	⇠	⇢
e	⇠	+	⇢	+		⇠	⇢
i	⇢	⇢	↦	↦	⇢		↦
o	⇠	⇠	⇠	⇠	⇠	⇠	

(b) $BP|_w$

Fig. 3. Net system S_2 and its $BP|_w$

Figure 3 presents an example showing that $BP|_w$ does not necessarily provide a detailed representation of the behavior of a WF-flow net. In this example, there is a WF-flow net system[5] and its behavioral profile $BP|_w$ aside. Let us draw you attention to transitions a and c, for which $BP|_w$ asserts an interleaving relation. However, in all the configurations where e occurs it is always the case that a precedes c. It is only in the set of configurations where e does not occur where a and c occur in any order. The fact is that these subtle kind of differences

---

[5] This net corresponds to the FES N presented in [8].

requires a diagnostic with contextual information in addition to the local information provided by a binary relation. It should be clear that it is possible to derive such sets of configurations from the $BP|_w^{fes}$.

A solution to disambiguate the situation presented in Fig. 3 is to reason not in terms of actions, but in terms of instances of actions (events), where it is possible to set a single relation between a pair of transitions (causality, conflict or concurrency). In this regard, alternative representations of the behavior of a WF-flow net, e.g., by means of a branching process [9], can

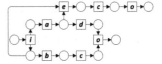

Fig. 4. Branching process of net system S_2 (Fig. 3(a))

result useful. For instance, the branching process of the net system in S_2 (Fig. 3) is displayed in Fig. 4. Although, the price to pay is that a branching process can contain several instances of a single activity, and the $O(|\Lambda|^2)$ size of the representation is no longer guaranteed.

Another approach to tackle the ambiguity of the $BP|_w$ is to use a larger set of behavioral relations. For instance, the 4C spectrum [4] defines a repertoire of eighteen basic behavioral relations that capture such behavioral phenomena as co-occurrence, conflict, causality, and concurrency. One can employ the relations of the 4C spectrum to construct an abstract representation of behavior of a process model, i.e., its behavioral profile. Note that due to the nature of the 4C spectrum, a pair of tasks can be associated with several behavioral relations. Nevertheless, behavioral profiles that are based on the relations of the 4C spectrum are guaranteed to be captured using $O(|\Lambda|^2)$ space. Even though this approach solves the problem of the ambiguity for the family of unlabeled net systems, it falls short when trying to generalize the solution to the case of net systems with silent transitions (as discussed in the next section).

4   Behavioral Profiles and Acyclic Labeled WF-flow Nets

This section extends the analysis of the behavioral profiles to labeled WF-flow nets. It is shown that for this family of nets neither the notion of classic behavioral profile nor its extensions, including that based on the relations of the 4C spectrum, provide behavior-preserving representations of process models.

Proponents of classic behavioral profiles search for providing a representation that only considers the observable behavior. When it comes to representing labeled net systems, the common approach is to omit the columns and rows in the matrix that would be associated with silent transitions. This decision, however, comes with a loss of accuracy of the representation. For example, consider the net system S_3 in Fig. 5. Its classic behavioral profile is isomorphic with the one of S_1, cf. Fig. 1. However, S_3 differs from S_1 in that it has two additional configurations: $\{a, b, d\}$ and $\{a, e, d\}$.

In order to preserve behavior, as for the case of unlabeled WF-flow nets, one possibility is to explicitly represent silent transitions in the matrix, as illustrated in Fig. 6. It is easy to see that, using this approach, the behavior of S_1 and S_3

would be represented with two non-isomorphic matrices. However, this approach does not provide a complete solution since multiple net systems may exist with different numbers of silent transitions exhibiting the same observable behavior.

The use of a larger number of behavior relations can be seen as a way to tackle the above problem. For instance, both causal behavioral profiles and behavioral profiles that are based on the relations of the 4C spectrum provide non-isomorphic representations for S_1 and S_3. However, none of them provides representations that distinguish the WF-flow net systems S_4 and S_5 in Fig. 7 w.r.t. configuration equiv-

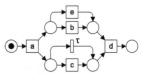

Fig. 5. Net system S_3

alence. Interestingly, there is only one configuration that distinguishes S_4 from S_5, namely $\{i, o\}$. It turns out that the set of configurations that is common to both systems, namely $\{\{i, a, o\}, \{i, b, o\}, \{i, a, b, o\}\}$, gives rise to the same representation based on the relations of the 4C spectrum.

Figure 8 shows two constructions that generalize the net systems in Fig. 7 with a variable amount of transitions n. It turns out that, for any fixed value of $n \in \mathbb{N}$, the system S_6 would comprise the set of configurations $\{\{i, a_1, a_2, \ldots, a_n, o\}\} \cup \{\{i, a_m, o\} \mid m \in [1 .. n]\}$, however, it would have the same representation as the system S_7 over the relations of the 4C spectrum. Note that system S_6 encodes $n + 1$ configurations, whereas system S_7 describes 2^n configurations. Therefore, there exist two net systems for which there is an exponential number of

	a	b	c	d	τ	e
a		<	<		<	<
b	<^{-1}			<		+
c	<^{-1}			<		+
d		<^{-1}	<^{-1}		<^{-1}	<^{-1}
τ	<^{-1}		+	<		
e	<^{-1}	+		<		

Fig. 6. $BP|_{fes}(S_3)$

configurations that are indistinguishable when using the representation based on the relations of the 4C spectrum; in specific, $2^n - n - 1$ indistinguishable configurations for systems in Fig. 8. This fact is captured in the next proposition.

Proposition 5. *There exist two labeled WF-flow net systems that have the same 4C relations over labels and the numbers of distinct configurations that the net systems describe differ in the value which is in the order of $O(2^n)$, where n is the number of distinct labels assigned to transitions of the net systems.*

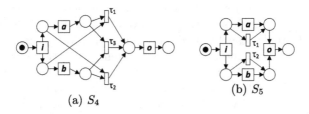

(a) S_4 (b) S_5

Fig. 7. Two net systems that have the same 4C relations over labels

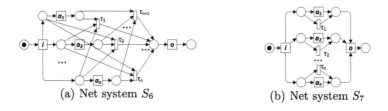

(a) Net system S_6 (b) Net system S_7

Fig. 8. Generalization of the net systems in Fig. 7

Observe that there also exist two net systems with no concurrent behavior on observable transitions that have the same 4C relations over labels but induce different configurations, cf. Fig. 9. Indeed, net systems S_8 and S_9 have the same 4C relations over labels, although net system S_9 describes configuration $\{i, o\}$ which is not captured by net system S_8.

The above observations confirm that existing behavioral profiles are lossy behavioral representations of labeled net systems. So, if one
relies on existing behavioral profiles in the context of process model comparison, then one
must tolerate inaccurate diagnosis. To address
this problem, one must either look for new
and more accurate behavioral profiles or, alternatively, explore behavior representations in
terms of occurrences of actions; however, the
size of such latter representations can be con-
siderably larger than $O(|\Lambda|^2)$.

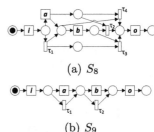

(a) S_8

(b) S_9

Fig. 9. Two net systems that have the same 4C relations over labels

5 Conclusion

This paper studies the idea of using behavioral profiles for the purpose of behavioral comparison of process models, i.e., deciding if two given models are behaviorally equivalent and, whenever required, providing a convenient representation
of their differences. The use of behavioral profiles allows reducing the problem
of behavioral comparison to that of matrix comparison, which provides a formal basis for tracing differences between process models that are grounded in
behavior. Moreover, the feasibility of the overall idea is validated by showing
that behavioral profiles can be used to decide configuration equivalence for a
restricted class of acyclic and unlabeled net systems. However, this result ceases
to hold (for any currently known notion of behavioral profile) once transitions of
net systems are allowed to 'wear' labels. Future works are called to contribute to
a better understanding of which behavioral profiles can be employed for the purpose of behavioral comparison of which families of process models under which
notions of behavioral equivalence.

The results of this paper have implications in the context of process mining algorithms that rely on matrix-based representations of behavior. A case in

point are alpha relations [10], which abstract an event log as an $O(|\Lambda|^2)$ matrix where each cell is annotated by a behavioral relation (direct causality, conflict or concurrency). Our results hint at the fact that such matrices may miss to encode an exponential number of computations. Thus, designers of process mining algorithms should consider using more faithful intermediate representations.

Alternatively, rather than relying on behavioral relations on tasks, one can consider behavioral comparison that is founded on binary behavioral relations on events, i.e., task occurrences. When viewing the set of binary relations as a matrix, this means that the matrix may be considerably larger than $O(|\Lambda|^2)$, since a task may occur in an exponential number of computations. In a separate work, we have explored the use of event structures as alternative representations for process model comparison [11]. It turns out that the most basic form of event structures requires maintaining a large number of events representing different occurrences of the same task. To tackle this problem, we apply reduction rules to obtain a canonical matrix representation of behavior [12,13]. However, achieving a quadratic or even a polynomial matrix-based representation of behavior appears to be elusive in the general case.

References

1. Weidlich, M., Mendling, J., Weske, M.: A foundational approach for managing process variability. In: Mouratidis, H., Rolland, C. (eds.) CAiSE 2011. LNCS, vol. 6741, pp. 267–282. Springer, Heidelberg (2011)
2. Kunze, M., Weidlich, M., Weske, M.: Behavioral similarity – a proper metric. In: Rinderle-Ma, S., Toumani, F., Wolf, K. (eds.) BPM 2011. LNCS, vol. 6896, pp. 166–181. Springer, Heidelberg (2011)
3. Weidlich, M., Polyvyanyy, A., Mendling, J., Weske, M.: Causal behavioural profiles – efficient computation, applications, and evaluation. Fundamenta Informaticae 113(3–4), 399–435 (2011)
4. Polyvyanyy, A., Weidlich, M., Conforti, R., La Rosa, M., ter Hofstede, A.H.M.: The 4C spectrum of fundamental behavioral relations for concurrent systems. In: Ciardo, G., Kindler, E. (eds.) PETRI NETS 2014. LNCS, vol. 8489, pp. 210–232. Springer, Heidelberg (2014)
5. van Glabbeek, R., Goltz, U.: Equivalence notions for concurrent systems and refinement of actions. In: van Glabbeek, R., Goltz, U. (eds.) Mathematical Foundations of Computer Science 1989. LNCS, vol. 379, pp. 237–248. Springer, Heidelberg (1989)
6. van der Aalst, W.M.P.: Verification of workflow nets. In: Azéma, P., Balbo, G. (eds.) ICATPN 1997. LNCS, vol. 1248, pp. 407–426. Springer, Heidelberg (1997)
7. van der Aalst, W.M.P.: Workflow verification: finding control-flow errors using Petri-net-based techniques. In: van der Aalst, W.M.P., Desel, J., Oberweis, A. (eds.) Business Process Management. LNCS, vol. 1806, p. 161. Springer, Heidelberg (2000)
8. Boudol, G.: Flow event structures and flow nets. In: Guessarian, I. (ed.) Semantics of Systems of Concurrent Processes. LNCS, vol. 469, pp. 62–95. Springer, Heidelberg (1990)
9. Engelfriet, J.: Branching processes of Petri nets. ACTA 28(6), 575–591 (1991)

10. van der Aalst, W.M.P., Weijters, T., Maruster, L.: Workflow mining: discovering process models from event logs. IEEE TKDE **16**(9), 1128–1142 (2004)
11. Armas-Cervantes, A., García-Bañuelos, L., Dumas, M.: Event structures as a foundation for process model differencing, part 1: acyclic processes. In: ter Beek, M.H., Lohmann, N. (eds.) WS-FM 2012. LNCS, vol. 7843, pp. 69–86. Springer, Heidelberg (2013)
12. Armas-Cervantes, A., Baldan, P., García-Bañuelos, L.: Reduction of event structures under hp-bisimulation. Technical report. http://arxiv.org/abs/1403.7181
13. Armas-Cervantes, A., Baldan, P., Dumas, M., García-Bañuelos, L.: Behavioral comparison of process models based on canonically reduced event structures. In: Sadiq, S., Soffer, P., Völzer, H. (eds.) BPM 2014. LNCS, vol. 8659, pp. 267–282. Springer, Heidelberg (2014)

Formal Verification of Petri Nets with Names

Marco Montali$^{(\boxtimes)}$ and Andrey Rivkin

Free University of Bozen-Bolzano, Piazza Domenicani 3, 39100 Bolzano, Italy
{montali,rivkin}@inf.unibz.it

Abstract. Petri nets with name creation and management have been recently introduced so as to make Petri nets able to model the dynamics of (distributed) systems equipped with channels, cyphering keys, or computing boundaries. While traditional formal properties such as boundedness, coverability, and reachability, have been thoroughly studied for this class of Petri nets, formal verification against rich temporal properties has not been investigated so far. In this paper, we attack this verification problem. We introduce sophisticated variants of first-order μ-calculus to specify rich properties that simultaneously account for the system dynamics and the names present in its states. We then analyse the (un)decidability boundaries for the verification of such logics, by considering different notions of boundedness. Notably, our decidability results are obtained via a translation to data-centric dynamic systems, a recently devised framework for the formal specification and verification of business processes working over relational database with constraints. In this light, our results contribute to the cross-fertilization between areas that have not been extensively related so far.

1 Introduction

Verifying the correctness of distributed systems, such as interacting web services, requires not only to check whether distributed components interoperate with each other in terms of their control- and message-flow, but also to consider the information they exchange. In the Petri net literature, several variants of colored nets have been thoroughly studied in the last decade so as to enrich classical P/T nets with information that go beyond the control-flow dimension. A notable class of colored Petri nets is constituted by ν-PNs [9,10], which are Petri nets with name creation and management. ν-PNs have been recently introduced so as to make Petri nets able to model the dynamics of (distributed) systems equipped with channels, cyphering keys, or computing boundaries [10]. Interestingly, variants of ν-PNs have been also investigated to express and verify message correlation for interacting web services [5].

At the same time, the field of database theory has produced a flourishing literature on the verification of database-driven dynamic systems and data-aware business processes [4]. In particular, the framework of data-centric dynamic systems (DCDSs for short) has been recently devised as a rich framework for the formal specification and verification of business processes working over full-fledged relational database with constraints [2].

© Springer International Publishing Switzerland 2016
T. Hildebrandt et al. (Eds.): WS-FM 2014/WS-FM 2015, LNCS 9421, pp. 29–47, 2016.
DOI: 10.1007/978-3-319-33612-1_3

While traditional formal properties such as boundedness, coverability, and reachability, have been extensively studied for ν-PNs, formal verification against rich temporal properties has instead not been investigated so far. The aim of this paper is to attack this verification problem, taking advantage from the interesting decidability results obtained for DCDSs [2]. Specifically we introduce two sophisticated variants of first-order μ-calculus to specify rich temporal properties that simultaneously account for the dynamics of ν-PNs and relate the names present in their states. We then characterise the (un)decidability boundaries for the verification of such logics over ν-PNs, by considering different notions of boundedness on the used names, on the amount of repetitions of the same name, and combinations of these two dimensions. Notably, the key decidability results obtained in this paper are obtained via a translation from ν-PNs to DCDSs that can provide the basis for the systematic transfer of (un)decidability and complexity results between variants of colored Petri nets and DCDSs.

2 ν-Petri Nets

ν-Petri nets (ν-PNs for short) are an extension of P/T nets [8] with pure name creation and management [9,10]. In a ν-PN, each token carries a name. Fresh names can be dynamically created, and transitions may impose matching restrictions on token names to fire. We briefly introduce ν-PNs, following the formulation in [10].

In the remainder of the paper, we consider the standard notion of *multiset*. Given a set A, the *set of finite multisets* over A, written $A^{\oplus}$, is the set of mappings of the form $m : A \to \mathbb{N}$. Given a multiset $S \in A^{\oplus}$ and an element $a \in A$, $S(a) \in \mathbb{N}$ denotes the number of times a appears in S. Given $a \in A$ and $n \in \mathbb{N}$, we write $a^n \in S$ if $S(a) = n$. The *support* of S is the set of elements that appear in S at least once: $supp(S) = \{a \in A \mid S(a) > 0\}$. We also consider the usual operations on multisets: given $S_1, S_2 \in A^{\oplus}$, we have: *(i)* $S_1 \subseteq S_2$ (resp., $S_1 \subset S_2$) if, for each $a \in A$, $S_1(a) \leq S_2(a)$ (resp., $S_1(a) < S_2(a)$); *(ii)* $S_1 + S_2 = \{a^n \mid a \in A \text{ and } n = S_1(a) + S_2(a)\}$; *(iii)* if $S_1 \subseteq S_2$, $S_2 - S_1 = \{a^n \mid a \in A \text{ and } n = S_2(a) - S_2(a)\}$.

Name management in ν-PNs is formalized by adding to ordinary tokens also a special form of colored tokens, each one carrying a name taken from a countably, unordered infinite set Id of names. In order to define behaviors that are affected not only by the presence of tokens in certain places, but also by the names they carry, all arcs in the net are labelled with matching variables, taken from a countably infinite set Var. Furthermore, to model the ability of an arc to create fresh names upon firing, a special subset $\Upsilon \subset Var$ of variables is introduced, with the constraint that a variable $\nu \in \Upsilon$ can only match with a fresh name, that is, a name not currently present in the net. To preserve usual P/T net notation in $\nu - PN$s, black, uncolored tokens are considered, by simply assuming that a special name $\bullet \in Id$ is used for them. We correspondingly introduce a special variable $\epsilon \in Var$, which only matches with black tokens. We have now all the ingredients to formally introduce ν-PNs and their execution semantics.

Definition 1. A ν-PN is a tuple $N = \langle P, T, F \rangle$, where: *(i)* P is a finite set of *places*; *(ii)* T is a finite set of *transitions*, disjoint from P; *(iii)* $F : (P \times T) \cup (T \times P) \to Var^{\oplus}$ is a *flow relation*, s.t., for every $t \in T$, we have $\Upsilon \cap pre(t) = \emptyset$ and $post(t) \setminus \Upsilon \subseteq pre(t)$, where $pre(t) = \bigcup_{p \in P} supp(F(p,t))$ and $post(t) = \bigcup_{p \in P} supp(F(t,p))$. ∎

The first condition for the flow relation indicates that new name variables cannot be associated to arcs that go from a place to a transition; in fact, by definition, a variable in Υ cannot match with any name present in the net. The second condition expresses instead that arcs that go from a transition t to a place can be decorated with fresh name variables and/or variables that appear in one of the incoming arcs pointing to t; the former case denotes the ability of t of generating new names upon firing, whereas the latter case models the matching between names of tokens consumed by t with names of tokens produced by t upon firing.

The usual notion of marking in Petri nets is suitably extended for ν-PNs so as to assign a name to each of the tokens present in the net.

Definition 2. Given a ν-PN $N = \langle P, T, F \rangle$, a *marking* m over N is a function $m : P \to Id^{\oplus}$. A *marked* ν-PN $\overline{N}$ is a tuple $\langle P, T, F, m \rangle$, where $N = \langle P, T, F \rangle$ is a ν-PN, and m is a marking over N. ∎

Given a place $p \in P$, $m(p)$ denotes the multiset of names assigned by m to p, and $Id(m)$ denotes the overall set of names present in m: $Id(m) = \bigcup_{p \in P} supp(m(p))$. Furthermore, given a place $p \in P$ and a name $a \in Id$, $m(p)(a)$ denotes the number if times a is assigned by m to p. Let us now discuss how the standard notion of firing in P/T nets is suitably extended to deal with names in ν-PN. Similarly to any class of colored Petri nets, the firing of a transition $t \in T$ is defined w.r.t. a *mode* $\sigma : Var(t) \to Id$, where $Var(t) = pre(t) \cup post(t)$. Intuitively, σ assigns a specific name to each of the variables that annotate the input or output arcs of t. However, to properly fire t, the mode σ must satisfy the different matching conditions expressed by new name variables and by variables that are repeated in the input and output transitions of t.

Definition 3. Consider a ν-PN $N = \langle P, T, F \rangle$, a transition $t \in T$, a marking m over N, and a mode σ for t. We say that t is *enabled in m with mode σ*, written $m[t, \sigma\rangle$, if: *(i)* the mode agrees with the distribution of named tokens in m, i.e., $\sigma(F(p,t)) \subseteq m(p)$ for every $p \in P$; *(ii)* the mode assigns fresh names to the new name variables attached to the output arcs of t, i.e., $\sigma(\nu) \notin Id(M)$ for every $\nu \in \Upsilon \cap Var(t)$.

An enabled transition can fire. In particular, given two markings m and m' over N, a transition $t \in T$, and a mode σ for t, we say that t *fires with mode σ in m producing m'*, written $m[t, \sigma\rangle m'$ if: *(i)* t is enabled in m with mode σ; *(ii)* m' is such that for every $p \in P$, we have $m'(p) = (m(p) - \sigma(F(p,t))) + \sigma(F(t,p))$. ∎

Execution Semantics. Starting from an initial marking, we define the execution semantics of a ν-PN N in terms of a possibly infinite-state transition system, whose states are labeled by reachable markings, and where each transition corresponds to the firing of a transition in N. Notice that the definition is different from the definition of reachability graph given in [10], in which a sort of *name abstraction* procedure (called α-equivalence in [10]) is applied while computing the reachable markings. As we will see in Sect. 3, applying α-equivalence when constructing the execution semantics of a ν-PN leads to a transition system that, in general, does not faithfully reproduce the behaviors of the net when it comes to verification of temporal properties that relate names over time.

Formally, the execution semantics of a marked ν-PN $\overline{N} = \langle P, T, F, m_0 \rangle$ is defined in terms of a transition system $\Gamma_{\overline{N}} = \langle M, m_0, \rightarrow \rangle$, where:

- M is a (possibly infinite) set of markings over N.
- $\rightarrow \subseteq M \times T \times M$ is a T-labelled transition relation between pairs of markings.
- M and $\rightarrow$ are defined by simultaneous induction as the smallest sets satisfying the following conditions: *(i)* $m_0 \in M$; *(ii)* if $m \in M$, then for every transition $t \in T$, mode σ and marking m' over N s.t. $m[t, \sigma \rangle m'$, we have $m' \in M$ and $m \xrightarrow{t} m'$.

A *run* τ over $\Gamma_{\overline{N}}$ is a possibly infinite sequence of markings $m_0, m_1, \cdots$ where, for every m_i, m_{i+1} in τ, there exists $t \in T$ s.t. $m_i \xrightarrow{t} m_{i+1}$.

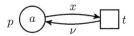

Fig. 1. A ν-PN that is width- and depth-bounded but not run-bounded.

Forms of Boundedness. Given a marked ν-PN $\overline{N}, \Gamma_{\overline{N}}$ could be infinite-state for different reasons: *(i)* *width-unboundedness* [10], i.e., accumulation of an unbounded number of different names in a state; *(ii)* *depth-unboundedness* [10], i.e., accumulation of an unbounded amount of tokens with the same name; *(iii)* *run-unboundedness*, i.e., presence of unboundedly many names along a run of $\Gamma_{\overline{N}}$; *(iv)* a combination of these conditions. We formally introduce the three corresponding notions of boundedness, and then relate them with the previous literature on ν-PNs.

Definition 4. A marked ν-PN $\overline{N} = \langle P, T, F, m_0 \rangle$ with transition system $\Gamma_{\overline{N}} = \langle M, m_0, \rightarrow \rangle$ is:

- *width-bounded* if there is $n \in \mathbb{N}$ s.t., for each $m \in M$, we have $|Id(m)| \leq n$;
- *depth-bounded* if there is $n \in \mathbb{N}$ s.t., for each $m \in M$, place $p \in P$, and name $a \in Id$, we have $m(p)(a) \leq n$;
- *run-bounded* if there is $n \in \mathbb{N}$ s.t., for every (possibly infinite) run τ over $\Gamma_{\overline{N}}$, we have $|\bigcup_{m \text{ in } \tau} Id(m)| \leq n$. ∎

Lemma 1. *If marked ν-PN is run-bounded, then it is width-bounded and depth-bounded.*

Proof. Immediate from Definition 4. $\square$

The converse implication does not hold: as witnessed by the following example, there are ν-PN that are width-bounded and depth-bounded, but not run-bounded. In this light, it is important to observe that in the original formulation of ν-PN reachability graph [10], run-unboundedness does not appear as a source of unboundedness, due to α-equivalence. However, what the authors call boundedness in [10] does not imply that $\Gamma_{\overline{N}}$ is finite-state, because it could still be run-unbounded.

Example 1. Consider the marked ν-PN in Fig. 1. The net is width- and depth-bounded: each marking in its transition system contains exactly one token. However, it is not run-bounded: there is an infinite run in which no name is repeated twice.   ∎

With the refined execution semantics we consider here, what is called boundedness in [10] corresponds in fact to the following notion of boundedness, which intuitively states that the amount of tokens present in each marking (and thus the corresponding set of names) is bounded.

Definition 5. A marked ν-PN $\overline{N} = \langle P, T, F, m_0 \rangle$ with transition system $\Gamma_{\overline{N}} = \langle M, m_0, \rightarrow \rangle$ is *state-bounded* if there is $n \in \mathbb{N}$ s.t., for each $m \in M$, we have $\sum_{p \in P, a \in Id} m(p)(a) \leq n$;   ∎

The following results reconstruct those in [10] by considering the notion of state boundedness as defined here.

Lemma 2. *A marked ν-PN is state-bounded if and only if it is width-bounded and depth-bounded.*

Proof. Immediate from Definitions 4 and 5. $\square$

Lemma 3. *A marked ν-PN is state-bounded if and only if its reachability graph, as defined in [10], is bounded.*

Proof. Immediate from Lemma 2 and Proposition 6 in [10]. $\square$

Theorem 6. *Checking whether a marked ν-PN is state-bounded is decidable.*

Proof. Immediate from Lemma 3 and Proposition 3 in [10]. $\square$

3   Verification of ν-PNs

We now consider formal verification of ν-PNs. To specify temporal properties of interest, the logic of choice must provide support for: *(i)* temporal modalities to predicate over the dynamics of the net; *(ii)* first-order (FO) local queries to predicate over the local states of the system, i.e., over markings; *(iii)* FO quantification across states, so as to allow one to relate names and places in different moments of the system evolution.

To support such fundamental requirements, we resort to a Petri net-variant of the $\mu\mathcal{L}_A$ logic defined in [2]. We call this logic $\mu\mathcal{L}_A^N$. Intuitively, $\mu\mathcal{L}_A^N$ allows for complex temporal formulae based on the μ-calculus, virtually the most expressive temporal logic used in verification, and for local queries inspecting the number of names present in the different places.

Definition 7. Given a marked ν-PN $\overline{N} = \langle P, T, F, m_0 \rangle$, a $\mu\mathcal{L}_A^N$ formula Φ over $\overline{N}$ is defined as:

$$\Phi ::= true \mid Z \mid [\#p \le c] \mid [\#p(x) \le c] \mid x = y \mid \Phi_1 \wedge \Phi_2 \mid \neg\Psi \mid \exists x.\mathrm{LIVE}(x) \wedge \Psi \mid \langle-\rangle\Psi \mid \mu Z.\Psi$$

where $p \in P$, $c \in \mathbb{N}$, x is either a variable or a constant name from $Id(m_0) \cup \{\bullet\}$, and Z is a second order predicate variable of arity 0. We make use of the following abbreviations: $[\#p \circledast c]$ and $[\#p(x) \circledast c]$, where $\circledast \in \{>, \ge, =, <\}$; $\forall x.\mathrm{LIVE}(x) \to \Psi = \neg(\exists x.\mathrm{LIVE}(x) \wedge \neg\Psi)$; $\Phi_2 \vee \Phi_2 = \neg(\neg\Phi_1 \wedge \neg\Phi_2)$; $[-]\Psi = \neg\langle-\rangle\neg\Psi$; $\nu Z.\Psi = \neg\mu.\neg\Psi\,[Z/\neg Z]$. ∎

The intuitive meaning of such formulae is: *(i)* $[\#p \le c]$ is true if the overall amount of tokens in p does not exceed c; *(ii)* $[\#p(x) \le c]$ is true if the overall amount of tokens in p that match name x does not exceed c; *(iii)* $\mathrm{LIVE}(x)$ is true if name x is present in the current marking; *(iv)* $\langle-\rangle\Psi$ is true if there exists a successor marking in which Ψ holds; *(v)* $[-]\Psi$ is true if in all successor markings, Ψ holds; *(vi)* $\mu Z.\Psi$ and $\nu Z.\Psi$ respectively represent the least and greatest fixpoint operator. As usual in the μ-calculus, for fixpoints we require the *syntactic monotonicity* of Ψ w.r.t. Z, that is, every occurrence of the variable Z in Ψ must be within the scope of an even number of negation signs. This guarantees that the least and greatest fixpoints always exist.

Formally, a $\mu\mathcal{L}_A^N$ formula Φ over $\overline{N} = \langle P, T, F, m_0 \rangle$ is interpreted over the transition system $\Gamma_{\overline{N}} = \langle \Sigma, m_0, \to \rangle$. Since Φ can contain both individual and predicate free variables, we introduce an individual variable valuation v mapping individual variables x to names in Id, and a predicate variable valuation V mapping predicate variables Z to subsets of Σ. The semantics of $\mu\mathcal{L}_A^N$ formulae is then defined through an *extension function* $|| \cdot ||_{v,V}^{\Gamma_{\overline{N}}}$ that maps formulae to subsets of Σ. The extension function is inductively defined as shown in Fig. 2.

When Φ is a closed formula, its valuation does not depend neither on V nor on v. Hence, we denote the extension of Φ by simply using $||\Phi||^{\Gamma_{\overline{N}}}$. Given a closed $\mu\mathcal{L}_A^N$ property Φ and a marked ν-PN $\overline{N} = \langle P, T, F, m_0 \rangle$, we say that $\overline{N}$ *verifies* Φ, written $\overline{N} \models \Phi$, if $m_0 \in ||\Phi||^{\Gamma_{\overline{N}}}$.

$$||\top||_{\mathcal{V},v}^{\Gamma_N} = \Sigma$$
$$||Z||_{\mathcal{V},v}^{\Gamma_N} = \mathcal{V}(Z)$$
$$||[\#p \le c]||_{\mathcal{V},v}^{\Gamma_N} = \{m \in \Sigma \mid m(p) \le c\}$$
$$||[\#p(x) \le c]||_{\mathcal{V},v}^{\Gamma_N} = \{m \in \Sigma \mid m(p)(xv) \le c\}$$
$$||\text{LIVE}(x)||_{\mathcal{V},v}^{\Gamma_N} = \{m \in \Sigma \mid x/d \in v \text{ implies } d \in Id(m)\}$$
$$||x = y||_{\mathcal{V},v}^{\Gamma_N} = \{m \in \Sigma \mid x/d \in v \text{ if and only if } y/d \in v\}$$
$$||\Phi_1 \wedge \Phi_2||_{\mathcal{V},v}^{\Gamma_N} = ||\Phi_1||_{\mathcal{V},v}^{\Gamma_N} \cap ||\Phi_2||_{\mathcal{V},v}^{\Gamma_N}$$
$$||\neg F||_{\mathcal{V},v}^{\Gamma_N} = X \setminus ||F||_{\mathcal{V},v}^{\Gamma_N}$$
$$||\exists x.\Phi||_{\mathcal{V},v}^{\Gamma_N} = \{m \in \Sigma \mid \exists a \in Id \text{ s.t. } m \in ||\Phi||_{\mathcal{V},v[x/a]}^{\Gamma_N}\}$$
$$||\langle - \rangle \Phi||_{\mathcal{V},v}^{\Gamma_N} = \{m \in \Sigma \mid \exists m' \in \Sigma \text{ s.t. } m \to m' \text{ and } m' \in ||\Phi||_{\mathcal{V},v}^{\Gamma_N}\}$$
$$||\mu Z.\Phi||_{\mathcal{V},v}^{\Gamma_N} = \bigcap \{Y \subseteq \Sigma \mid ||\Phi||_{\mathcal{V}[Z/Y],v}^{\Gamma_N} \subseteq Y\}$$

Fig. 2. Semantics of $\mu\mathcal{L}_A^N$

Example 2. Formula $\Phi_d = \nu Z.(\forall x.[\#p(x) = 1] \to \nu Y.[\#p(x) = 0] \wedge \langle - \rangle Y) \wedge [-] Z$ holds in the ν-PN of Fig. 1. Φ_d expresses that it is always the case that, whenever place p contains exactly one token named x, then there exists an ongoing run in which x never reappears. Notice that, Φ_d is a $\mu\mathcal{L}_A^N$ formula, because $[\#p(x) = 1]$ implies $\text{LIVE}(x)$. ∎

We observe that there cannot be any finite-state representation of the transition system for the ν-PN in Fig. 1 in which the $\mu\mathcal{L}_A^N$ property in Example 2 holds. In fact, the net always has a successor, and if the transition system is finite-state, infinite runs should sooner or later go back visiting a marking that was visited before, violating the fact that there must exist a run in which names never reappear. Since the ν-PN of Fig. 1 is bounded in the sense of [10], its reachability graph is finite-state, hence it does not properly represent the execution semantics of the ν-PN when it comes to verification of $\mu\mathcal{L}_A^N$ properties. The intuitive reason is that $\mu\mathcal{L}_A^N$ properties can "store" visited names inside a FO quantifier, and check the presence or absence of such names in markings that are arbitrarily far away from the state in which the quantifier was bound. Consequently, the name renaming allowed by α-equivalence in [10] does not preserve $\mu\mathcal{L}_A^N$ properties.

4 Undecidability Results

We prove here two key undecidability results related to the verification of $\mu\mathcal{L}_A^N$ properties over ν-PNs. This motivates the fine-grained study presented in Sect. 5.

Theorem 8. *Verification of $\mu\mathcal{L}_A^N$ properties over ν-PNs is undecidable even when formulae do not make use of FO quantification, and only employ a single, constant name.*

Proof. Consider marked ν-PNs that only use the special name $\bullet$ and the special variable ϵ. This class of ν-PNs coincides with classical P/T nets. Now consider $\mu\mathcal{L}_A^N$ properties that do not make use of FO quantification, and whose local predicates only employ the special name $\bullet$. This class of formulae resembles the propositional μ-calculus whose verification over P/T nets is shown to be undecidable in [7].   □

One could wonder what happens when the considered ν-PN obeys to some boundedness criterion among those discussed in Sect. 2. The following negative result, however, holds for the important class of state-bounded ν-PNs.

Theorem 9. *Verification of $\mu\mathcal{L}_A^N$ properties over state-bounded ν-PNs is undecidable.*

Proof. The proof resembles the proof of Theorem 5.1 in [1], and is based on a reduction from satisfiability of LTL with freeze quantifier over infinite data words, shown to be undecidable in [6], to verification of (linear-time) $\mu\mathcal{L}_A^N$ properties over state-bounded ν-PNs. An infinite data word is an infinite sequence of pairs (σ_i, d_i), where σ_i is a label taken from a finite set $\mathcal{L}$, and d_i is a datum taken from a countably infinite set $\mathcal{D}$ (which, without loss of generality, we consider here to coincide with Id)[1].

The idea is to construct a "universal" ν-PN whose transition system runs correspond to all possible data words, and then reduce satisfiability to verification over such transition system. Given a finite set $\mathcal{L} = \{\sigma_1, \dots, \sigma_n\}$, we construct the marked ν-PN $\overline{U}^{\mathcal{L}} = \langle P, T, F, m_0 \rangle$ as follows: *(i)* $P = \{p_0, p_{\sigma_1}, \dots, p_{\sigma_n}\}$, i.e., P contains a starting place p_0 and one dedicated place for each $\sigma_i \in \mathcal{L}$; *(ii)* $T = \{t_{0i} \mid i \in \{1, \dots, n\}\} \cup \{t_{ij}^=, t_{ij}^{\neq} \mid i, j \in \{1, \dots, n\}\}$; *(iii)* m_0 assigns a single, black token $\bullet$ to p_0; *(iv)* F is such that:

- for each transition t_{0i}, $F(p_0, t_{0i}) = \emptyset$ and $F(t_{0i}, p_{\sigma_i}) = \{\nu\}$; this models an initial pure nondeterministic choice from p_0, in which a fresh name is put in one of p_{σ_i}.
- for each transition $t_{ij}^=$, $F(p_{\sigma_i}, t_{ij}^=) = F(t_{ij}^=, (p_{\sigma_j})) = \{x\}$; this models the situation where a token currently present in p_{σ_i} is moved into p_{σ_j}, maintaining its name.
- for each transition $t_{ij}^{\neq}$, $F(p_{\sigma_i}, t_{ij}^{\neq}) = \emptyset$ and $F(t_{ij}^{\neq}, (p_{\sigma_j})) = \{\nu\}$; this models the situation where a token present in p_{σ_i} is moved into p_{σ_j}, by changing its name.

Figure 4 in the appendix shows the marked ν-PN obtained by following this procedure when $\mathcal{L} = \{\sigma_1, \sigma_2\}$. We observe that $\overline{U}^{\mathcal{L}}$ is state-bounded: every marking in $\Gamma_{\overline{U}^{\mathcal{L}}}$ assigns a single token to one of the places, leaving all other places empty.

Now consider an LTL formula φ with freeze quantifier. We first apply the following transformation rules to obtain a $\mu\mathcal{L}_A^N$ formula φ_N:

---

[1] For a detailed description of LTL with freeze quantifier, the interested reader can refer to [6].

- Temporal modalities in φ are expressed in their corresponding μ-calculus form (recall that μ-calculus subsumes both CTL and LTL).
- Boolean connectives are maintained unaltered.
- Each freeze-quantifier $\downarrow_n$ in φ corresponds to $\exists x_n.\text{LIVE}(x_n)$ in φ_N.
- Each occurrence of $\uparrow_n$ in φ corresponds to $\text{LIVE}(x_n)$ in φ_N.
- Each proposition $\sigma_i \in \mathcal{L}$ appearing in φ becomes $[\#p_{\sigma_i} = 1]$ in φ_N.

For example, property $\downarrow_1 \mathbf{X}(\mathbf{F}(\sigma_1 \rightarrow \uparrow_1))$ becomes

$$\exists x_1.\text{LIVE}(x_1) \wedge \mu Z.([\#p_{\sigma_1} = 1] \rightarrow \text{LIVE}(x_1)) \vee \ominus Z$$

We now take φ_N and we set $\Phi_N = \langle - \rangle \neg \varphi_N$. Intuitively, $\langle - \rangle$ is applied to move one step away from the initial marking, which does not correspond to a proper data word element. It is now easy to see that an LTL formula φ with freeze quantifier is *unsatisfiable* over infinite data words and labels $\mathcal{L}$ if and only if $\Gamma_{\overline{U}^{\mathcal{L}}} \models \Phi_N.\square$

5 Decidability of Verification

In this section, we provide the two key decidability results of this paper. We start overviewing the salient features of DCDSs, and proposing a translation mechanism from ν-PNs to DCDSs, that is instrumental towards such decidability results.

5.1 Data-Centric Dynamic Systems

We recall the main aspects of Data-Centric Dynamic Systems (DCDSs) [2]. A DCDS is a pair $\mathcal{S} = \langle \mathcal{D}, \mathcal{P} \rangle$ where $\mathcal{D}$ is a *data layer* and $\mathcal{P}$ is a *process layer*. Both layers are interacting as follows: the data layer stores all the data of interest, while the process layer modifies and evolves such data.

Definition 10. A *data layer* is a tuple $\mathcal{D} = \langle \mathcal{C}, \mathcal{R}, \mathcal{E}, \mathcal{I}_0 \rangle$ where:

- $\mathcal{C}$ is a countably infinite set of constants/values;
- $\mathcal{R} = \{R_1, \ldots, R_n\}$ is a database schema, constituted by a finite set of relation schemas;
- $\mathcal{E}$ is a finite set $\{\mathcal{E}_1, \ldots, \mathcal{E}_m\}$ of equality constraints. Each $\mathcal{E}_i$ has the form $Q_i \rightarrow \bigwedge_{j=1,\ldots,k} z_{ij} = y_{ij}{}^2$, where Q_i is a domain independent FOL query over $\mathcal{R}$ using constants from $\text{ADOM}(\mathcal{I}_0)^3$ whose free variables are $\vec{x}$, and z_{ij} and y_{ij} are either variables in $\vec{x}$ or constants in $\text{ADOM}(\mathcal{I}_0)^4$;

---

[2] Instead of $z_{ij} = y_{ij}$ we can also use $z_{ij} \neq y_{ij}$ or $\bot$ (forming a full denial constraint).

[3] Given a database instance $\mathcal{I}$, its active domain $\text{ADOM}(\mathcal{I})$ is the subset of $\mathcal{C}$ such that $u \in \text{ADOM}(\mathcal{I})$ if and only if u occurs in $(\mathcal{I})$.

[4] For convenience, and without loss of generality, we assume that all constants used inside formulas appear in $\mathcal{I}_0$.

- $\mathcal{I}_0$ is a database instance that represents the initial state of the data layer, which conforms to the schema $\mathcal{R}$ and satisfies the constraints $\mathcal{E}$: namely, for each constraint $Q_i \to \bigwedge_{j=1,\ldots,k} z_{ij} = y_{ij}$ and for each tuple (i.e., substitution for the free variables) $\theta \in ans(Q_i, \mathcal{I}_0)$, it holds that $z_{ij}\theta = y_{ij}\theta$. ∎

The process layer constitutes the progression mechanism for the DCDS. It is assumed that at every time the current instance of the data layer can be both arbitrarily queried and updated (through action executions), possibly involving external service calls to get new values from the environment.

Definition 11. A *process layer* $\mathcal{P}$ over a data layer $\mathcal{D} = \langle \mathcal{C}, \mathcal{R}, \mathcal{E}, \mathcal{I}_0 \rangle$ is a tuple $\mathcal{P} = \langle \mathcal{F}, \mathcal{A}, \rho \rangle$. $\mathcal{F}$ is a finite set of *functions*, each representing the interface to an external service. Such services can be called, and as a result the function is activated and the answer is produced. How the result is actually computed is unknown to the DCDS since the services are indeed external.

$\mathcal{A}$ is a finite set of *actions*, whose execution updates the data layer, and may involve external service calls. Formally, an *action* $\alpha \in \mathcal{A}$ is an expression $\alpha(p_1, \ldots, p_n) : \{e_1, \ldots, e_m\}$ where:

- $\alpha(p_1, \ldots, p_n)$ is the action *signature*, constituted by a name α and a sequence $p_1, \ldots, p_n$ of *parameters*, to be substituted with values when the action is invoked;
- $\{e_1, \ldots, e_m\}$, also denoted as **EFFECT**(α), is a set of *specifications of effects*, which are assumed to take place simultaneously. Each e_i has the form $q_i^+ \wedge Q_i^- \rightsquigarrow E_i$. The formula $q_i^+ \wedge Q_i^-$ is a query over $\mathcal{R}$ whose terms are variables, action parameters, and constants from $\mathtt{ADOM}(\mathcal{I}_0)$, where q_i^+ is a union of conjunctive queries, and Q_i^- is an arbitrary FOL formula whose free variables are among those of q_i^+. Intuitively, q_i^+ selects the tuples to instantiate the effect, and Q_i^- filters away some of them. E_i is the *effect*, i.e., a set of facts for $\mathcal{R}$, which includes as terms the following: terms in $\mathtt{ADOM}(\mathcal{I}_0)$, free variables of q_i^+ and Q_i^- (including action parameters), and Skolem terms formed by applying a function $f \in \mathcal{F}$ to one of the previous kinds of terms. Such Skolem terms involving functions represent external (nondeterministic) service calls and are interpreted as the returned value chosen by an external user/environment when executing the action.

Finally, ρ is a finite set of *condition-action rules* (of the form $Q \to \alpha$, where $\alpha \in \mathcal{A}$ and Q is a FOL query[5] over $\mathcal{R}$) that form the specification of the overall *process*, which tells at any moment which actions can be executed. ∎

Execution Semantics. The execution semantics of a DCDS $\mathcal{S}$ is defined in terms of a possibly infinite transition system $\Lambda_\mathcal{S}$ whose states are labeled by databases. Such a transition system represents all possible computations that the process layer can do on the data layer. Formally, $\Lambda_\mathcal{S} = \langle \Delta, \mathcal{R}, \Sigma, s_0, db, \Rightarrow \rangle$,

---

[5] Its free variables are exactly the parameters of α, and other terms can be quantified variables or constants in $\mathtt{ADOM}(\mathcal{I}_0)$.

where: *(i)* Δ is a countably infinite set of values; *(ii)* Σ is a set of states; *(iii)* $s_0 \in \Sigma$ is the initial state; *(iv)* db is a function such that for each state $s \in \Sigma$ returns a database $D \subseteq \Delta$ conforming to $\mathcal{R}$; *(v)* $\Rightarrow \subseteq \Sigma \times \Sigma$ is a transition relation over states.

Given a DCDS $\mathcal{S} = \langle \mathcal{D}, \mathcal{P} \rangle$ with $\mathcal{D} = \langle \mathcal{C}, \mathcal{R}, \mathcal{E}, \mathcal{I}_0 \rangle$ and $\mathcal{P} = \langle \mathcal{F}, \mathcal{A}, \rho \rangle$ one can construct $\Lambda_{\mathcal{S}}$ following the next steps. Starting from $\mathcal{I}_0$, condition-action rules in ρ are evaluated and the set of all possible executable actions with corresponding ground parameter assignments is defined. Then, nondeterministically, one such action with parameter assignments $\alpha \vec{p}$ (α is partially grounded with the parameter assignment $\vec{p}$) is selected and executed over $\mathcal{I}_0$ by calculating all the answers of action's left-hand side and grounding the right-hand side accordingly. In case that the right-hand side is containing service calls, the latter are issued nondeterministically returning values from $\mathcal{C}$. Then, every service call is substituted with its actual result (i.e., the values yielded on the previous step). The overall set of ground facts obtained is constituting the next database instance. Hence, the transition system construction is determined as process of all possible successors extraction, each of which is obtained by selecting one of the executable actions with corresponding parameters, and one result perch each service call involved. The construction proceeds recursively over the newly generated states. For a formal description of the execution semantics, one can check [2].

5.2   From ν-PNs to DCDSs

In this section we discuss how a ν-PN $\overline{N}$ can be encoded into a DCDS $\tau(\overline{N}) = \langle \mathcal{D}_N, \mathcal{P}_N \rangle$ that faithfully reproduces the execution semantics of $\overline{N}$. We discuss the translation using the marked ν-PN $\overline{N}$ shown in Fig. 3. The example is simple but illustrates all the main difficulties of the translation. The general translation is provided in the appendix. Specifically, there are two fundamental critical issue in the translation. First, ν-PNs have a bag semantics, whereas DCDSs rely on set semantics. Hence, the only way for faithfully reconstructing the execution semantics of $\overline{N}$ in terms of a DCDS, is to introduce implicit token identifiers that are in the DCDS to distinguish two distinct tokens that belong to the same place and carry the same name. The same strategy must be consistently maintained when, upon firing, two distinct tokens with the same name must be inserted into the same place.

Second, to inject new data (corresponding, in our case, to token names and token identifiers) in the system, DCDSs employ the notion of service call. However, an issued service call may not necessarily return a fresh value, but could (nondeterministically) return a value that is currently used in the system. To properly reconstruct the fresh name generation of ν-PNs, temporary relations and specific database constraints must be employed.

In the remainder of the section, we use the following typographical conventions: v for variables, v for constants.

Data Layer. The data layer is $\mathcal{D}_N = \langle \mathcal{C}_N, \mathcal{R}_N, \mathcal{E}_N, \mathcal{I}_0^N \rangle$. The data domain $\mathcal{C}_N$ contains the overall set Id of names, together with additional constants used to denote the different elements of $\overline{N}$: $Id \cup T \cup P \cup Var \subseteq \mathcal{C}_N$.

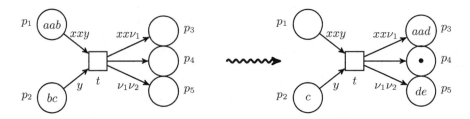

Fig. 3. A marked ν-PN, where t is fired with mode σ: $\sigma(x) = a$, $\sigma(y) = b$, $\sigma(\nu_1) = d$, $\sigma(\nu_2) = e$, where d and e are fresh names

The relation schema is $\mathcal{R}_N = \{p_i/2 \mid i \in \{1,\ldots,5\}\} \cup NewID/5 \cup FL/0$. Relation $p_i(\mathsf{id}, \mathsf{n})$ represents that p_i currently contains a token with identifier id and name n;

$NewID(\mathsf{t}, \mathsf{p}, \mathsf{v}, \mathsf{d}, \mathsf{id})$ is a temporary relation used to store that transition t is has produced a token with identifier id and name d, that this token is matched with variable v, and that the destination of this token in the next step is place p. Relation FL is a flag distinguishing between the two modes in which the DCDS $\tau(\overline{N})$ operates to simulate the firing of a transition t: *(i)* the first consisting in the consumption of tokens from the input places of t, and the contemporary generation of token identifiers and names, to be stored in the temporary relations $NewID$ of t; *(ii)* the second consisting in the forwarding of tokens from such temporary relations to the output places of t, provided that the previous step has completed correctly, i.e., without violating any constraint in $\mathcal{E}_N$.

The relation schema $\mathcal{C}_N$ is subject to constraints $\mathcal{E}_N = \{\mathcal{E}_1, \mathcal{E}_2, \mathcal{E}_3, \mathcal{E}_4\}$. Constraint $\mathcal{E}_1$ and $\mathcal{E}_2$ ensures that identifiers present in the temporary relation $NewID$ are unique, i.e., distinct from all identifiers stored in the place relations (cf. $\mathcal{E}_1$), and from those stored in other tuples of $NewID$ (cf. $\mathcal{E}_2$):

$$\mathcal{E}_1 = \forall id. NewID(\_, \_, \_, id, \_) \wedge \bigvee_{i \in \{1,\ldots,5\}} p_i(id, \_) \rightarrow \bot$$
$$\mathcal{E}_2 = \forall id, t, p, v, n, t', p', v', n'. NewID(t, p, v, id, n) \wedge NewID(t', p', v', id, n')$$
$$\rightarrow t = t' \wedge p = p' \wedge v = v' \wedge n = n'$$

$\mathcal{E}_3$ and $\mathcal{E}_4$ mirror $\mathcal{E}_1$ and $\mathcal{E}_2$ by considering names stored in $NewID$ tuples that refer to new name variables in Υ, i.e., in our case ν_1 and ν_2 (which are constants in the DCDS):

$$\mathcal{E}_3 = \forall n. \bigvee_{c \in \{\nu_1, \nu_2\}} NewID(\_, \_, c, \_, n) \wedge \bigvee_{i \in \{1,\ldots,5\}} p_i(\_, n) \rightarrow \bot$$
$$\mathcal{E}_4 = \forall n_1, n_2. NewID(\_, \_, \nu_1, \_, n_1) \wedge NewID(\_, \_, \nu_2, \_, n_2) \rightarrow n_1 \neq n_2$$

Finally, $\mathcal{I}_0^N$ encodes m_0 by maintaining the name distribution of tokens, as well as their cardinality. The latter requirement is enforced by picking pairwise distinct identifiers from $\mathcal{C}_N$. It is worth noting that identifiers and names are always treated separately by the DCDS, and therefore also identifiers can be picked from the set Id of names. Consequently, a suitable choice for $\mathcal{I}_0^N$ is $\{p_1(a, a), p_1(b, a), p_1(c, a), p_2(d, b), p_2(e, b)\}$.

Process Layer. The process layer of $\tau(\overline{N})$ is defined as $\mathcal{P}_N = \langle \mathcal{F}_N, \mathcal{A}_N, \rho_N \rangle$. $\mathcal{F}_N$ contains service calls that are used to inject token identifiers and names into the system. In particular, each time a transition t fires, tokens are generated according to the arcs that have t as input. The generation of a new identifier depends on: *(i)* the considered arc, which is in turn determined by the input transition and output place; *(ii)* the variable name; *(iii)* the occurrence of the variable name. For this reason, we introduce a service call $genID/4$, where $genID(\mathsf{t}, \mathsf{p}, \mathsf{v}, \mathsf{i})$ represents the new id generation for the i-th occurrence of variable v on the arc that connects t to p. Name generation depends instead only on the considered new name variable in Υ. Therefore, we introduce a service call $genName/1$, where $genFresh(\nu)$ represents the generation of a name for ν.

The process and action components ρ_N and $\mathcal{A}_N$ contain an action gen_t for each transition t of $\overline{N}$, and an additional action $transf$. Intuitively, the firing of t is simulated in the corresponding DCDS by the serial execution of gen_t and $transf$. The first action is executable only when t is enabled, and its execution leads to consume the named tokens in the input places of t (in accordance with the variables attached to the arcs), and to generate (and store in the temporary relation $NewID$) the named tokens produced by t (again in accordance with the variables attached to the arcs). Action $transf$ then takes care of transferring such newly generated tokens into the corresponding output places.

Formally, in our example we have a single transition, hence $\mathcal{A}_N = \{gen_t\}$. The process ρ_N expresses the executability of gen_t as follows:

$$p_1(id_1, x) \wedge p_1(id_2, x) \wedge p_1(id_3, y) \wedge p_2(id_4, y) \wedge \bigwedge_{i,j \in \{1,4\}, i \neq j} id_i \neq id_j \wedge \neg FL$$
$$\mapsto gen_t(id_1 id_2, id_3, id_4, x, y)$$

Observe also the consistent usage of variables x and y w.r.t. the ν-PN in Fig. 3, and the fact that gen_t takes in input the pairs identifiers of selected tokens, as well as the matched names. This allows us to make gen_t able to consume the selected tokens (without touching the unselected ones), and at the same time able to transfer the matched names to the output. Specifically, gen_t works as follows (notice the difference between constant x and parameter x):
$gen_t(id_1 id_2, id_3, id_4, x, y) =$

$$\{p_1(id, n) \wedge \bigwedge_{i \in \{1,2,3\}} id \neq id_i \rightsquigarrow \{p_1(id, n)\}$$
$$p_2(id, n) \wedge id \neq id_4 \rightsquigarrow \{p_2(id, n)\}$$
$$p_i(id, n) \rightsquigarrow \{p_i(id, n)\} \qquad \text{for } i \in \{3, 4, 5\}$$
$$true \rightsquigarrow \{NewID(\mathsf{t}, \mathsf{p_3}, \mathsf{x}, genID(\mathsf{t}, \mathsf{p_3}, \mathsf{x}, 1), x),$$
$$NewID(\mathsf{t}, \mathsf{p_3}, \mathsf{x}, genID(\mathsf{t}, \mathsf{p_3}, \mathsf{x}, 2), x)\}$$
$$NewID(\mathsf{t}, \mathsf{p_3}, \nu_1, genID(\mathsf{t}, \mathsf{p_3}, \nu_1, 1), genName(\nu_1))\}$$
$$true \rightsquigarrow \{NewID(\mathsf{t}, \mathsf{p_4}, \epsilon, genID(\mathsf{t}, \mathsf{p_3}, \epsilon, 1), \bullet)\}$$
$$true \rightsquigarrow \{NewID(\mathsf{t}, \mathsf{p_5}, \nu_1, genID(\mathsf{t}, \mathsf{p_5}, \nu_1, 1), genName(\nu_1)),$$
$$NewID(\mathsf{t}, \mathsf{p_5}, \nu_1, genID(\mathsf{t}, \mathsf{p_5}, \nu_2, 1), genName(\nu_2))\}$$
$$true \rightsquigarrow FL \}$$

The first block of effects is dedicated to maintain those tokens that are not consumed by the transition t. For places that are input of t, this requires to properly filter out those tokens that were selected in the precondition of gen_t (which has non-empty answers only if t is enabled). The second block of effects is instead focused on the generation of one distinct token for each of the variables that decorate the output arcs of t, with the corresponding restrictions over matching names. The last effect switches the flag from false to true, inhibiting the possibility of reapplying actions of the type gen_t; this is imposed in the precondition of gen_t, which contains $\neg FL$ among its conjuncts.

Observe that, once gen_t is applied, the newly obtained database must conform to all constraints in $\mathcal{E}$. Consequently, only states that correctly assign new identifiers and fresh names in the case of Υ variables are kept as valid successors. This explains why this two-step approach is needed when formalizing the firing of t.

Let us now turn to the action $transf$. It is independent of the specific transition, because what it only needs to do is transfer the tokens generated in a generation step from the temporary relations $NewID$ to the proper output places. The only precondition of $transf$ is then just to check whether FL is true (which attests that a generation action has been applied in the previous computation step). I.e., ρ_N contains the following condition-action rule: $FL \mapsto transf()$. In the case illustrated by Fig. 3, we then have:

$$transf() = \{ \quad\quad p_i(id, n) \rightsquigarrow \{p_i(id, n)\} \quad\quad \text{for } i \in \{1, \ldots, 5\}$$
$$NewId(\_, \mathsf{p}_j, \_, id, n) \rightsquigarrow \{p_j(id, n)\} \quad\quad \text{for } j \in \{1, \ldots, 5\} \}$$

Notice that since FL is not explicitly copied by $transf$, it is implicitly toggled, making $transf$ not applicable anymore (it will be again applicable after a generation step).

From $\mu\mathcal{L}_A^N$ to $\mu\mathcal{L}_A$. We now continue the correspondence between verification problems in ν-PNs and verification problems in DCDSs, by considering the temporal logics used to specify properties. As already mentioned in Sect. 3, $\mu\mathcal{L}_A^N$ has been inspired by the $\mu\mathcal{L}_A$ logic for DCDSs. We now establish a precise translation ξ that takes a $\mu\mathcal{L}_A^N$ property Φ and produces a corresponding $\mu\mathcal{L}_A$ property $\xi(\Phi)$:

$$\xi(\Phi) = \begin{cases} \Phi & \text{if } \Phi \in \{true, x = y, Z\} \\ \forall i_1, \ldots, i_c, i_{c+1}. \bigwedge\limits_{j \in \{1,..,c+1\}} p(i_j, \_) \rightarrow \bigvee\limits_{k,l \in \{1,..,c+1\}, k<l} i_k = i_l & \text{if } \Phi = [\#p \leq c] \\ \forall i_1, \ldots, i_c, i_{c+1}. \bigwedge\limits_{j \in \{1,..,c+1\}} p(i_j, x) \rightarrow \bigvee\limits_{k,l \in \{1,..,c+1\}, k<l} i_k = i_l & \text{if } \Phi = [\#p(x) \leq c] \\ \neg\xi(Psi) & \text{if } \Phi = \neg\Psi \\ \xi(\Phi_1) \vee \xi(\Phi_2) & \text{if } \Phi = \Phi_1 \vee \Phi_2 \\ \exists x.\xi(\Psi) & \text{if } \Phi = \exists x.\Psi \\ \langle-\rangle\langle-\rangle\xi(\Psi) & \text{if } \Phi = \langle-\rangle\Psi \\ \mu Z.\xi(\Psi) & \text{if } \Phi = \mu Z.\Psi \end{cases}$$

The only non-trivial cases are local queries, which are expressed as counting queries over the current database, and the case of $\langle-\rangle$, which is translated by doubling the $\langle-\rangle$ operator since every step in the transition system of a marked ν-PN corresponds to a sequence of two steps (generation and transfer) in the transition system of the corresponding DCDS.

5.3   Decidability Results

We are now in the position of formally assessing the connection between ν-PNs and DCDSs, leveraging on the translation functions τ and ξ.

Theorem 12. *For every marked ν-PN $\overline{N}$ and every closed $\mu\mathcal{L}_A^N$ formula Φ, $\overline{N} \models \Phi$ if and only if $\tau(\overline{N}) \models \xi(\Phi)$.*

Proof. Let $\overline{N} = \langle P, T, F, m_0 \rangle$, and $\tau(\overline{N}) = \langle \mathcal{D}_N, \mathcal{P}_N \rangle$. Recall that for each transition $t \in T$ there are an action gen_t and a condition-action rule $Q(\vec{x}) \mapsto gen_t$ in $\mathcal{P}_N$. In addition, also $transf$ is an action in $\mathcal{P}_N$.

The proof is a variation of the simpler proof given in [3] for the comparison between P/T nets and (lossy) DCDSs. To compare the states of $\Gamma_{\overline{N}}$ with those of $\Lambda_{\tau(\overline{N})}$, we define the following *name cardinality-equivalence* relation: given a marking m in $\Gamma_{\overline{N}}$ and a state s in $\Lambda_{\tau(\overline{N})}$, we say that m is name cardinality-equivalent to s, written $m \approx s$, if, for each place $p_i \in P$ and name $a \in Id$, $m(p)(a) = n$ if and only if $db(s)$ contains n tuples $\langle \_, a \rangle$ in relation p. By definition, $m_0 \approx s_0$. It can then be shown, inductively, that, given m in $\Gamma_{\overline{N}}$ and s in $\Lambda_{\tau(\overline{N})}$ such that $m \approx s$, for every transition $t \in T$ (and corresponding action gen_t in $\tau(\overline{N})$): *(i)* for every t, σ and m' s.t. $m[t, \sigma)m'$, there exists a sequence $s \rightarrow s' \rightarrow s''$ in $\Lambda_{\tau(\overline{N})}$, where s' is produced by the application of gen_t with parameter substitution σ', and where s'' is produced from s' by the application of $transf$, s.t. $m' \approx s''$; *(ii)* for every sequence $s \rightarrow s' \rightarrow s''$ produced by the application of action gen_t with parameter substitution σ, followed by the application of $transf$, there exists σ' and m' s.t. $m[t, \sigma')m'$ and $m' \approx s''$. The proof concludes by making the following two observations. First, the two transition systems have the same structure, apart from the fact that each transition in $\Gamma_{\overline{N}}$ corresponds to a sequence of two transitions in $\Lambda_{\tau(\overline{N})}$, a feature that is correctly mirrored by ξ. Second, name cardinality-equivalence preserves the answers of local queries, i.e., given m and s s.t. $m \approx s$:

- for every number $n \in \mathbb{N}$ and every boolean $\mu\mathcal{L}_A^N$ query of the form $[\#p \leq c]$, $[\#p \leq c]$ is true in m if and only if $\xi([\#p \leq c])$ is true in $db(s)$;
- for every number $n \in \mathbb{N}$, every open $\mu\mathcal{L}_A^N$ query of the form $[\#p(x) \leq c]$, and every substitution $\theta = [x/n]$, $[\#p(x) \leq c]\theta$ is true in m if and only if $\xi([\#p(x) \leq c]\theta)$ is true in $db(s)$. $\qquad\square$

With Theorem 12 at hand, we can now prove the following key decidability result.

Theorem 13. *Verification of $\mu\mathcal{L}_A^N$ properties over run-bounded marked ν-PNs is decidable, and reducible to finite-state model checking.*

Proof. From the proof of Theorem 12, we know that given a marked ν-PN $\overline{N}$, $\tau(\overline{N})$ faithfully reconstruct the execution semantics of $\overline{N}$. In particular, the states of $\Gamma_{\overline{N}}$ and those of $\Lambda_{\tau(\overline{N})}$ are connected by the name cardinality-equivalence relation. This immediately leads to the fact that if $\overline{N}$ is run-bounded, then $\tau(\overline{N})$ is a run-bounded DCDS (in the sense defined in [2]). The claim is then obtained by combining Theorem 12 with the fact that verification of $\mu\mathcal{L}_A$ properties over run-bounded DCDSs is decidable, and reducible to finite-state model checking [2]. □

The notion of run-boundedness is quite restrictive, because it does not allow for infinite runs triggering unboundedly many times an arc decorated with a new name variable from Υ. In [2] also a decidability result for the verification of state-bounded DCDSs is given, by limiting the power of $\mu\mathcal{L}_A$ when using FO quantification that spans across system states. In particular, decidability is proven for the logic $\mu\mathcal{L}_P$, in which FO quantification only applies to those objects that *persist* in the current active domain. When quantification is applied to an object that disappears from the active domain, then it is possible to control whether the property, applied to that object, trivializes to *true* or *false*. By incorporating this idea in the setting considered here, we obtain the logic $\mu\mathcal{L}_P^N$.

Definition 14. Given a marked ν-PN $\overline{N} = \langle P, T, F, m_0 \rangle$, a $\mu\mathcal{L}_P^N$ formula Φ over $\overline{N}$ is defined as:

$$\Phi ::= true \mid Z \mid [\#p \leq c] \mid [\#p(x) \leq c] \mid x = y \mid \Phi_1 \wedge \Phi_2 \mid \neg\Psi \mid$$
$$\exists x.\text{LIVE}(x) \wedge \Psi \mid \text{LIVE}(\vec{x}) \wedge \langle-\rangle\Psi \mid \text{LIVE}(\vec{x}) \wedge \boxminus\Psi \mid \mu Z.\Psi$$

with the usual assumptions done for $\mu\mathcal{L}_A^N$, and the additional assumption that in $\text{LIVE}(\vec{x}) \wedge \langle-\rangle\Psi$ and $\text{LIVE}(\vec{x}) \wedge \boxminus\Psi$, variables $\vec{x}$ are exactly the free variables of Φ, once we replace each bound predicate variable Z in Φ with its bounding formula $\mu Z.\Phi'$. Beside the usual abbreviations, we also make use of $\text{LIVE}(\vec{x}) \rightarrow \langle-\rangle\Psi = \neg(\text{LIVE}(\vec{x}) \wedge \langle-\rangle\neg\Psi)$ and $\text{LIVE}(\vec{x}) \rightarrow \boxminus\Psi = \neg(\text{LIVE}(\vec{x}) \wedge \boxminus\neg\Psi)$. ∎

As shown by the following example, $\mu\mathcal{L}_P^N$ properties are particularly useful in all those cases where names maintain an identity only if they persist in the system.

Example 3. The $\mu\mathcal{L}_P^N$ formula

$$\nu Z.(\exists n.[\#p_1(n) = 1] \wedge \mu Y.([\#p_2(n) = 1]) \vee (\text{LIVE}(n) \wedge \langle-\rangle Y)) \wedge \boxminus Z$$

expresses that in every state of the system, place p_1 must contain a single name n that persists in the system until it is the unique name present in p_2. Instead, formula

$$\nu Z.(\exists n.[\#p_1(n) = 1] \wedge \mu Y.([\#p_2(n) = 1]) \vee (\text{LIVE}(n) \rightarrow \langle-\rangle Y)) \wedge \boxminus Z$$

expresses that in every state of the system, place p_1 must contain a single name n that either disappears from the system or becomes eventually the unique name present in p_2. ∎

By exploiting again Theorem 12, we finally obtain:

Theorem 15. *Verification of $\mu\mathcal{L}_P^N$ properties over state-bounded marked ν-PNs is decidable, and reducible to finite-state model checking.*

Proof. Let $\overline{N}$ be a ν-PN. By adopting the same line of reasoning of the proof for Theorem 13, we get that if $\overline{N}$ is state-bounded, then the DCDS $\tau(\overline{N})$ is state-bounded (in the sense defined in [2]). It is easy to see that if the translation function ξ is applied to a $\mu\mathcal{L}_P^N$ formula $\varPhi$, the resulting formula $\xi(\varPhi)$ is in $\mu\mathcal{L}_P$. The claim is then obtained by combining Theorem 12 with the fact that verification of $\mu\mathcal{L}_P$ properties over state-bounded DCDSs is decidable, and reducible to finite-state model checking [2].   □

6   Conclusion

We have studied the decidability boundaries related to the verification of ν-PNs against rich temporal properties specified using first-order variants of the μ-calculus. The decidability results are obtained via a translation to DCDSs, showing that interesting, new results can be obtained by cross-fertilizing research areas that have not been extensively related so far. It is interesting to observe that checking whether a DCDS is state-bounded is undecidable even when it is very restricted [3]. Thanks to the decidability of state-boundedness for ν-PNs, the DCDSs obtained from our translation mechanism represent an interesting DCDS fragment for which state-boundedness is indeed decidable to check. We plan to continue the combined investigation of these research areas, and foresee a systematic transfer of results between classes of colored Petri nets and DCDSs, leveraging on the connections drawn in this paper.

A   From ν-PNs to DCDSs

We define a translation function τ that, given a marked ν-PN $\overline{N} = (P, T, F, m_0)$, produces a DCDS $\tau(\overline{N}) = \langle \mathcal{D}_N, \mathcal{P}_N \rangle$, whose execution semantics faithfully reproduces that of $\varGamma_{\overline{N}}$. The data layer of $\tau(N)$ is $\mathcal{D}_N = \langle \mathcal{C}_N, \mathcal{R}_N, \mathcal{E}_N, \mathcal{I}_0^N \rangle$, where:

1. $\mathcal{C}_N = Id \cup T \cup P \cup Var$
2. $\mathcal{R}_N$ contains:
   - $p_i/2$ for each $p_i \in P$
   - $NewID/5 = NewID(\mathsf{t}, \mathsf{p}, \mathsf{v}, \mathsf{d}, \mathsf{id})$
   - $FL/0$
3. $\mathcal{E}_N$ is constituted by the following constraints:
   - $\mathcal{E}_1$ and $\mathcal{E}_2$ ensure that the new identifiers from $NewID$ are unique:

$$\mathcal{E}_1 = \forall id. NewID(\_, \_, \_, id, \_) \wedge \bigvee_{p_i \in \mathcal{R}_N} p_i(id, \_) \rightarrow \bot$$

$$\mathcal{E}_2 = \forall id, t, p, v, n, t', p', v', n'. \; NewID(t, p, v, id, n) \wedge NewID(t', p', v', id, n')$$
$$\rightarrow t = t' \wedge p = p' \wedge v = v' \wedge n = n'$$

- $\mathcal{E}_3$ and $\mathcal{E}_4$ ensure the uniqueness of the fresh names stored in *NewID* (here Υ_N contains all the fresh variables present in N):

$$\mathcal{E}_3 = \forall n. \bigvee_{c \in \Upsilon_N} NewID(\_, \_, c, \_, n) \wedge \bigvee_{i \in \{1,\dots,5\}} p_i(\_, n) \to \bot$$

$$\mathcal{E}_4 = \forall n_1, n_2. \bigvee_{\nu_1, \nu_2 \in \Upsilon_N, \nu_1 \neq \nu_2} \Big(NewID(\_, \_, \nu_1, \_, n_1) \wedge NewID(\_, \_, \nu_2, \_, n_2)$$
$$\to n_1 \neq n_2 \Big)$$

4. for each $p \in P$ such that $M_0(p) \neq \emptyset$, $\mathcal{I}_0^N$ is containing the following set of facts:

$$\Big\{ p(\mathrm{id}_k^p, \mathsf{d}) : \mathsf{d} \in M_0(p), \mathrm{id}_k^p \in X_p \subset \mathbb{N}, \forall i, j, .i \neq j \text{ we have } \mathrm{id}_i^p \neq \mathrm{id}_j^p,$$
$$\text{and } \forall p, p'. X_p \cap X_{p'} = \emptyset \Big\}$$

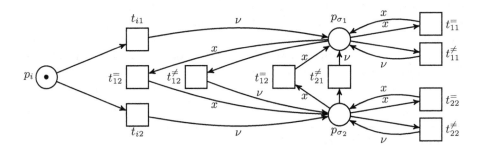

Fig. 4. Marked ν-PN representing all possible infinite data words with labels $\{\sigma_1, \sigma_2\}$.

The process layer of $\tau(N)$ is $\mathcal{P}_N = \langle \mathcal{F}_N, \mathcal{P}_N, \rho_N \rangle$, where:

1. $\mathcal{F}_N$ includes the following non-deterministic services:
   - a new id generator $genID(\mathsf{t}, \mathsf{p}, \mathsf{v}, \mathsf{i})$,
   - a fresh data generator $genFresh(\nu)$.
2. Sets of process and action components ρ_N and $\mathcal{A}_N$ are constructed as follows:
   - for each transition $t \in T$ we define *(i)* a process

$$\bigwedge_{CA_G^1} (p_j(\mathrm{id}_k^j, v) \wedge \mathrm{id}_k^j \neq \mathrm{id}_m^j) \wedge \neg FL \mapsto gen_t(\vec{v}, \vec{\mathrm{id}}),$$

where $CA_G^1 = \left\{p_j \in^{\bullet} t,\, m,k \in \{1,\ldots,|pre(t,p_j)|\},\, m \neq k,\, v \in pre(t,p_j)\right\}$ is the guard condition, and *(ii)* a corresponding action $gen_t(\vec{v},\vec{id}) =$

$$\{p_j(id,n) \wedge \bigwedge_{i\in I_{p_j}} id \neq id_i^j \rightsquigarrow \{p_j(id,n)\} \quad \text{for} p_j \in {}^{\bullet}t$$

$$\text{and } I_{p_j} = \{1,\ldots,|pre(t,p_j)|\}\}$$

$$p_i(id,n) \rightsquigarrow \{p_i(id,n)\} \quad \text{for} p_i \in P \setminus {}^{\bullet}t$$

$$true \rightsquigarrow \{NewID(\mathsf{t},\mathsf{p_k},\mathsf{x},genID(\mathsf{t},\mathsf{p_k},\mathsf{x},\mathsf{num_x}),v) : A_1\},$$

$$true \rightsquigarrow \{NewID(\mathsf{t},\mathsf{p_k},\nu,genID(\mathsf{t},\mathsf{p_k},\nu,1),$$
$$genName(\nu)) : A_2\},$$

$$true \rightsquigarrow FL\ \},$$

where A_1 and A_2 are two conditions which are defined as follows:

(a) $A_1 = \left\{p_k \in t^{\bullet}, \mathsf{x} \in post(t,p_j) \setminus \Upsilon, \mathsf{num_x} = \{1,\ldots,post(t,p_j)(var)\}\right\}$,

(b) $A_2 = \left\{p_k \in t^{\bullet}, \nu \in post(t,p_j) \cap \Upsilon\right\}$;

– define an additional action

$$transf() = \{ \qquad p_i(id,n) \rightsquigarrow \{p_i(id,n)\} \qquad \text{for } p_i \in P$$
$$NewId(\_,\mathsf{p_j},\_,id,n) \rightsquigarrow \{p_j(id,n)\} \qquad \text{for } p_j \in P\ \}$$

and a condition-action rule corresponding to it:

$$FL \mapsto transf()$$

References

1. Bagheri Hariri, B., Calvanese, D., De Giacomo, G., Deutsch, A., Montali, M.: Verification of relational data-centric dynamic systems with external services. CoRR Technical report, arXiv.org e-Print archive (2012). http://arxiv.org/abs/1203.0024
2. Bagheri Hariri, B., Calvanese, D., De Giacomo, G., Deutsch, A., Montali, M.: Verification of relational data-centric dynamic systems with external services. In: Proceedings of PODS, pp. 163–174. ACM (2013)
3. Bagheri Hariri, B., Calvanese, D., Deutsch, A., Montali, M.: State boundedness in data-aware dynamic systems. In: Proceedings of KR (2014)
4. Calvanese, D., De Giacomo, G., Montali, M.: Foundations of data aware process analysis: a database theory perspective. In: Proceedings of PODS (2013)
5. Decker, G., Weske, M.: Instance isolation analysis for service-oriented architectures. In: Proceedings of SCC, pp. 249–256. IEEE Computer Society (2008)
6. Demri, S., Lazic, R.: LTL with the freeze quantifier and register automata. ACM Trans. Comput. Log **10**(3), 16 (2009)
7. Esparza, J.: On the decidability of model checking for several μ-calculi and petri nets. In: Tison, S. (ed.) CAPP 1994. LNCS, vol. 787, pp. 115–129. Springer, Heidelberg (1994)
8. Reisig, W., Rozenberg, G. (eds.): Lectures on Petri Nets I: Basic Models. Advances in Petri Nets. LNCS, vol. 1491. Springer, Heidelberg (1998)
9. Rosa-Velardo, F., de Frutos-Escrig, D.: Name creation vs. replication in petri net systems. Fundam. Inform. **88**(3), 329–356 (2008)
10. Rosa-Velardo, F., de Frutos-Escrig, D.: Decidability and complexity of petri nets with unordered data. Theor. Comput. Sci. **412**(34), 4439–4451 (2011)

Service-Oriented Systems

Modeling and Formal Analysis of a Client-Server Application for Cloud Services

Paolo Arcaini[1](✉), Roxana-Maria Holom[2], and Elvinia Riccobene[3]

[1] Dipartimento di Ingegneria, Università degli Studi di Bergamo, Bergamo, Italy
paolo.arcaini@unibg.it
[2] Christian-Doppler Laboratory for Client-Centric Cloud Computing Hagenberg,
Johannes Kepler University Linz, Linz, Austria
roxana.chelemen@cdcc.faw.jku.at
[3] Dipartimento di Informatica, Università degli Studi di Milano, Milan, Italy
elvinia.riccobene@unimi.it

Abstract. In the context of Cloud computing, a service can be invoked by distinct devices having different HW/SW characteristics; therefore, the content must be adapted to each device profile. A solution consists in having a middleware server that receives requests from the clients, forwards them to the cloud, and adapts the answers coming from the cloud on the base of device profiles. This paper proposes a formalization of this framework using Abstract State Machines (ASMs). The modeling process is based on the ASMs refinement method, and has been guided and supported by several validation and verification activities to guarantee consistency, correctness, and reliability properties.

1 Introduction

Cloud computing is emerging as an important trend in the area of software architecture and computing. Most of the attention of the research community is focused on the side of Cloud providers [5], but many problems still remain to be addressed for the client side of Cloud computing. In particular, we are considering those arising from device fragmentation and variety of operating systems. Nowadays, a typical architecture of a cloud system presumes many different end-devices (desktop computers, laptops, tablets, smartphones, etc.), running different operating systems, owning distinct hardware characteristics (e.g., processor speed, size screen, resolution, etc.), using different browsers, connected with the Cloud, and asking for the same cloud service. An end-user should be able to access the same cloud service from any kind of device (s)he is using. Creating specific applications for each type of device is not a solution.

To tackle this problem, the long term goal of the project presented in [17] – context in which this work has been done – is to develop a framework where all the services available inside the Cloud are adapted on-the-fly to the different end-devices, i.e., Cloud services must be adapted to the different devices contexts. We here present only aspects related to the adaptation in the presentation layer.

© Springer International Publishing Switzerland 2016
T. Hildebrandt et al. (Eds.): WS-FM 2014/WS-FM 2015, LNCS 9421, pp. 51–66, 2016.
DOI: 10.1007/978-3-319-33612-1_4

A preliminary solution was presented in [9] in terms of a Web application (WA), accessible from everywhere, that should act as *middleware* between clients' devices and the services provided by the Cloud. In this way, a service is accessible from any device, without the need to install any extra tool for using it; the middleware is responsible for adapting the content coming from the cloud to the different devices profiles. However, WAs are related to different standards and implementation frameworks [11], therefore they do not have a precise definition or a precise model to follow. Furthermore, reliability properties must be guaranteed in order to ensure that, e.g., the client will receive the same (or as similar as possible) output independently of the device (s)he is using. Formal modeling and verification must be involved to ensure development of correct and reliable WAs [11,15].

In [9], Abstract State Machines (ASMs) [7] are used for presenting in a rigorous way the proposed WA. ASMs permit to design and analyze asynchronous multiple-agent distributed systems, as the cloud framework we deal with; moreover, thanks to refinement mechanism [7], they allow to create a chain of coherent system models that can possibly bring to the implementation; finally, they provide a high level notation that permits to concisely describe complex systems and that can be easily understood by all the stakeholders (ASMs can be seen as pseudo-code working over abstract data structures [7]). The method also supports rigorous model validation and verification.

The work in [9], however, merely presents the preliminary two client/server models of the proposed framework, without exploiting in deep the potentiality of the ASM method. In this paper, we fully exploit the capabilities of the ASMs as formal rigorous system engineering approach to develop correct distributed applications. Using the ASMs refinement method, we have produced, starting from a high level model of the framework – originally presented in [9] –, more detailed models, each one adding further details. Each refinement step has been proved correct. Indeed, our long term goal is to obtain correct executable code from specifications through a chain of models correctly refined.

These precise high-level specifications allow model analysis already at early stages of system design. Validation techniques (simulation, scenario construction) available for ASMs have been used to check if the application under development behaves as expected, and if the models correctly capture the intended requirements. Model checking of properties has been performed to guarantee application independent properties, as consistency and minimality, and application dependent properties (derived from the system requirements), as correctness and reliability. As application dependent properties we have checked, for example, that all the clients' requests are eventually satisfied, and that the middleware correctly identifies a device profile and correctly stores the device characteristics in a local database for further requests.

Regarding verification of properties, we show how model abstraction is necessary to keep the size and the complexity of specifications under control and make proof of properties feasible. All models have been improved on the base of the results of model validation and verification; for example, we discovered some consistency errors contained in the original models presented in [9].

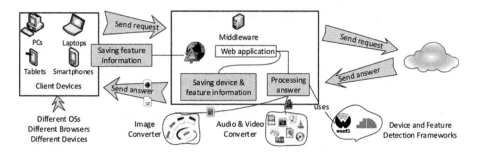

Fig. 1. Framework architecture

In Sect. 2 we present the general architecture of the WA solution we propose. Background on ASMs and tool support for validation and verification is given in Sect. 3. The ASM formal specifications for the client-server cloud application are presented in Sect. 4. Sections 5 and 6 describe the validation and verification activities we have performed on the formal specifications. Some related work is introduced in Sect. 7. Conclusions are outlined in Sect. 8.

2   Client-Server Cloud Application

The proposed framework, initially presented in [9], is shown in Fig. 1. It is composed of three actors: the client (represented by a device), the middleware, and the cloud. The middleware software realizes the communication between the client and the cloud (the connection between the client and the middleware is realized through a WA). The client starts the interaction by selecting a service made available by the cloud. The middleware forwards all client requests to the cloud and waits for the answers. Meanwhile, a *device profile* is created on the server, using the modernizr framework[1] for detecting device properties. It creates some JavaScript tests that are afterwards executed on the client-side, and whose results are sent back to the server using a cookie[2]. On server-side a profile for each device is created, based on the properties discovered on client-side; such profile is used to adapt the content coming from the cloud that finally can be forwarded to the client (e.g., the problem of missing browser functionalities can be solved by using replacement code done in JavaScript, the so called "polyfills"; if the format of images and/or videos is not accepted, then third-party tools can be used to generate other formats). The device profile is also saved locally on the server, to be able to reuse the information when the user logs in again from the same device.

---

[1] http://modernizr.com/.

[2] If we need some extra information regarding the device, and we cannot get it using modernizr, then we use a device detection database tool, as WURFL. However, this feature is not considered in this work.

3   ASM Formal Modeling Framework

Abstract State Machines (ASMs) [7] are a system engineering method that guides the development of software systems seamlessly from requirements capture to their implementation [7]. The method is built upon the following three main concepts: *ASMs*, *ground model*, and *model refinement*.

ASMs are an extension of FSMs: unstructured control states are replaced by states with arbitrary complex data. The *states* of an ASM are multi-sorted first-order structures, i.e., domains of objects with functions and predicates defined on them. ASM states are modified by *transition rules* describing the modification of the function interpretations from one state to the next one. The basic form of a transition rule is the *guarded update*: "**if** *Condition* **then** *Updates*", where *Updates* is a set of function updates of the form $f(t_1, \ldots, t_n) := t$ which are simultaneously executed when *Condition* is true. f is an arbitrary n-ary function and $t_1, \ldots, t_n, t$ are first-order terms. Besides **if-then**, there is a limited but powerful set of *rule constructors*: **par** for simultaneous parallel actions, **seq** for sequential actions, **choose** for nondeterminism (existential quantification), **forall** for unrestricted synchronous parallelism (universal quantification).

ASMs allow to model any kind of computational paradigm, from a *single* agent executing simultaneous parallel actions, to distributed *multiple* agents interacting in a synchronous or asynchronous way. Functions that never change during any run of the machine are *static*. Those updated by agent actions are *dynamic*, and distinguished between *monitored* (only read by the machine and modified by the environment), and *controlled* (read and written by the machine).

For our purposes, we here use a particular class of ASMs, called *control state ASMs* [7], useful to explicitly describe different system *modes*. Figure 2 shows the graphical representation and the form of transition rules for a control state ASM.

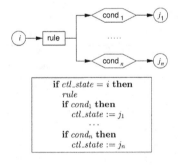

Fig. 2. Control state ASMs

Using ASMs, the process of *requirements capture* results in constructing rigorous **ground models** which are precise but concise high-level system blueprints ("system contracts"), formulated in domain-specific terms, using an application-oriented language which can be understood by all stakeholders. From the ground model, by **step-wise refined models** [7], further details can be added to capture the major design decisions. In this way the complexity of the system can be always taken under control, and it is possible to bridge, in a seamless manner, the gap between specification and code. Along the chain of refined models, each refined model can be proved correct w.r.t. the abstract one.

Still from its ground level, an ASM model can be *validated* and *verified* in order to, respectively, ensure that the specification really reflects the statements about the system, and guarantee the expected properties. Tools allowing different forms of model analysis are available for the ASM method: the ASMETA (ASM mETAmodeling) framework[3] [4] provides basic functionalities for ASM models creation and manipulation (as editing, storage, interchange, access, etc.), as well as advanced model analysis techniques (as validation, verification, testing, model review, requirements analysis, runtime monitoring, etc.). The tools are strongly integrated to permit reusing information about models for different activities.

4   Formal Specification

In this section we describe how the ASM method has been used to model the client-server framework described in Sect. 2. We have improved the first two preliminary models presented in [9] by refining them into more detailed models, for example, explicitly representing the content of the cookie, of the JavaScript tests, and of the server database. Moreover, we have added the communication part between the client and the middleware (server), and corrected some mistakes found in the initial specification. We here show the graphical representation of the control state ASMs for the client and for a request considered by the server.

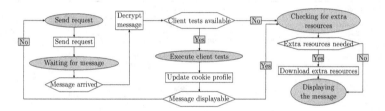

Fig. 3. Client – control state ASM

Figure 3 describes the client's device activity. There are five states through which the client goes: the initial state *Send request*, *Waiting for message*, *Execute client tests*, *Checking for extra resources*, and the final state *Displaying the message*. The client initiates the communication by sending a request to the server and then waits for the answer. If a message arrives, then it is automatically decrypted by the browser (therefore we keep this macro abstract) and the guard *Client tests available* checks if JavaScript (modernizr) tests exist in the received message. If so, they are executed and the result is used to update the cookie ("key X value" entries); in this way the server, when will receive the cookie, will be aware of the new values of the device properties.

The messages coming from the server are labeled with a flag saying if a message should be displayed or it should be sent back to the server for further processing (an improvement with respect to the models presented in [9]). The *Message displayable* guard checks the flag. A message is sent back to the server (as additional request) if extra device information was asked by the server

---

[3] http://asmeta.sourceforge.net/.

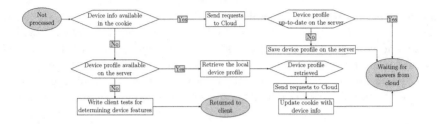

Fig. 4. Request on the server – control state ASM

(the information was not available in the cookie nor in the local database); otherwise the message is processed to be displayed.

The client reaches state *Checking for extra resources* if no modernizr test is available or if the message must be displayed after the test execution. In this state, if extra resources are needed, they are downloaded by the browser, and then the client reaches the final state *Displaying the message* where it can display the message on the device.

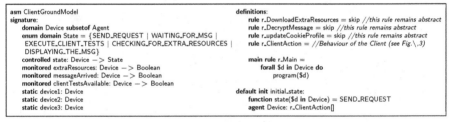

Code 1. Ground model of the client

The server keeps on waiting for requests from the clients and, when a request arrives, it handles it (actually the server can handle multiple requests in parallel). In the following we only describe the request states, as reported in Fig. 4: *Not processed, Returned to client, Waiting for answers from cloud*. When a request is available and not yet processed, the server searches for the device information, first in the cookie and, if not available in the cookie, on the server (the information can be stored locally in a database or in a file). In case device information is not available neither in the cookie nor on the server, modernizr tests are created in JavaScript, and the state of the request is set to *Returned to client* (i.e., the request is sent back to the client for executing the JavaScript code and updating the device information in the cookie). Otherwise, if the information has been found, the request is forwarded to the cloud, and the request enters the state *Waiting for answers from cloud*. If the device profile has been retrieved from the cookie, it is updated on the server (if necessary), otherwise, if it has been retrieved from the server, the cookie is updated.

Code 1 shows the ground model of the client written in AsmetaL [10], the textual notation for ASM models in ASMETA. The behavior of each client (described in Fig. 3) is modeled by rule **r_ClientAction**; the mapping from the graphical notation to the textual notation is done according to the definition of control state ASM, as shown in Fig. 2. For example, each action, reported with a rectangle in Fig. 3, becomes a rule in the AsmetaL code.

Code 2 shows the first refinement for the client model in which we added the modeling of the cookies and of the modernizr. In the refined model, rule r_updateCookieProfile is no more abstract but it updates the cookie using the information contained in the modernizr. Another refinement (not reported here) introduces also the modeling of the content of the web page (e.g., checking if a web page contains modernizr tests). Refined models have been proved to be correct w.r.t. the abstract ones, but without any automatic support. For the lack of space, we do not even report the modeling of the server and of the communication between the client and the server[4]. In the following, to describe the performed validation activities, we mainly focus on the client model, while for describing the verification activities we also consider the server model.

```
asm ClientWithCookie
signature:
    ...
    controlled cookie: Prod(Device, String) −> String
    controlled modernizr: Device −> Seq(Prod(String, Boolean, Seq(Prod(String, Boolean))))
definitions:
    ...
    rule r_updateCookieProfile = r_updateCookieWithModernizr[cookie(self,"deviceProfile"), modernizr(self)] //rule for updating the cookies
    ...
default init initial_state:
    function modernizr($d in Device) = switch $d
                case device2:[("canvas", true, undef), ("textshadow", true, undef), ("opacity", true, undef),
                        ("touch", false, undef), ("audio", undef, [("ogg", false), ("mp3", true)])]
            endswitch
    ...
```

Code 2. First refinement of the client

5   Validation

We have performed the following validation activities over the ASM model by using the framework ASMETA.

5.1   Simulation

As first validation activity, we have executed the ASM specification by the AsmetaS simulator [10]. Simulation has been useful to gain confidence that the specification actually captured the intended behavior. Moreover, the AsmetaS simulator permits to check if some invariants are satisfied during simulation. We added some invariants specifying some safety requirements; for example, the following invariant of the client model

(**forall** \$d **in** Device **with** (state(\$d) = DISPLAYING_THE_MESSAGE and modernizr(\$d) != undef) implies
cookie(\$d,"deviceProfile") != undef)

---

[4] All the specifications are available at http://www.cdcc.faw.jku.at/publications/ rchelemen/WS_FM_FASOCC2014_models.zip.

```
<State 1 (controlled)>                          <State 2 (monitored)>
state(device1)=WAITING_FOR_MSG                  extraResources(device1)=false
state(device2)=WAITING_FOR_MSG                  messageArrived(device3)=false
state(device3)=WAITING_FOR_MSG                  </State 2 (monitored)>
</State 1 (controlled)>                          <State 3 (controlled)>
Insert a boolean constant for messageArrived(device1):   cookie(device2,"deviceProfile")="canvas:true|..."
true                                            modernizr(device2)=[("canvas",true,undef),...]
Insert a boolean constant for clientTestsAvailable(device1):  state(device1)=DISPLAYING_THE_MSG
false                                           state(device2)=CHECKING_FOR_EXTRA_RESOURCES
Insert a boolean constant for messageArrived(device2):   state(device3)=WAITING_FOR_MSG
true                                            </State 3 (controlled)>
Insert a boolean constant for clientTestsAvailable(device2):  Insert a boolean constant for extraResources(device2):
true                                            true
Insert a boolean constant for messageArrived(device3):   Insert a boolean constant for messageArrived(device3):
false                                           false
<State 1 (monitored)>                           <State 3 (monitored)>
messageArrived(device1)=true                    extraResources(device2)=true
messageArrived(device2)=true                    messageArrived(device3)=false
messageArrived(device3)=false                   </State 3 (monitored)>
</State 1 (monitored)>                           <State 4 (controlled)>
<State 2 (controlled)>                           cookie(device2,"deviceProfile")="canvas:true|..."
state(device1)=CHECKING_FOR_EXTRA_RESOURCES      modernizr(device2)=[("canvas",true,undef),...]
state(device2)=EXECUTE_CLIENT_TESTS             state(device1)=DISPLAYING_THE_MSG
state(device3)=WAITING_FOR_MSG                   state(device2)=DISPLAYING_THE_MSG
</State 2 (controlled)>                           state(device3)=WAITING_FOR_MSG
Insert a boolean constant for extraResources(device1):   </State 4 (controlled)>
false
Insert a boolean constant for messageArrived(device3):
false
```

Fig. 5. Example of simulation of the client model (first refinement in Code 2)

states that if a device is displaying a message and the modernizr is defined, then its cookie must be defined as well (since it has been updated during the test).

Figure 5 shows a simulation of the client model initialized with three clients. The simulator, at each step, asks the user for the values of the monitored functions. In the example, the monitored function `messageArrived` models the arrival of a message for a device, `clientTestsAvailable` the presence of tests to be executed, and `extraResources` the need of extra resources.

5.2 Scenario-Based Validation

Although simulation is useful in the first stages of the model development, when the model becomes particularly big, following a long simulation can be a tedious task for the developer. Scenario-based validation by the tool AsmetaV [8] permits to specify *scenarios* describing the interaction between a user (i.e., the environment) and the machine. The Avalla language provides constructs to **set** the values of the monitored functions, to execute a **step** of simulation of the ASM, and to **check** that a given closed first order formula (*assertion*) holds in a given state. The validator AsmetaV simulates (using the simulator AsmetaS) the ASM model according to the commands of the scenario, and checks if all the assertions are satisfied. As soon as an assertion is not satisfied, the simulation is interrupted reporting the violation.

We have produced some scenarios of interaction sequences with suitable checks describing our expectations about the model states (similarly to what is done with unit testing in code development). Moreover, such scenarios have been executed every time we modified and/or enhanced our models to check that no faults were introduced (in a kind of regression testing).

```
scenario interactionWithThreeClients
load ClientWithCookie.asm

step
check state(device1)=WAITING_FOR_MSG and state(device2)=WAITING_FOR_MSG and state(device3)=WAITING_FOR_MSG;

set messageArrived(device1) := true; set clientTestsAvailable(device1) := false; set messageArrived(device2) := true;
set clientTestsAvailable(device2) := true; set messageArrived(device3) := false;
step
check state(device1)=CHECKING_FOR_EXTRA_RESOURCES and state(device2)=EXECUTE_CLIENT_TESTS and state(device3)=WAITING_FOR_MSG;

set extraResources(device1) := false; set messageArrived(device3) := false;
step
check state(device1)=DISPLAYING_THE_MSG and state(device2)=CHECKING_FOR_EXTRA_RESOURCES and state(device3)=WAITING_FOR_MSG;
check cookie(device2,"deviceProfile")="canvas:true|textshadow:true|opacity:true|touch:false|audio:/ogg:false/mp3:true";

set extraResources(device2) := true; set messageArrived(device3) := false;
step
check state(device1)=DISPLAYING_THE_MSG and state(device2)=DISPLAYING_THE_MSG and state(device3)=WAITING_FOR_MSG;
```

Code 3. Example of scenario

Code 3 shows a scenario in which, after a step of simulation, all the three devices have sent a request and are waiting for a reply message from the server. After another step of simulation, device1 does not have any test to execute and so it can check for extra resources, while device2 must execute a test. In this state, the monitored location extraResources(device1) is set to *false*, in order to say that there are no extra resources for device1. After another step of simulation, we expect that device1 can display the message, whereas device2 must check for extra resources; moreover, we expect that the cookie of device2 has a particular content. In this state, the monitored location extraResources(device2) is set to *true*, in order to say that there are extra resources for device2. After another step of simulation, we expect that also device2 can display the message. Along all the scenario, device3 keeps on waiting for a message that, however, is not provided by the server.

6 Verification

As further analysis activity, we have verified the specifications through model checking. AsmetaSMV [2] is a tool that translates ASM specifications into models of the NuSMV model checker, and so it allows the verification of *Computation Tree Logic* (CTL) and *Linear Temporal Logic* (LTL) formulae. As underlined also in [13], declaring a property for a high level-model of the system is definitely easier than writing the same property for a low-level model, as the one we would obtain directly using the syntax provided by model checkers (e.g., Promela, the input language of SPIN, or the input syntax of NuSMV).

Since model checking requires a finite number of states to verify, we have slightly modified our models in order to make them suitable for model checking. For example, we have modified the signature of functions cookie and modernizr of the client model as follows:

controlled cookie: Prod(Device, Key) −> Boolean
controlled modernizr: Prod(Device, Key) −> Boolean

being Key an enumerative domain representing the possible keys of a cookie. cookie(d,k) is true if the device d ∈ Device has the key k ∈ Key in its cookie;

`modernizr(d,k)` is true if the modernizr associates the key `k` to the device `d`. Two other functions record the sub-keys of the cookie keys.

controlled cookieSub: Prod(Device, Key, SubKey) −> Boolean
controlled modernizrSub: Prod(Device, Key, SubKey) −> Boolean

We have checked two different kinds of properties:

- general properties like *completeness*, *minimality*, and *consistency*, that any ASM model should guarantee (described in Sect. 6.1);
- properties related to the proposed web application, to guarantee correctness and reliability (described in Sect. 6.2).

We verified all the properties on a Linux machine, Intel(R) Core(TM) i7 CPU @ 2.67 GHz, 4 GB RAM.

6.1 Model Review

The aim of *model review* is to determine if a model is of sufficient *quality* to be easy to develop, maintain, and enhance. This technique allows to identify defects early in the system development, reducing the cost of fixing them, so it should be applied also on models just sketched. The `AsmetaMA` tool [3] (based on `AsmetaSMV`) allows *automatic* review of ASMs. Typical vulnerabilities and defects that can be introduced during the modeling activity using ASMs are checked as violations of suitable *meta-properties* (*MPs*, defined in [3] as CTL formulae). The violation of a meta-property means that a quality attribute (minimality, completeness, consistency) is not guaranteed, and it may indicate the presence of an actual fault (i.e., the ASM is indeed faulty), or only of a *stylistic defect* (i.e., the ASM could be written in a better way). An inconsistent update (meta-property MP1), for example, is a signal of a real fault in the model; the presence of functions that are never read nor updated (meta-property MP7), instead, may simply indicate that the model is not minimal, but not that it is faulty.

During the development process, we have executed `AsmetaMA` on all the models. The verification of all the meta-properties took around 25 s.

In the first refinement of the client model (`ClientWithCookie` shown in Code 2) we have found several violations of meta-property MP4, requiring that *no assignment is always trivial* [7]: an update rule $l := t$ is always trivial if, when the rule is applied, l is always already equal to t. In order to check if an update is trivial, we verify the temporal property $\mathbf{EF}(cond) \rightarrow \mathbf{EF}(cond \wedge l \neq t)$, being *cond* the condition (possibly the conjunctions of a set of conditions) that guards the update rule. In our model we always update all the keys of a cookie through the modernizr, even if they are already up to date, as shown in Code 4. In this way, the locations of function *cookie* that refer to keys that never change, will be always updated to the same value. Although this is not a real error, it gave us a more deep understanding of the behavior of our specification. In a further refinement of our model, we could avoid updating keys that are already up to date; surely this kind of control should be done in the final implementation, in order to improve the performances.

```
forall $k in Key do
  par
    cookie(self, $k) := modernizr(self, $k)
    forall $c in SubKey with keyParentalRel($k, $c) do cookieSub(self, $k, $c) := modernizrSub(self, $k, $c)
  endpar
```

Code 4. Rule `r_updateCookieProfile`

A more serious error that we have discovered in our first specification was the presence of an inconsistent update (a consistency violation). In an ASM two updates are inconsistent if they update the same location to two different values at the same time [7]. In our case, we found that the client specification published in [9] actually contained an error: indeed, upon some conditions, the machine could simultaneously update a location of the function `state` (`ctl_state` in [9]) to two different values. Although sometimes inconsistent updates can be easily discovered by simulation or by scenario-based validation (see Sect. 5), when the model becomes particularly complex, they may be more difficult to find and an automatic approach as that provided by the model reviewer is helpful.

In different models we have found minimality violations, since some functions were declared but never used (meta-property MP7): we discovered that some of these functions were indeed unuseful (and so they could be removed), while some others were useful, but we forgot to use (read or update) them.

6.2 Verification of Case Study Requirements

We have then verified classical temporal properties to guarantee correctness and reliability of the web application. We present the properties verified for the client and for the server, distinguishing between *reachability*, *liveness*, and *safety* properties. In this section, we focus on the verification of the single agents (i.e., the client and the server), and not on their communication. The verification of all the properties took around 6 s.

Client

Reachability. As first property we have verified that each device can reach a state in which it displays a message[5].

(**forall** $d **in** Device **with** ef(state($d) = DISPLAYING_THE_MSG))

This simple property permits to verify that each device can actually receive some information.

---

[5] Note that we have actually checked a slightly different property, because in NuSMV (the model checker used by AsmetaSMV) a CTL formula holds if it holds in all initial states. More information can be found in the NuSMV FAQ http://nusmv.fbk.eu/faq.html#007.

Liveness. Through liveness properties we check that requests are eventually satisfied. As first liveness property we have checked that, whenever a message has arrived and it contains a test (and the device is waiting for the message), then in the next state the device executes the test.

(**forall** $d **in** Device **with** ag((state($d) = WAITING_FOR_MSG and messageArrived($d) and
                    clientTestsAvailable($d)) implies ax(state($d) = EXECUTE_CLIENT_TESTS)))

As further liveness property, we have verified that, if a device executes a test, then afterwards it has some information in its cookie (i.e., at least a key of its cookie is defined).

(**forall** $d **in** Device **with** ag((state($d) = EXECUTE_CLIENT_TESTS) implies
                    (**exists** $k **in** Key **with** ax(cookie($d, $k) != undef))))

Such property guarantees that the execution of a test provides the information requested by the server. However, the property is quite general and does not check that the information copied in the cookie is indeed correct. The following property checks that during a test the cookie is updated with the information contained in the modernizr.

(**forall** $d **in** Device **with** ag(state($d) = EXECUTE_CLIENT_TESTS implies
                    (**forall** $k **in** Key **with** ax(cookie($d, $k) = modernizr($d, $k)))))

Safety. The following property checks that, once a device has displayed a message, it does not change its state (indeed, at this stage of modeling, we only check one session of communication with the server).

(**forall** $d **in** Device **with** ag((state($d) = DISPLAYING_THE_MSG) implies
                    ag(state($d) = DISPLAYING_THE_MSG)))

Server

The signature of the server contains functions `cookie` and `cookieSub` as declared for the client; moreover, it contains functions `deviceProfileDB` and `deviceProfileDBsub`[6], representing the server database that stores the device profiles.

Liveness. As first liveness property for the server, we have checked that every request received from the client is eventually considered (it is either sent to the cloud or returned to the client).

(**forall** $r **in** Request **with** ag(requestState($r) = NOT_PROCESSED implies
    ef(requestState($r) = WAITING_CLOUD_ANSWERS or requestState($r) = RETURNED_TO_CLIENT)))

The server has a database for memorizing the devices profiles extracted from the cookies. The following three properties check that the memorization mechanism behaves correctly. First of all, we have checked that, if a key is present in a cookie, it will be eventually present in the database as well.

(**forall** $d **in** Device, $k **in** Key **with** ag(cookie($d, $k) != undef implies ef(deviceProfileDB($d, $k) != undef)))

---

[6] **controlled** deviceProfileDB: Prod(Device, Key) $->$ Boolean

   controlled deviceProfileDBsub: Prod(Device, Key, SubKey) $->$ Boolean.

The previous property does not check that the value stored in the database is correct. So, we have proved that the key value of a cookie (top-level key or sub-key) is eventually copied in the database.

```
(forall $d in Device, $k in Key with
    ag(cookie($d, $k) != undef implies ef(deviceProfileDB($d, $k) = cookie($d, $k))) )
(forall $d in Device, $k in Key, $c in SubKey with
    ag(cookieSub($d, $k, $c) != undef implies ef(deviceProfileDBsub($d, $k, $c) = cookieSub($d, $k, $c))))
```

The device configurations stored in the database can also be used to update a cookie if this does not report any information about the device (i.e., the corresponding location is *undef*). So, the following property checks that a device information stored in the database (as top-level key or sub-key) is eventually copied in the undefined cookie location.

```
(forall $d in Device, $k in Key with ag((deviceProfileDB($d, $k) != undef and cookie($d, $k) = undef) implies
                                ef(cookie($d, $k) = deviceProfileDB($d, $k)) ) )
(forall $d in Device, $k in Key, $c in SubKey with ag((deviceProfileDBsub($d, $k, $c) != undef and
    cookieSub($d, $k, $c) = undef) implies ef(cookieSub($d, $k, $c) = deviceProfileDBsub($d, $k, $c))))
```

Safety. In the server model, we assume that the information about a device does not change. So, the following property checks that, once a cookie gets a value for one of its keys (top-level or sub-key), it cannot change it.

```
(forall $d in Device, $k in Key, $b in Boolean with ag(cookie($d, $k) = $b implies ag(cookie($d, $k) = $b)) )
(forall $d in Device, $k in Key, $c in SubKey, $b in Boolean with
    ag(cookieSub($d, $k, $c) = $b implies ag(cookieSub($d, $k, $c) = $b)) )
```

Since we abstract from modeling the communication with the cloud, a request from the client is considered fulfilled when it has been sent to the cloud. The following property checks that, if the server is waiting for an answer for a particular request, it cannot change the request state.

```
(forall $r in Request with ag(requestState($r) = WAITING_CLOUD_ANSWERS implies
                    ag(requestState($r) = WAITING_CLOUD_ANSWERS)) )
```

7   Related Work

In the past years several papers regarding analysis and verification of WAs appeared, but not many of them are based on formal approaches. The research literature splits into two groups: on one side there are papers proposing forward engineering methods (starting by specifying the requirements, then going to the design phase and from this building the WA), and on the other side there are papers using reverse engineering methods to extract from an existing WA the corresponding models, and afterwards to verify the models. There are also several analysis methods [1] that are used, like modeling the navigational aspects of WAs, or modeling the behavior and the features of WAs, or modeling, validation and verification of the completeness and correctness of web pages. The survey in [1] presents the desirable properties for WA modeling, and compares and categorizes some existing modeling methods based on the level of WA modeling.

Several research papers are using reverse engineering methods. In the approach presented in [12], a WA is monitored while it is explored by a user or a program and traces are collected: in this way the WA behavior is modeled. A finite automata model is built in order to validate the WA (the task of property verification is delegated to an existing model checker). The system presented in [6] verifies if (partial) correctness and completeness properties are fulfilled by a web site. The system uses a rule-based language for the specification and the verification of syntactic and semantic properties of collections of XML/XHTML documents. Note that the approach in [6] verifies the WA, whereas we verify a model of the WA; indeed, we think that the use of validation and verification in the design phase helps to ensure the WA reliability.

Other works are using forward engineering methods in order to check if the WA satisfies the requirements. UML is used in [15] to build the navigation model which would then be verified using NuSMV. Since UML can't be directly used for automated verification, the navigation model is manually defined as a Kripke structure and the properties are defined using CTL in NuSMV syntax (as mentioned before, it is more complicated to declare a property directly using the syntax provided by the model checkers than declaring it for a high-level model). Another proposal to WA navigation model is presented in [14], where the model is represented by using two finite-state automata, a page automaton and an internal state automaton, and then expressed using Promela, the input language for SPIN model checker. A drawback would be that they don't use a tool to automatically transform the models into Promela. A non-formal model of the presentation layer of a WA is presented in [16] with the aim of testing the application; however, the model does not support asynchronous server-client interactions and concurrency, and it is based on a static technique.

8   Conclusions

We have presented the formalization process, using Abstract State Machines (ASMs), of a framework for the adaptation, at the presentation layer, of the content coming from the cloud; the framework consists in a middleware server that receives requests from the clients, forwards them to the cloud, and adapts the answers coming from the cloud based on the profiles of the clients' devices. A device profile is discovered by means of JavaScript tests created by the modernizr and executed on the device; the devices profiles are also stored at the server-side for further communications with the client.

We have modeled the client and the server with two ASMs. Each ASM has been obtained through a chain of refinements, starting from a high level model to more detailed ones. Validation activities as simulation and scenario-based validation have given us the confidence that the produced models actually capture the informal requirements. Such activities have been particularly useful to reason about the requirements with the stakeholders of the system. Thanks to the modular nature of ASMs, we have been able to reason both on the single components and on their communication. All the validation activities have been performed along all the model development, using an iterative process between model specification and model validation.

More in-depth analyses are permitted by model checking. Apart the verification of the application dependent properties that we specified starting from the requirements, we found particularly useful the verification of the application independent properties provided by model review. Indeed, thanks to this technique, we were able to discover real errors in our models (inconsistencies); moreover, other meta-properties violations, although were not real faults, allowed us to find some weaknesses of the models (e.g., locations that were always trivially updated). In order to be model checked, we had to apply some abstractions to our models, for example by replacing infinite domains with finite ones. Such kind of transformations do not diminish the expressive power of our models, but simply rewrite them in a form more suitable for verification purposes. Note that, however, some models could not be handled at all: for example, models extending domains. Although some limitations exist on the class of ASMs that can be model checked, the alternative would be to encode the system under development directly in the model checker syntax, arising two problems: (i) the model checkers syntaxes usually have a low expressive power and it may be difficult to model complex systems with them, (ii) we could produce a model not equivalent with the ASM specification.

This paper presents results about the validation and verification of a preliminary design of the proposed framework. The current version of the specification mainly focuses on the communication between the client and the middleware in order to retrieve information regarding the client's device. Future versions will also consider the communication between the middleware and the Cloud.

The long term goal of the project presented in [17] is to develop, in a controlled and verified way, through a chain of refinements, the implementation of a prototype. As future work we plan to formally prove the correctness of the refinement in an automatic way. Regarding the verification of properties we intend to adapt the AsmetaSMV tool to work with an infinite-state model checker.

References

1. Alalfi, M.H., Cordy, J.R., Dean, T.R.: Modelling methods for web application verification and testing: state of the art. Softw. Test. Verif. Reliab. **19**(4), 265–296 (2009)
2. Arcaini, P., Gargantini, A., Riccobene, E.: AsmetaSMV: a way to link high-level ASM models to low-level NuSMV specifications. In: Frappier, M., Glässer, U., Khurshid, S., Laleau, R., Reeves, S. (eds.) ABZ 2010. LNCS, vol. 5977, pp. 61–74. Springer, Heidelberg (2010)
3. Arcaini, P., Gargantini, A., Riccobene, E.: Automatic review of abstract state machines by meta property verification. In: Muñoz, C. (ed.) Proceedings of the Second NASA Formal Methods Symposium (NFM), pp. 4–13. NASA (2010)
4. Arcaini, P., Gargantini, A., Riccobene, E., Scandurra, P.: A model-driven process for engineering a toolset for a formal method. Softw. Pract. Experience **41**, 155–166 (2011)

5. Ardagna, D., Di Nitto, E., Mohagheghi, P., Mosser, S., Ballagny, C., D'Andria, F., Casale, G., Matthews, P., Nechifor, C.-S., Petcu, D., Gericke, A., Sheridan, C.: Modaclouds: a model-driven approach for the design and execution of applications on multiple clouds. In: 2012 ICSE Workshop on Modeling in Software Engineering (MISE), pp. 50–56, June 2012

6. Ballis, D., Garca-Viv, J.: A rule-based system for web site verification. Electron. Notes Theor. Comput. Sci. **157**(2), 11–17 (2006)

7. Börger, E., Stärk, R.: Abstract State Machines: A Method for High-Level System Design and Analysis. Springer, Heidelberg (2003)

8. Carioni, A., Gargantini, A., Riccobene, E., Scandurra, P.: A scenario-based validation language for ASMs. In: Börger, E., Butler, M., Bowen, J.P., Boca, P. (eds.) ABZ 2008. LNCS, vol. 5238, pp. 71–84. Springer, Heidelberg (2008)

9. Chelemen, R.-M.: Modeling a web application for cloud content adaptation with ASMs. In: 2013 International Conference on Cloud Computing and Big Data (CloudCom-Asia), pp. 44–51, December 2013

10. Gargantini, A., Riccobene, E., Scandurra, P.: A metamodel-based language and a simulation engine for abstract state machines. J. Univ. Comput. Sci. **14**(12), 1949–1983 (2008)

11. Gervasi, R.-M., Börger, E., Cisternino, A.: Modeling web applications infrastructure with ASMs. Sci. Comput. Programm. **94**, 69–92 (2014)

12. Haydar, M., Petrenko, A., Boroday, S., Sahraoui, H.: A formal approach for runtime verification of web applications using scope-extended LTL. Inf. Softw. Technol. **55**(12), 2191–2208 (2013)

13. Heitmeyer, C.L.: On the need for *practical* formal methods. In: Ravn, A.P., Rischel, H. (eds.) FTRTFT 1998. LNCS, vol. 1486, pp. 18–26. Springer, Heidelberg (1998)

14. Homma, K., Izumi, S., Abe, Y., Takahashi, K., Togashi., A: Using the model checker spin for web application design. In: 2010 10th IEEE/IPSJ International Symposium on Applications and the Internet (SAINT), pp. 137–140, July 2010

15. Mao-shan, S., Yi-hai, C., Sheng-bo, C., Mei-Jia: A model checking approach to web application navigation model with session mechanism. In: 2010 International Conference on Computer Application and System Modeling (ICCASM), vol. 5, pp. V5–398–V5–403, October 2010

16. Offutt, J., Wu, Y.: Modeling presentation layers of web applications for testing. Softw. Syst. Model. **9**(2), 257–280 (2010)

17. Schewe, K.-D., Bósa, K., Lampesberger, H., Ma, H., Vleju, M.B.: The Christian Doppler laboratory for client-centric cloud computing. In: 2nd Workshop on Software Services (WoSS 2011), Timisoara, Romania, June 2011

An Event-Based Approach to Runtime Adaptation in Communication-Centric Systems

Cinzia Di Giusto[1] and Jorge A. Pérez[2(✉)]

[1] I3S, UMR 7271, University of Nice Sophia Antipolis,
Sophia Antipolis, Nice, France
[2] Johann Bernoulli Institute for Mathematics and Computer Science,
University of Groningen, Groningen, The Netherlands
j.a.perez@rug.nl

Abstract. This paper presents a model of session-based concurrency with mechanisms for *runtime adaptation*. Thus, our model allows to specify communication-centric systems whose session behavior can be dynamically updated at runtime. We propose an *event-based* approach: adaptation requests, issued by the system itself or by its environment, are assimilated to events which may trigger runtime adaptation routines. Based on type-directed checks, these routines naturally enable the reconfiguration of processes with active sessions. We develop a type system that ensures *communication safety* and *consistency* properties: while the former guarantees absence of runtime communication errors, the latter ensures that update actions do not disrupt already established sessions.

1 Introduction

Context. Modern software systems are built as assemblies of heterogeneous artifacts which must interact following predefined protocols. Correctness in these *communication-centric* systems largely depends on ensuring that dialogues are consistent. *Session-based concurrency* is a type-based approach to ensure conformance of dialogues to prescribed protocols: dialogues are organized into units called *sessions*; interaction patterns are abstracted as *session types* [9], against which specifications may be checked.

As communication-centric systems operate on open infrastructures, *runtime adaptation* appears as a crucial feature to ensure continued system operation. Here we understand runtime adaptation as the dynamic modification of (the behavior of) the system in response to an exceptional event, such as, e.g., a varying requirement or a local failure. These events are not necessarily catastrophic but are hard to predict. As such, protocol conformance and dynamic reconfiguration are intertwined concerns: although the specification of runtime adaptation is not strictly tied to that of structured protocols, steps of dynamic reconfiguration have a direct influence in a system's interactive behavior.

We are interested in integrating forms of runtime adaptation into models of session-based concurrency. As a first answer to this challenge, in previous work [8] we extended a typed process framework for binary sessions with basic

© Springer International Publishing Switzerland 2016
T. Hildebrandt et al. (Eds.): WS-FM 2014/WS-FM 2015, LNCS 9421, pp. 67–85, 2016.
DOI: 10.1007/978-3-319-33612-1_5

constructs from the model of *adaptable processes* [2]. In this work, with the aim of extending the applicability and expressiveness of the approach in [8], we propose adaptation mechanisms which depend on the state of the session protocols active in a given location. As a distinctive feature, we advocate an *event-based* approach: by combining constructs for *dynamic type inspection* and *non-blocking event detection* (as put forward by Kouzapas et al. [11,13]), adaptation requests, both internal or external to the location, can be naturally assimilated to events.

A Motivating Example. Here we consider a standard syntax for binary session types [9]:

$$\alpha, \beta ::= \ ?(T).\beta \qquad\qquad\qquad \text{input a value of type} T, \text{continue as } \beta$$

$$| \ !(T).\beta \qquad\qquad\qquad\quad \text{output a value of type} T, \text{continue as } \beta$$

$$| \ \&\{n_1{:}\alpha_1 \ldots n_m{:}\alpha_m\} \ \ \text{branching (external choice)}$$

$$| \ \oplus\{n_1{:}\alpha_1 \ldots n_m{:}\alpha_m\} \ \ \text{selection (internal choice)}$$

$$| \ \varepsilon \quad | \quad \mu t.\alpha \ | \ t \qquad\ \ \text{terminated and recursive session}$$

where T stands for both basic types (e.g., booleans, integers) and session types α. Also, $n_1, \ldots, n_m$ denote *labels*. To illustrate session types, consider a buyer B and a seller S which interact as follows. First, B sends to S the name of an item and S replies back with its price. Then, depending on the amount, B either adds the item to its shopping cart or closes the transaction. In the latter case the protocol ends. In the former case B must further choose a paying method. From B's perspective, this protocol may be described by the session type $\alpha = !\mathsf{item}. ?\mathsf{amnt}. \alpha_{\mathsf{pay}}$, where item and amnt are base types and

$$\alpha_{\mathsf{pay}} = \oplus\{\mathsf{addItem} : \ \oplus\{\mathsf{ccard} : \ \alpha_{\mathsf{cc}}, \ \mathsf{payp} : \ \alpha_{\mathsf{pp}}\}, \ \mathsf{cancel} : \ \varepsilon\}.$$

Thus, session type α says that protocol α_{pay} may only be enabled after sending a value of type item and receiving a value of type amnt. Also, addItem, ccard, cc, and payp denote labels in the internal choice. Types α_{cc} and α_{pp} denote the behavior of each payment method. Following the protocol abstracted by α, code for B may be specified as a π-calculus process. Processes P and R below give two specifications for B:

$$P = \overline{x}(\mathsf{book}).x(a).\text{if } a < 50 \text{ then } x \triangleleft \mathsf{addItem}; x \triangleleft \mathsf{ccard}; P^c \text{ else } x \triangleleft \mathsf{cancel}; \mathbf{0}$$

$$R = \overline{x}(\mathsf{game}).x(b).\text{if } b < 80 \text{ then } x \triangleleft \mathsf{addItem}; x \triangleleft \mathsf{payp}; R^p \text{ else } x \triangleleft \mathsf{cancel}; \mathbf{0}$$

Thus, although both P and R implement α, their behavior is rather different, for they purchase different items using different payment methods (which are abstracted by processes P^c and R^p). Let us now analyze the situation for the seller S. To ensure protocol compatibility and absence of communication errors, the session type for S, denoted β, should be *dual* to α. This is written $\alpha \perp_c \beta$. Intuitively, duality decrees that every action from B must be matched by a complementary action from S, e.g., every output of a string in α is matched by an input of a string in β. In our example, we let $\beta = ?\mathsf{item}. !\mathsf{amnt}. \beta_{\mathsf{pay}}$, where β_{pay} and a process implementation for S are as follows:

$$\beta_{\mathsf{pay}} = \&\{\mathsf{addItem} : \ \&\{\mathsf{ccard} : \ \beta_{\mathsf{cc}}, \ \mathsf{payp} : \ \beta_{\mathsf{pp}}\}, \ \mathsf{cancel} : \ \varepsilon\}$$

$$Q = y(i).\overline{y}(price(i)).y \triangleright \{\mathsf{addItem} : y \triangleright \{\mathsf{ccard} : Q^c \ \| \ \mathsf{ppal} : Q^p\} \ \| \ \mathsf{cancel} : \mathbf{0}\}$$

where *price* stands for an auxiliary function. Also, β_{cc} and β_{pp} are the duals of α_{cc} and α_{pp}; they are realized by processes Q_y^c and Q_y^p. The interaction of P and Q is defined using *session initialization* constructs: process $\overline{u}(x{:}\alpha).P$ denotes the *request* of a session of type α; dually, $u(x{:}\alpha).P$ denotes the *acceptance* of a session of type α. In both cases, u denotes a *(shared) name* used for synchronization. In our example, we may have

$$Sys = \overline{u}(x{:}\alpha).P \mid u(y{:}\beta).Q \longrightarrow (\nu\kappa)(P[{^{\kappa^+}}\!/x] \mid Q[{^{\kappa^-}}\!/y]) = S'$$

Thus, upon synchronization on u, a new session κ is established. Intuitively, in process S' session κ is "split" into two *session channels* (or *endpoints*) κ^+ and κ^-: we write $+$ and $-$ to denote their opposing *polarities*, which make their complementarity manifest. The use of restriction $(\nu\kappa)$ covers both channels, thus ensuring an interference-free medium for executing the session protocols described by α and β.

In this work, we are interested in ways of expressing and reasoning about the dynamic modification of session-typed processes such as P and Q above. Such modifications may be desirable to react to exceptional runtime conditions (say, an error) or to implement new requirements. For instance, the type below defines a new payment method for S:

$$\beta_{\texttt{gift}} = \&\{\texttt{addItem} : \&\{\texttt{giftc} : \beta_{gc}, \texttt{ccard} : \beta_{cc}, \texttt{payp} : \beta_{pp}\}, \texttt{cancel} : \varepsilon\}$$

Intuitively, $\beta_{\texttt{gift}}$ *extends* $\beta_{\texttt{pay}}$ with a new alternative on label $\texttt{giftc}$. As such, it is safe to use a process implementing $\beta_{\texttt{gift}}$ wherever a process implementing $\beta_{\texttt{pay}}$ is required. The *safe substitution* principle that connects $\beta_{\texttt{gift}}$ and $\beta_{\texttt{pay}}$ is formalized by a *subtyping* relation on session types [7], denoted $\leq_c$. In our example, we have $\beta_{\texttt{pay}} \leq_c \beta_{\texttt{gift}}$.

In previous work [8] we studied how to update processes when sessions have not yet been established; this suffices to analyze runtime adaptation for processes such as Sys above. In this paper, we go further and address the runtime adaptation of processes such as S' above, which contain already established session protocols. As we would like to guarantee that adaptation preserves overall system correctness, a key challenge is ensuring that adaptation does not jeopardize such protocols. Continuing our example, let S'' be the process resulting from S' above, after the first step stipulated by α and β (i.e., an exchange of a value of type item). Intuitively, at that point, the buyer part of S' will have session type ?amnt. $\alpha_{\texttt{pay}}$, whereas the seller part of S' will have session type !amnt. $\beta_{\texttt{pay}}$. Suppose we wish to modify at runtime the part of S'' realizing the buyer behavior. To preserve protocol correctness, a candidate new implementation must conform, up to $\leq_c$, to the type ?amnt. $\alpha_{\texttt{pay}}$; a process realizing any other type will fail to safely interact with the part of S'' implementing the seller. In [8] we defined the notion of *consistency* to formalize the correspondence between declared session protocols and the processes installed by steps of runtime adaptation. As we will see, consistency is still appropriate for reasoning about runtime adaptation of processes with active sessions.

Our Approach. Having motivated the context of our contributions, we move on to describe some technical details. We rely on a process language which extends session π-calculi with *locations*, *located processes*, and *update processes* [2]. We use *locations* as explicit delimiters for process behavior: these are transparent, possibly nested computation sites. Given a location loc and a process P, the *located process* loc$[P]$ denotes the fact that P resides in loc (or, alternatively, that P has scope loc). This way, e.g., process

$$W = \mathsf{sys}\big[\,\mathsf{buyer}\big[\overline{u}(x{:}\alpha).P\big] \mid \mathsf{seller}\big[u(y{:}\beta).Q\big]\,\big]$$

represents an explicitly distributed variant of Sys above: the partners now reside in locations buyer and seller; location sys encloses the whole system. An *update process*, denoted loc$\{U\}$, intuitively says that the behavior currently enclosed by loc should be replaced according to the adaptation routine U. Since a location may enclose one or more session channels, update processes allow for flexible specifications of adaptation routines. This way, e.g., one may specify an update on buyer that does not involve seller (and vice versa); also, a system-level adaptation could be defined by adding a process sys$\{U_s\}$ in parallel to W, given an U_s that accounts for both buyer and seller behaviors.

The integration of runtime adaptation into sessions is delicate, and involves defining not only *what* should be the state of the system after adaptation but also *when* an adaptation step should be triggered. To rule out careless adaptation steps which jeopardize established protocols, communication and adaptation actions should be harmonized. As hinted at above, in previous work [8] we proposed admitting adaptation actions only when locations do not enclose running sessions. This is a simple solution that privileges communication over adaptation, in the sense that adaptation is enabled only when sessions are not yet active. Still, in realistic applications it may be desirable to give communication and adaptation a similar status. To this end, in this paper we admit the adaptation of locations with running sessions. We propose update processes loc$\{U\}$ in which U is able to dynamically check the current state of the session protocols running in loc. In their simplest form, our update processes concern only one session channel and are of the shape

$$\mathsf{loc}\{\mathsf{case}\, x\, \mathsf{of}\, \{(x{:}\beta^i) : U_i\}_{i \in I}\}$$

where I is a finite index set, x denotes a channel variable, each β^i and U_i denotes a session type and an *alternative* (process) U_i, respectively. (We assume x occurs free in U_i.) The informal semantics for this construct is better understood by considering its interaction with a located process loc$[Q]$ in which Q implements a session of type α along channel κ^p. The two processes may interact as follows. If there is a $j \in I$ such that types α and β^j "match" (up to $\leq_c$), then there is a reduction to process loc$[U_j[\kappa^p/x]]$. Otherwise, if no β^j validates a match, then there is a reduction to process loc$[Q]$, keeping the behavior of loc unchanged and consuming the update.

In general, update processes may define adaptation for locations enclosing more than one session channel. In the distributed buyer-seller example, the process below defines a runtime update which depends on the current state of the two channels at location sys:

$$U_{xy} = \text{sys} \left\{ \text{case } x, y \text{ of} \left\{ \begin{array}{l} (x{:}\alpha \,;\, y{:}\beta) : \text{buyer}[R] \mid \text{seller}[Q] \\ (x{:}\alpha_{\mathsf{pay}} \,;\, y{:}\beta_{\mathsf{pay}}) : \text{buyer}[P^*] \mid \text{seller}[Q^*] \end{array} \right\} \right\} \quad (1)$$

U_{xy} defines two possibilities for runtime adaptation. If the protocol has just been established (i.e., current types are α and β) then only the buyer is updated—its new behavior will be given by R above. If both item and price information have been already exchanged then implementations P^* and Q^*, compliant with types α_{pay} and β_{pay}, are installed.

Update processes rely on the protocol state at a given location to assess the suitability of adaptation routines. Our semantics for update relies on (a) *monitors* which store the current type for each running session; and (b) a type-directed test on the monitors enclosed in a given location. This test generalizes the typecase construct in [11].

While expressive, our typeful update processes by themselves do not specify *when* adaptation should be available. Even though update processes could be embedded within session communication prefixes (thus creating causal dependencies between communication and adaptation), such a specification style would only allow to handle exceptional conditions which can be fully characterized in advance. Other kinds of exceptional conditions, in particular contextual and/or unsolicited runtime conditions, are much harder to express by interleaving update processes within structured protocols.

To offer a uniform solution to this issue, we propose a *event-based* approach to trigger updates. We endow each location with a *queue* of adaptation requests; such requests may be internal or external to the location. In our example, an external request could be, e.g., a warning message from the buyer's bank indicating that an exchange with the bank is required before committing to the purchase with the seller.

Location queues are independent from session behavior. Their identity is visible to processes; they are intended as interfaces with other processes and the environment. To issue an adaptation request r for location loc, our process syntax includes *adaptation signals*, written $\overline{\text{loc}}(r)$. Similar to ordinary communication prefixes, these signals are orthogonal to sessions. Then, we may detect the presence of request r in the queue of loc using the *arrival predicate* arrive(loc, r) [11]. As an example, let upd_E denote an *external* adaptation request. To continuously check if an external request has been queued for sys, the process below combines process U_{xy} in (1) with arrival predicates, conditionals, and recursion:

$$U^*_{xy} = \mu \mathcal{X}.\text{if arrive}(\text{sys}, \mathsf{upd}_E) \text{ then } U_{xy} \text{ else } \mathcal{X} \quad (2)$$

We couple our process model for session-based concurrency and runtime adaptation with a type system that ensures the following key properties:

- *Safety*: well-typed programs do not exhibit communication errors (e.g., mismatched messages).

- *Consistency*: well-typed programs do not allow adaptation actions that disrupt already established sessions.

Safety is the typical guarantee expected from any session type discipline, here considered in a richer setting that combines session communication with runtime adaptation. In contrast, consistency is a guarantee unique to our setting: it connects the behavior of the adaptation mechanisms with the preservation of prescribed typed interfaces. We show that well-typed programs are safe and consistent (Theorem 3.6): this ensures that specified session protocols are respected, while forbidding incautious adaptation steps that could accidentally remove or disrupt the session behavior of interacting partners.

Organization. The rest of the paper is organized as follows. Next we present our event-based process model of session communication with typeful constructs for runtime adaptation (Sect. 2). Then, we present our session type system, which ensures safety and consistency for processes with adaptation mechanisms (Sect. 3). In Sect. 4 we discuss a process model of communication and adaptation with explicit compartments; it distills the main features of the model in Sect. 2. At the end, we discuss related works and draw some concluding remarks (Sect. 5). The appendix gives full sets of reduction and typing rules. Additional technical details and omitted definitions can be found in an online technical report [5].

2   The Process Model: Syntax and Semantics

Syntax. We rely on base sets for *names*, ranged over by $u, a, b \ldots$; *(session) channels*, ranged over by $k, \kappa^p, \ldots$, with *polarity* $p \in \{+, -\}$; *labels*, ranged over by $n, n', \ldots$; and *variables*, ranged over by $x, y, \ldots$. *Values*, ranged over by $v, v', \ldots$, may include booleans (written **false** and **true**), integers, names, and channels. We use r to range over *adaptation messages*: two instances are upd_I and upd_E, for internal and external requests. We use $\tilde{\cdot}$ to denote finite sequences. Thus, e.g., $\tilde{x}$ is a sequence of variables $x_1, \ldots, x_n$. We use ϵ to denote the empty sequence.

Table 1 reports the syntax of expressions and processes. Processes include usual constructs for input, output, and labeled choice. Common forms of recursion, parallel composition, conditionals, and restriction are also included. As illustrated in Sect. 1, constructs for session establishment are annotated with a session type α, which is useful in derived static analyses. A prefix for closing a session, inherited from [8], is convenient to structure specifications. Variable x is bound in processes $\overline{u}(x{:}\alpha).P$, $u(x{:}\alpha).P$, and $k(x).P$. Binding for name and channel restriction is as usual. Also, recursion variable $\mathcal{X}$ is bound in process $\mu\mathcal{X}.P$. Given a process P, its sets of free/bound channels, names, variables, and recursion variables—noted $\mathsf{fc}(P)$, $\mathsf{fn}(P)$, $\mathsf{fv}(P)$, $\mathsf{fpv}(P)$, $\mathsf{bc}(P)$, $\mathsf{bn}(P)$, $\mathsf{bv}(P)$, and $\mathsf{bpv}(P)$, respectively—are as expected. We always rely on usual notions of α-conversion and (capture-avoiding) substitution, denoted $[k/x]$ (for channels) and $[P/\mathcal{X}]$ (for processes). We write $[k_1, \ldots, k_n/x_1, \ldots, x_n]$ to stand for an n-ary simultaneous substitution. Processes without free variables or free channels are called *programs*.

Table 1. Process syntax. Above, annotation α denotes a session type.

$$
\begin{aligned}
e \ ::=& \ v \ \big| \ x, y, z \ \big| \ k = k \ \big| \ a = a & \text{expressions} \\
& \big| \ \mathsf{arrive}(\mathsf{loc}, r) & \text{arrival predicate} \\
P \ ::=& \ \overline{u}(x : \alpha).P \ \ \big| \ \ u(x : \alpha).P \ \ \big| \ \ \mathsf{close}\,(k).P & \text{session request / acceptance / closure} \\
& \big| \ \overline{k}(e).P \ \ \big| \ \ k(x).P & \text{data output /input} \\
& \big| \ k \triangleleft n; P \ \ \big| \ \ k \triangleright \{n_i{:}P_i\}_{i\in I} & \text{selection / branching} \\
& \big| \ \mu \mathcal{X}.P \ \ \big| \ \ \mathcal{X} & \text{recursion / rec. variable} \\
& \big| \ P \mid P \ \ \big| \ \ \mathbf{0} & \text{parallel composition / inaction} \\
& \big| \ (\nu \kappa) P \ \ \big| \ \ (\nu u) P \ \ \big| \ \ \mathsf{if}\ e\ \mathsf{then}\ P\ \mathsf{else}\ Q & \text{channel / name hiding / conditional} \\
& \big| \ k \lfloor \alpha \rfloor & \text{session monitor} \\
& \big| \ \mathsf{loc}[P] & \text{located process} \\
& \big| \ \mathsf{loc}\{\mathsf{case}\ \widetilde{x}\ \mathsf{of}\ \{(x_1{:}\beta_1^i; \cdots ; x_m{:}\beta_m^i) : Q_i\}_{i\in I}\} & \text{typeful update process} \\
& \big| \ \overline{\mathsf{loc}}(r) \ \big| \ \mathsf{loc}\lfloor \widetilde{r} \rfloor & \text{adaptation signal / queue}
\end{aligned}
$$

Up to here, the language is a synchronous π-calculus with sessions. Building upon *locations* $\mathsf{loc}, l_1, l_2, \ldots$, constructs for adaptation are: *located processes*, denoted $\mathsf{loc}[P]$; *update processes*, denoted $\mathsf{loc}\{\mathsf{case}\ x_1, \ldots, x_m\ \mathsf{of}\ \{(x_1{:}\beta_1^i; \cdots ; x_m{:}\beta_m^i) : Q_i\}_{i\in I}\}$; *(session) monitors*, denoted $\kappa^p \lfloor \alpha \rfloor$; *location queues*, denoted $\mathsf{loc}\lfloor \widetilde{r} \rfloor$; and *adaptation signals*, denoted $\overline{\mathsf{loc}}(r)$. Moreover, expressions include the *arrival predicate* $\mathsf{arrive}(\mathsf{loc}, r)$.

We now comment on these elements. *Located processes* and *update processes* have been motivated in Sect. 1. Here we just remark that update processes are assumed to refer to at least one variable x_i and to offer at least one alternative Q_i. Also, variables $x_1, \ldots, x_m$ are bound in $\mathsf{loc}\{\mathsf{case}\ x_1, \ldots, x_m\ \mathsf{of}\ \{(x_1{:}\beta_1^i; \cdots ; x_m{:}\beta_m^i) : Q_i\}_{i\in I}\}$; this process is often abbreviated as $\mathsf{loc}\{\mathsf{case}\ \widetilde{x}\ \mathsf{of}\ \{(x_1{:}\beta_1^i; \cdots ; x_m{:}\beta_m^i) : Q_i\}_{i\in I}\}$. Update processes generalize the `typecase` introduced in [11], which defines a case-like choice based on a single channel; in contrast, to specify adaptation for locations with multiple open sessions, our update processes define type-directed checks over one or more channels.

Update processes go hand-in-hand with *monitors*, runtime entities which keep the current protocol state at a given channel. We write $\kappa^p \lfloor \alpha \rfloor$ to denote the monitor which stores the protocol state α for channel κ^p. In [11], a similar construct is used to store in-transit messages in asynchronous communication. For simplicity, here we consider synchronous communication; monitors store only the current protocol state. This choice is aligned with our goal of identifying the core elements from the eventful session framework that are central in defining runtime adaptation (cf. Remark 3.7).

Location queues, not present in [11], handle adaptation requests, modeled as a possibly empty sequence of messages $\widetilde{r}$. Location queues enable us to give a unified treatment to adaptation requests, internal and external. Given $\mathsf{loc}\lfloor \widetilde{r} \rfloor$, it is worth observing that messages $\widetilde{r}$ are not related to communication as abstracted

Table 2. Reduction semantics: selected rules. Both α and β denote session types.

$\langle\textsc{r:Open}\rangle$ $C\{u(x:\alpha).P\} \mid D\{\overline{u}(y:\beta).Q\} \longrightarrow$
$$(\nu\kappa)(C\{P[^{\kappa^{p}}/x] \mid \kappa^{p}\lfloor\alpha\rfloor\} \mid D\{Q[^{\kappa^{\overline{p}}}/y] \mid \kappa^{\overline{p}}\lfloor\beta\rfloor\}) \quad (\alpha \perp_{\mathsf{c}} \beta)$$

$\langle\textsc{r:Com}\rangle$ $C\{\overline{\kappa}^{p}(v).P \mid \kappa^{p}\lfloor!(T).\alpha\rfloor\} \mid D\{\kappa^{\overline{p}}(x).Q \mid \kappa^{\overline{p}}\lfloor?(T).\beta\rfloor\} \longrightarrow$
$$C\{P \mid \kappa^{p}\lfloor\alpha\rfloor\} \mid D\{Q[^{v}/x] \mid \kappa^{\overline{p}}\lfloor\beta\rfloor\}$$

$\langle\textsc{r:Sel}\rangle$ $C\{\kappa^{p} \triangleright \{n_{j}:P_{j}\}_{j\in J} \mid \kappa^{p}\lfloor\&\{n_{j}:\alpha_{j}\}_{j\in J}\rfloor\} \mid D\{\kappa^{\overline{p}} \triangleleft n_{i}; Q \mid \kappa^{\overline{p}}\lfloor\oplus\{n_{j}:\beta_{j}\}_{j\in J}\rfloor\}$
$$\longrightarrow C\{P_{i} \mid \kappa^{p}\lfloor\alpha_{i}\rfloor\} \mid D\{Q \mid \kappa^{\overline{p}}\lfloor\beta_{i}\rfloor\} \quad (i \in J)$$

$\langle\textsc{r:Clo}\rangle$ $C\{\mathsf{close}\,(\kappa^{p}).P \mid \kappa^{p}\lfloor\varepsilon\rfloor\} \mid D\{\mathsf{close}\,(\kappa^{\overline{p}}).Q \mid \kappa^{\overline{p}}\lfloor\varepsilon\rfloor\} \longrightarrow C\{P\} \mid D\{Q\}$

$\langle\textsc{r:UReq}\rangle$ $C\{\mathsf{loc}\lfloor\widetilde{r}_{1}\rfloor\} \mid D\{\overline{\mathsf{loc}}(r)\} \longrightarrow C\{\mathsf{loc}\lfloor\widetilde{r}_{1} \cdot r\rfloor\} \mid D\{\mathbf{0}\}$

$\langle\textsc{r:Arr1}\rangle$
$$\frac{\widetilde{r} = r_{1} \cdot \widetilde{r}_{0}}{C\{\mathsf{E}[\mathsf{arrive}(\mathsf{loc}, r_{1})]\} \mid D\{\mathsf{loc}\lfloor\widetilde{r}\rfloor\} \longrightarrow C\{\mathsf{E}[\mathbf{true}]\} \mid D\{\mathsf{loc}\lfloor\widetilde{r}_{0}\rfloor\}}$$

$\langle\textsc{r:Arr2}\rangle$
$$\frac{(\widetilde{r} = r_{2} \cdot \widetilde{r}_{0} \wedge r_{1} \neq r_{2}) \vee \widetilde{r} = \epsilon}{C\{\mathsf{E}[\mathsf{arrive}(\mathsf{loc}, r_{1})]\} \mid D\{\mathsf{loc}\lfloor\widetilde{r}\rfloor\} \longrightarrow C\{\mathsf{E}[\mathbf{false}]\} \mid D\{\mathsf{loc}\lfloor\widetilde{r}\rfloor\}}$$

$\langle\textsc{r:Upd}\rangle$
$$\frac{\begin{array}{c}\mathsf{fc}(P) = \{\kappa_{1}^{p}, \ldots, \kappa_{m}^{p}\} \quad \forall j \in [1, .., m].(\kappa_{j}^{p}\lfloor\alpha_{j}\rfloor \in P) \\ (V = P) \bigvee \exists l.(\mathsf{match}_{I}(l, \{\alpha_{1}, \ldots, \alpha_{m}\}, \{\beta_{1}^{i}, \ldots, \beta_{m}^{i}\}_{i\in I}) \wedge \\ V = Q_{l}[\kappa_{1}^{p}, \ldots, \kappa_{m}^{p}/x_{1}, \ldots, x_{m}])\end{array}}{C\{\mathsf{loc}[P]\} \mid D\{\mathsf{loc}\{\mathsf{case}\,\widetilde{x}\,\mathsf{of}\,\{(x_{1}{:}\beta_{1}^{i}; \cdots; x_{m}{:}\beta_{m}^{i}) : Q_{i}\}_{i\in I}\}\} \longrightarrow \\ C\{\mathsf{loc}[V]\} \mid D\{\mathbf{0}\}}$$

by session types. This represents the fact that we handle adaptation requests and structured session exchanges as orthogonal issues. An *adaptation signal* $\overline{\mathsf{loc}}(r)$ enqueues request r into the location queue of loc. To this end, as detailed below, the operational semantics defines synchronizations between adaptation signals and location queues. To connect runtime adaptation and communication, our language allows the coupling of update processes with the *arrival predicate on locations*, denoted $\mathsf{arrive}(\mathsf{loc}, r)$. Inspired by the `arrive` predicate in [11], this predicate detects if a message r has been placed in the queue of loc.

Our language embodies several concerns related to runtime adaptation: using adaptation signals and location queues we may formally express *how* an adaptation request is issued; arrival predicates enable us to specify *when* adaptation will be handled; using update processes and monitors we may specify *what* is the goal of an adaptation event.

Semantics. The semantics of our language is given by a *reduction semantics*, the smallest relation generated by the rules in Table 5 (Appendix A). We write $P \longrightarrow P'$ for the reduction from P to P'. Reduction relies on a standard notion of structural congruence, denoted $\equiv$ (see [8, Def. 1]). It also relies on *evaluation* and *location* contexts:

$$\mathsf{E} ::= - \mid \overline{k}(-).P \mid \mathsf{if} - \mathsf{then}\,P\,\mathsf{else}\,Q \qquad C, D ::= - \mid \mathsf{loc}[C \mid P]$$

Given $C\{-\}$ (resp. $\mathsf{E}[-]$), we write $C\{P\}$ (resp. $\mathsf{E}[e]$) to denote the process (resp. expression) obtained by filling in occurrences of hole $-$ in C with P (resp. in E with e).

Table 2 gives a selection of reduction rules; we comment on these rules below. The first four rules formalize session behavior within hierarchies of nested locations. Using duality for session types, denoted $\perp_c$ (see [7] and Sect. 3), in rule $\langle \text{R:OPEN} \rangle$ the synchronization on a name u leads to establish a session on fresh channels κ^p and $\kappa^{\overline{p}}$; also, two monitors with the declared session types are created. Duality for polarities p is as expected: $\overline{+} = -$ and $\overline{-} = +$. Monitors are *local* by construction: they are created in the same contexts in which the session is established. Rule $\langle \text{R:COM} \rangle$ represents communication of a value: we require both complementary prefixes and that the monitors support input and output actions. After reduction, prefixes in processes and monitors are consumed. Similarly, rule $\langle \text{R:SEL} \rangle$ for labeled choice is standard, augmented with monitors. Rule $\langle \text{R:CLO} \rangle$ formalizes session termination, discarding involved monitors. The monitors in these three rules allow us to track the evolution of active session protocols.

The remaining rules in Table 2 define our event-based approach to runtime adaptation. Rule $\langle \text{R:UREQ} \rangle$ treats the issue of an adaptation request r as a synchronization between a location queue and an adaptation signal. The queue and the signal may be in different contexts; this enables "remote" requests. Rules $\langle \text{R:ARR1} \rangle$ and $\langle \text{R:ARR2} \rangle$ resolve arrival predicates by querying the (possibly remote) queue $\tilde{r}$. Rule $\langle \text{R:UPD} \rangle$ defines the typeful update of the current protocol state at loc, which is given by an indexed set of open sessions with their associated monitors. The rule attempts to match such protocol state with the first suitable option offered by an update process for loc. If there is no matching alternative the current protocol state at loc is kept unchanged. By an abuse of notation, we write $P_1 \in P$ to indicate that P_1 occurs in P, i.e., if $P = C[P_1]$ for some C. Formally, given an index set I over the update process, suitability with respect to the behavior at loc is defined by predicate match_I in Definition 2.1 below. Using subtyping $\leq_c$ (see [7] and Sect. 3), the predicate holds for an $l \in I$ which defines a new protocol state.

In addition to the rules in Table 2, our semantics includes standard and/or self-explanatory treatments for reduction under evaluation contexts, parallel composition, located context, and restriction. Also, it accounts for applications of structural congruence, recursion and conditionals. The full set of rules is in Table 5 (Appendix A).

Definition 2.1 (Matching). *Given an index set I, session types $\alpha_1, \ldots, \alpha_m$, an indexed sequence of session types $\{\beta_1^i, \ldots, \beta_m^i\}_{i \in I}$, and an $l \in I$, we write*

$$\text{match}_I(l, \{\alpha_1, \ldots, \alpha_m\}, \{\beta_1^i, \ldots, \beta_m^i\}_{i \in I})$$

if and only if $\forall n < l.(\exists j \in [1..m]. \beta_j^n \not\leq_c \alpha_j) \wedge (\bigwedge_{h \in [1..m]} \beta_h^l \leq_c \alpha_h).$

Example 2.2. Recall process W given in the Introduction. According to our semantics:

$$W \longrightarrow (\nu\kappa)\big(\mathsf{sys}\big[\,\mathsf{buyer}\big[P[\kappa^p/x]\mid \kappa^p\lfloor\alpha\rfloor\big]\mid \mathsf{seller}\big[Q[\kappa^{\overline{p}}/y]\mid \kappa^{\overline{p}}\lfloor\beta\rfloor\big]\big]\big)$$
$$\longrightarrow^2 (\nu\kappa)\big(\mathsf{sys}\big[\,\mathsf{buyer}\big[P'\mid \kappa^p\lfloor\alpha_{\mathsf{pay}}\rfloor\big]\mid \mathsf{seller}\big[Q'\mid \kappa^{\overline{p}}\lfloor\beta_{\mathsf{pay}}\rfloor\big]\big]\big)$$

Suppose that following an external request the seller must offer a new payment method. (a gift card). Precisely, we would like S to act according to the type β_{gift} given in Sect. 1. Let α_{gift} be the dual of β_{gift}. We then may define the following update process R^1_{xy}:

$$\mathsf{sys}\big\{\mathsf{case}\,x,y\,\mathsf{of}\,\{(x{:}\alpha_{\mathsf{pay}}\,;\,y{:}\beta_{\mathsf{pay}}):\mathsf{buyer}\big[P'\mid x\lfloor\alpha_{\mathsf{gift}}\rfloor\big]\mid \mathsf{seller}\big[Q''\mid y\lfloor\beta_{\mathsf{gift}}\rfloor\big]\}\big\}$$

Thus, R^1_{xy} keeps the expected implementation for the buyer (P'), but updates its associated monitor. For the seller, both the implementation and monitor are updated; above, Q'' stands for a process offering the three payment methods. We may then specify the whole system as: $W \mid \mu\mathcal{X}.\mathsf{if\ arrive}(\mathsf{sys}, \mathsf{upd}_E)$ then R^1_{xy} else $\mathcal{X}$. The type system introduced next ensures, among other things, that updates such as R^1_{xy} consider both a process and its associated monitors, ruling out the possibility of discarding the monitors that enable reduction.

3   Session Types for Eventful Runtime Adaptation

This section introduces a session type system for the process language of Sect. 2. Our main result (Theorem 3.6) is that well-typed programs enjoy both *safety* (absence of runtime communication errors) and *consistency* properties (update actions do not disrupt established sessions). Our development follows the lines of the typed framework in [8].

The syntax of session types (ranged over by $\alpha, \beta, \ldots$) has been already presented in the Introduction. We consider *basic types* (ranged over by $\tau, \sigma, \ldots$) and write $T, S, \ldots$ to range over τ, α. Therefore, although our process language copes with runtime adaptation, our type syntax is standard and retains the intuitive meaning of session types [9], which we now briefly recall. Type $?(\tau).\alpha$ (resp. $?(\beta).\alpha$) abstracts the behavior of a channel which receives a value of type τ (resp. a channel of type β) and then continues as α. Dually, type $!(\tau).\alpha$ (resp. $!(\beta).\alpha$) represents the behavior of a channel which sends a value of type τ and then continues as α. Type $\&\{n_1 : \alpha_1 \ldots n_m : \alpha_m\}$ describes a branching behavior: it offers m behaviors, and if the j-th alternative is selected then it behaves as described by type α_j ($1 \leq j \leq m$). In turn, type $\oplus\{n_1 : \alpha_1 \ldots n_m : \alpha_m\}$ describes the behavior of a channel which may select a single behavior among $\alpha_1, \ldots, \alpha_m$ and then continues as α_j. We use ε to type a channel with no communication behavior. Type $\mu t.\alpha$ describes recursive behavior; as usual, we consider recursive types under equi-recursive and contractive assumptions.

Along the paper we have informally appealed to *duality* and *subtyping* over session types (denoted $\perp_\mathsf{c}$ and $\leq_\mathsf{c}$, resp.). For the sake of space, we omit their full definitions; we just remark that since our session type structure is standard, we may rely on the (coinductive) definitions given by Gay and Hole [7], which are standard and well-understood.

Our typing judgments generalize usual notions with an *interface* $\mathcal{I}$. Based on the syntactic occurrences of session establishment prefixes $\bar{a}(x{:}\alpha)$, and $a(x{:}\alpha)$, the interface of a process describes the services appearing in it. We annotate services with a *qualification* q, which may be 'lin' (linear) or 'un' (unrestricted). Thus, the interface of a process gives an "upper bound" on the services that it may execute. The typing system uses interfaces to control the behavior contained by locations after an update. We have:

Definition 3.1 (Interfaces). *We define an* interface *as the multiset whose underlying set of elements is* $\mathrm{I} = \{\mathsf{q}\,u{:}\alpha \mid \mathsf{q} \in \{\mathsf{lin}, \mathsf{un}\}\}$ *(i.e., a set of assignments from names to qualified session types). We use* $\mathcal{I}, \mathcal{I}', \ldots$ *to range over interfaces. We write* $dom(\mathcal{I})$ *to denote the set* $\{u \mid u : \alpha_\mathsf{q} \in \mathcal{I}\}$ *and* $\#_\mathcal{I}(a) = h$ *to mean that* a *occurs* h *times in* $\mathcal{I}$.

The union of two interfaces is essentially the union of their underlying multisets. We sometimes write $\mathcal{I} \uplus a : \alpha_\mathsf{lin}$ and $\mathcal{I} \uplus a : \alpha_\mathsf{un}$ to stand for $\mathcal{I} \uplus \{\mathsf{lin}\,a{:}\alpha\}$ and $\mathcal{I} \uplus \{\mathsf{un}\,a{:}\alpha\}$, respectively. Moreover, we write $\mathcal{I}_\mathsf{lin}$ (resp. $\mathcal{I}_\mathsf{un}$) to denote the subset of $\mathcal{I}$ involving only assignments qualified with lin (resp. un). We now define an ordering relation over interfaces, relying on subtyping:

Definition 3.2 (Interface Ordering). *Given interfaces* $\mathcal{I}$ *and* $\mathcal{I}'$, *we write* $\mathcal{I} \sqsubseteq \mathcal{I}'$ *iff*

1. $\forall(\mathsf{lin}\,a{:}\alpha)$ *such that* $\#_{\mathcal{I}_\mathsf{lin}}(\mathsf{lin}\,a{:}\alpha) = h$ *with* $h > 0$, *then one of the following holds:*
   (a) *there exist* h *distinct elements* $(\mathsf{lin}\,a{:}\beta_i) \in \mathcal{I}'_\mathsf{lin}$ *such that* $\alpha \leq_\mathsf{c} \beta_i$ *for* $i \in [1..h]$;
   (b) *there exists* $(\mathsf{un}\,a{:}\beta) \in \mathcal{I}'_\mathsf{un}$ *such that* $\alpha \leq_\mathsf{c} \beta$.
2. $\forall(\mathsf{un}\,a{:}\alpha) \in \mathcal{I}_\mathsf{un}$ *then* $(\mathsf{un}\,a{:}\beta) \in \mathcal{I}'_\mathsf{un}$ *and* $\alpha \leq_\mathsf{c} \beta$, *for some* β.

We now define our typing environments. We write q to range over qualifiers lin and un.

$$\Delta ::= \emptyset \mid \Delta, k : \alpha \mid \Delta, k : \lfloor\alpha\rfloor \qquad\qquad \text{typing with active sessions}$$
$$\Gamma ::= \emptyset \mid \Gamma, e : \tau \mid \Gamma, u : \langle\alpha_\mathsf{q}, \beta_\mathsf{q}\rangle \quad \text{first-order environment (with } \alpha_\mathsf{q} \perp_\mathsf{c} \beta_\mathsf{q})$$
$$\Theta ::= \emptyset \mid \Theta, \mathcal{X} : \Delta; \mathcal{I} \mid \Theta, \mathrm{loc} : \mathcal{I} \qquad\qquad \text{higher-order environment}$$

We consider typings Δ and environments Γ and Θ. Typing Δ collects assignments from channels to session types; it describes currently active sessions. In our system, Δ also includes *bracketed assignments*, denoted $\kappa^p : \lfloor\alpha\rfloor$, which represent the type for monitors. Subtyping extends to these assignments ($\lfloor\alpha\rfloor \leq_\mathsf{c} \lfloor\beta\rfloor$ if $\alpha \leq_\mathsf{c} \beta$) and thus to typings. We write $dom(\Delta)$ to denote the set $\{k^p \mid k^p : \alpha \in \Delta \vee k^p : \lfloor\alpha\rfloor \in \Delta\}$. We write $\Delta, k : \alpha$ where $k \notin dom(\Delta)$. Furthermore, we write $\Delta, k : \langle\!\langle\alpha\rangle\!\rangle$ to abbreviate $\Delta, k : \alpha, k : \lfloor\alpha\rfloor$. That is, $k : \langle\!\langle\alpha\rangle\!\rangle$ describes both a session and its associated monitor.

Table 3. Well-typed processes: selected rules.

$$\frac{}{\Theta, loc : \mathcal{I} \vdash loc \triangleright \mathcal{I}} \; \langle \text{T.LocEnv} \rangle \qquad \frac{}{\Gamma; \Theta \vdash k\lfloor \alpha \rfloor \triangleright k : \lfloor \alpha \rfloor; \emptyset} \; \langle \text{T.Que} \rangle$$

$$\frac{}{\Gamma \vdash r_1 \triangleright msg} \; \langle \text{T.Msg} \rangle \qquad \frac{\Gamma \vdash \widetilde{r} \triangleright msg \quad \Gamma \vdash r_1 \triangleright msg}{\Gamma \vdash r_1; \widetilde{r} \triangleright msg} \; \langle \text{T.LocQ} \rangle$$

$$\frac{\Theta \vdash loc \triangleright \mathcal{I} \quad \Gamma \vdash r \triangleright msg}{\Gamma; \Theta \vdash \mathsf{arrive}(loc, r) \triangleright \mathsf{bool}} \; \langle \text{T.Arrive} \rangle \qquad \frac{\Gamma \vdash r \triangleright msg}{\Gamma; \Theta \vdash \overline{loc}(r) \triangleright \emptyset; \emptyset} \; \langle \text{T.Sig} \rangle$$

$$\frac{\Theta \vdash loc \triangleright \mathcal{I} \quad \Gamma; \Theta \vdash P \triangleright \Delta; \mathcal{I}' \quad \mathcal{I}' \sqsubseteq \mathcal{I}}{\Gamma; \Theta \vdash loc[P] \triangleright \Delta; \mathcal{I}'} \; \langle \text{T.Loc} \rangle \qquad \frac{\Gamma \vdash \widetilde{r} \triangleright msg}{\Gamma; \Theta \vdash loc[\widetilde{r}] \triangleright \emptyset; \emptyset} \; \langle \text{T.QLoc} \rangle$$

$$\frac{\alpha \perp_c \beta \quad \Gamma \vdash u \triangleright \langle \alpha_{\mathsf{lin}}, \beta_{\mathsf{lin}} \rangle \quad \gamma \leq_c \alpha \quad \Gamma; \Theta \vdash P \triangleright \Delta, x : \gamma; \mathcal{I}}{\Gamma; \Theta \vdash u(x : \gamma).P \triangleright \Delta; \mathcal{I} \uplus u : \gamma_{\mathsf{lin}}} \; \langle \text{T.Accept} \rangle$$

$$\frac{\alpha \perp_c \beta \quad \Gamma \vdash u \triangleright \langle \alpha_{\mathsf{q}}, \beta_{\mathsf{lin}} \rangle \quad \gamma \leq_c \beta \quad \Gamma; \Theta \vdash P \triangleright \Delta, x : \gamma; \mathcal{I}}{\Gamma; \Theta \vdash \overline{u}(x : \gamma).P \triangleright \Delta; \mathcal{I} \uplus u : \gamma_{\mathsf{lin}}} \; \langle \text{T.Request} \rangle$$

$$\frac{\Gamma; \Theta \vdash P \triangleright \Delta; \mathcal{I} \quad k \notin dom(\Delta)}{\Gamma; \Theta \vdash \mathsf{close}\,(k).P \triangleright \Delta, k : \varepsilon; \mathcal{I}} \; \langle \text{T.Clo} \rangle \qquad \frac{\Gamma; \Theta \vdash P \triangleright \Delta_1; \mathcal{I}_1 \quad \Gamma; \Theta \vdash Q \triangleright \Delta_2; \mathcal{I}_2}{\Gamma; \Theta \vdash P \mid Q \triangleright \Delta_1 \cup \Delta_2; \mathcal{I}_1 \uplus \mathcal{I}_2} \; \langle \text{T.Par} \rangle$$

$$\frac{\begin{array}{c} \Theta \vdash loc \triangleright \mathcal{I} \quad \forall j \in J, \; \mathsf{fv}(Q_j) \setminus \{x_1, \ldots, x_m\} = \emptyset \\ \Gamma; \Theta \vdash Q_j \triangleright x_1 : \langle\!\langle \beta_1^j \rangle\!\rangle; \cdots; x_m : \langle\!\langle \beta_m^j \rangle\!\rangle; \mathcal{I}_j \quad \mathcal{I}_j \sqsubseteq \mathcal{I} \end{array}}{\Gamma; \Theta \vdash loc\{\mathsf{case}\, \widetilde{x}\, \mathsf{of}\, \{(x_1 : \beta_1^j; \cdots; x_m : \beta_m^j) : Q_j\}_{j \in J}\} \triangleright \emptyset; \emptyset} \; \langle \text{T.Adapt} \rangle$$

$$\frac{\Gamma; \Theta \vdash P \triangleright \Delta, \kappa^p : \langle\!\langle \alpha_1 \rangle\!\rangle, \kappa^{\overline{p}} : \langle\!\langle \alpha_2 \rangle\!\rangle; \mathcal{I} \quad \alpha_1 \perp_c \alpha_2}{\Gamma; \Theta \vdash (\nu\kappa)P \triangleright \Delta; \mathcal{I}} \; \langle \text{T.CRes} \rangle$$

$$\frac{\Gamma; \Theta \vdash P \triangleright \Delta; \mathcal{I} \quad \Delta \leq_c \Delta' \quad \mathcal{I} \sqsubseteq \mathcal{I}'}{\Gamma; \Theta \vdash P \triangleright \Delta'; \mathcal{I}'} \; \langle \text{T.Sub} \rangle \qquad \frac{\Gamma; \Theta \vdash P \triangleright \Delta; \mathcal{I} \cup \mathcal{I}_u \quad u \notin dom(\mathcal{I})}{\Gamma; \Theta \vdash (\nu u)P \triangleright \Delta; \mathcal{I}} \; \langle \text{T.NRes} \rangle$$

Γ is a first-order environment which maps expressions to basic types and names to pairs of qualified session types. As motivated earlier, a session type is qualified with 'un' if it is associated to a unrestricted/persistent service; otherwise, it is qualified with 'lin'. The higher-order environment Θ collects assignments of typings to process variables and interfaces to locations. While the former concerns recursive processes, the latter concerns located processes. As we explain next, by relying on the combination of these two pieces of information the type system ensures that runtime adaptation actions preserve the behavioral interfaces of a process. We write $vdom(\Theta) = \{\mathsf{X} \mid \mathsf{X} : \mathcal{I} \in \Theta\}$ to denote the variables in the domain of Θ. Given these environments, a *type judgment* is of form

$$\Gamma; \Theta \vdash P \triangleright \Delta; \mathcal{I}$$

meaning that, under environments Γ and Θ, process P has active sessions declared in Δ and interface $\mathcal{I}$. Selected typing rules are shown in Table 3; remaining rules can be found in Table 6 (Appendix B). Below we comment on some of the rules in Table 3: the rest are standard and/or self explanatory. Rule $\langle \text{T:Adapt} \rangle$ types update processes. Notice that the typing rule ensures that each process Q_i has exactly the same active sessions that those declared in the respective case. Also, we require that alternatives contain both processes and monitors. With $\mathcal{I}_j \sqsubseteq \mathcal{I}$ we guarantee that the process behavior does not "exceed" the expected behavior within the location. Rule $\langle\text{T:SUB}\rangle$ takes care of subtyping both for typings Δ and interfaces. Rule $\langle\text{T:CRES}\rangle$ types channel restriction that ensures typing duality among partners of a session and their respective queues. Typing of queues is given by rule $\langle\text{T:QUE}\rangle$ that simply assigns type $k : \lfloor\alpha\rfloor$ to queue $k\lfloor\alpha\rfloor$. Finally, rule $\langle\text{T:NRES}\rangle$ types hiding of service names, by simply removing their declarations from the interface $\mathcal{I}$ of the process. In the rule, $\mathcal{I}_u$ contains only declarations for u, i.e., $\forall v \neq u, v \notin \text{dom}(\mathcal{I}_u)$.

Our type system enjoys the standard *subject reduction* property. We rely on *balanced* typings: Δ is balanced iff for all $\kappa^p : \alpha \in \Delta$ (resp. $\kappa^p : \lfloor\alpha\rfloor \in \Delta$) then also $\kappa^{\overline{p}} : \beta \in \Delta$ (resp. $\kappa^{\overline{p}} : \lfloor\beta\rfloor \in \Delta$), with $\alpha \perp_{\mathsf{c}} \beta$. The proof proceeds by induction on the last rule applied in the reduction; it adapts the one given in [8].

Theorem 3.3 (Subject Reduction). *If $\Gamma \,;\, \Theta \vdash P \triangleright \Delta; \mathcal{I}$ with Δ balanced and $P \longrightarrow Q$ then $\Gamma \,;\, \Theta \vdash Q \triangleright \Delta'; \mathcal{I}'$, for some $\mathcal{I}'$ and balanced Δ'.*

We now define and state *safety* and *consistency* properties. While safety guarantees adherence to prescribed session types and absence of runtime errors, consistency ensures that sessions are not jeopardized by careless runtime adaptation actions. Defining both properties requires the following notions of κ-*processes*, κ-*redexes*, and *error process*.

Definition 3.4 (κ-processes, κ-redexes, Errors). *A process P is a κ-process if it is a prefixed process with subject κ^p, i.e., P is one of the following:*

$$\kappa^p(x).P' \qquad \overline{\kappa}^p(v).P' \qquad \mathsf{close}\,(\kappa^p).P' \qquad \kappa^p \triangleright \{n_i{:}P_i\}_{i\in I} \qquad \kappa^p \triangleleft n.P'$$

Process P is a κ-redex if it contains the composition of exactly two κ-processes with opposing polarities. P is an error if $P \equiv (\nu\tilde{\kappa})(Q \mid R)$ where, for some κ, Q contains <u>either</u> exactly two κ-processes that do not form a κ-redex <u>or</u> three or more κ-processes.

Informally, a process P is called *consistent* if whenever it has a κ-redex then update actions do not destroy such a redex. Below, we formalize this intuition. Let us write $P \longrightarrow_{\text{upd}} P'$ for any reduction inferred using rule $\langle\text{R:UPD}\rangle$. We then define:

Definition 3.5 (Safety, Consistency). *Let P be a process. We say P is safe if it never reduces into an error. We say P is update-consistent if and only if, for all P' and κ such that $P \longrightarrow^* P'$ and P' contains a κ-redex, if $P' \longrightarrow_{\text{upd}} P''$ then P'' contains a κ-redex.*

We now state our main result; it follows as a consequence of Theorem 3.3.

Theorem 3.6 (Typing Ensures Safety and Consistency). *If $\Gamma \,;\, \Theta \vdash P \triangleright \Delta; \mathcal{I}$ with Δ balanced then program P is update consistent and safe.*

Remark 3.7 (Asynchronous Communication). We have focused on *synchronous* communication: this allows us to give a compact semantics, relying on a standard type structure. To account for asynchrony, we would require a runtime syntax for programs with queues for in-transit messages (values, sessions, labels). The type system must be extended to accommodate these new runtime processes. In our case, an extension with asynchrony would rely on the machinery defined in [11].

4   Discussion: A Compartmentalized Model of Communication and Adaptation

Given that the process model in Sect. 2 enables the interplay of communication and adaptation, how can we organize specifications to reflect a desirable separation of concerns? In ongoing work, with the aim of specifying systems at a high-level of abstraction, we have developed a model which defines *compartments* to isolate communication behavior and adaptation routines. Here we briefly describe this model, which is given in Table 4.

In a nutshell, programs of Sect. 2 are now organized into *systems*. A system G is the composition of a set of *applications* $A_1, \ldots, A_n$ each comprising three elements: a *behavior* R, a *state* S, and a *manager* $\mathcal{M}$. As a simple example of a system, we may consider the operating system of a smartphone, which is meant to manage a number of applications that may interact among them. Applications in our model can communicate between each other or exhibit intra-application communication. The behavior R is specified as a process; we distinguish between located processes representing service definitions from located processes which make use of such definitions. A reduction semantics (omitted) ensures that locations enclosing service definitions do not contain open (active) sessions. This may be convenient for defining adaptation strategies, since updates to service definitions may now be performed without concerns of disruption of active sessions. The state S collects session monitors and location queues and it is kept separate from R. As a simple example, the buyer-seller scenario given in Sect. 1 can be casted in our model as

$$\mathsf{byr}\langle \mathsf{buyer}\big[\,\overline{u@\mathsf{slr}}(x : \alpha).P\big] \,;\, \mathsf{S_b} \,;\, \mathcal{M}_b\rangle \parallel \mathsf{slr}\langle \mathsf{seller}\big[*\,u(y{:}\beta).Q\big] \,;\, \mathsf{S_s} \,;\, \mathcal{M}_s\rangle$$

That is, buyer and seller are implemented as separate applications, named byr and slr, respectively. Above, we have $\mathsf{S_b} = \mathsf{buyer}\lfloor\epsilon\rfloor$ and $\mathsf{S_s} = \mathsf{seller}\lfloor\epsilon\rfloor$.

While the manager $\mathcal{M}$ implements adaptation at the application (local) level, a *handler* $\mathcal{H}$ defines adaptation at the system (global) level. As we wish to describe communication behavior separately from adaptation routines, update processes are confined to handlers and managers. A manager is meant to react upon the arrival of an internal adaptation message upd_I. As in Sect. 2, managers may act upon the issue of an internal update request upd_I for some location, whereas handlers may act upon the arrival of an external update request or an application upgrade request (denoted upd_E and upg, respectively). A handler may either **update** or **upgrade** the behavior at some location loc within

Table 4. A compartmentalized model of communicating systems: syntax.

$$G ::= A \mid \mathcal{H} \mid (\nu\kappa)A \mid G_1 \parallel G_2 \mid \mathbf{0} \qquad A ::= a\langle R\,;\, \mathsf{S}\,;\, \mathcal{M}\rangle$$

$$\mathcal{H} ::= *\,\mathsf{if}\ \mathsf{arrive}(l_1@a, \mathsf{upd}_E)\ \mathsf{then}\ l_1\big\{\mathsf{case}\ \widetilde{x}\ \mathsf{of}\ \{(x_1{:}\beta_1^i\,;\cdots\,;x_m{:}\beta_m^i) : Q_i\}_{i\in I}\big\}$$

$$\mid\ *\,\mathsf{if}\ \mathsf{arrive}(l_1@a, \mathsf{upg})\ \mathsf{then}\ l_1\big\{\!\big\{P\big\}\!\big\}$$

$$R ::= \mathsf{loc}\big[u(x{:}\alpha).P\big] \mid \mathsf{loc}\big[*\,u(x{:}\alpha).P\big] \mid \mathsf{loc}\big[P^-\big] \mid R_1 \mid R_2$$

$$\mathsf{S} ::= \kappa^p\lfloor\alpha\rfloor \mid \mathsf{loc}\lfloor\widetilde{r}\rfloor \mid \mathsf{S}_1 \diamond \mathsf{S}_2 \mid \mathbf{0}$$

$$\mathcal{M} ::= *\,\mathsf{if}\ \mathsf{arrive}(l_1, \mathsf{upd}_I)\ \mathsf{then}\ l_1\big\{\mathsf{case}\ \widetilde{x}\ \mathsf{of}\ \{(x_1{:}\beta_1^i\,;\cdots\,;x_m{:}\beta_m^i) : Q_i\}_{i\in I}\big\} \mid \mathcal{M}_1 \circ \mathcal{M}_2 \mid \mathbf{0}$$

application a; this is written loc@a. Upgrades are denoted $l_1\{\!\{P\}\!\}$; they are a particular form of update intended for service definitions only. In Table 4 we write $*\mathsf{if}\ e\ \mathsf{then}\ P$ and $*u(x{:}\alpha).P$ as shorthands for persistent conditionals and services, respectively.

Our compartmentalized model induces specifications in which communication, runtime adaptation, and state (as in, e.g., asynchronous communication) are jointly expressed, while keeping a desirable separation of concerns. Notice that the differences between "plain" processes (as given in Sect. 2) and systems (as defined in Table 4) are mostly conceptual, rather than technical. In fact, the higher level of abstraction that is enforced by our model does not result in additional technicalities. We conjecture that a reduction-preserving translation of application-based specifications into processes does not exist—a main difficulty being, unsurprisingly, properly representing the separation between behavior and state. This difference in terms of expressiveness does not appear to affect the type system. In future work we plan to extend the typing discipline in Sect. 3 (and its associated safety and consistency guarantees) to systems.

5   Related Work and Concluding Remarks

Related Work. The combination of static typing and type-directed tests for dynamic reconfiguration is not new. For instance, Seco and Caires [14] study this combination for a calculus for object-oriented component programming. To the best of our knowledge, ours is the first work to develop this combination for a session process language. As already discussed, we build upon constructs proposed in [10–13]. The earliest works on eventful sessions, covering theory and implementation issues, are [10,12]. Kouzapas's PhD thesis [11] provides a unified presentation of the eventful framework, with case studies including event selectors (a building block in event-driven systems) and transformations between multithreaded and event-driven programs. At the level of types, the work in [11] introduces session set types to support the typecase construct. We use dynamic session type inspection only for runtime adaptation; in [11] typecase is part of the process syntax. This choice enables us to retain a standard session type syntax. Runtime adaptation of session typed processes—the main contribution of this paper—seems to be an application of eventful session types not previously identified.

Previous works on runtime adaptation for session types (binary and multi-party) include [1,3,8]. We have already commented on how our current approach enhances that in our previous work [8]. Both [1] and [3] study adaptation for multiparty communications, which already sets a substantial difference with respect to our work. In [3], a set of monitors which govern the behavior of participants are derived from a global specification. Self-adaptation for monitored processes is triggered by an external adaptation function, which is often left unspecified. As in our work, the operational semantics for adaptation in [3] uses (local) types and monitors; key differences include the use of type-directed checks for selecting adaptation routines that preserve consistency, and the use of events and queues to handle adaptation requests. The work [1] studies dynamic update for message passing programs; a form of consistency for updates over threads is ensured using multiparty session types, following an asynchronous communication discipline.

Concluding Remarks. Building upon [11], we have introduced an eventful approach to runtime adaptation of session typed processes. We identified the strictly necessary eventful process constructs that enhance and refine known mechanisms for runtime adaptation. Adaptation requests, both internal and external, are handled via event detectors and queues associated to locations. Our approach enables us to specify rich forms of updates on locations with running sessions; this represents a concrete improvement with respect to previous works [8]. We notice that expressing both internal and external exceptional events is useful in practice; for instance, both kinds of events coexist in BPMN 2.0 (see, e.g., [6, Chap. 4]). To rule out update steps that jeopardize running session protocols, we also introduced a type system that ensures communication safety and update consistency for session programs. We have also outlined a high-level model of structured interaction which organizes communication and adaptation components into a sensible structure.

Adaptation in our framework is "monotonic" or "incremental" in that changes always preserve/extend active session protocols, exploiting subtyping for enhanced flexibility. Interestingly, our framework can be modified so that arbitrary protocols are installed as a result of an update. One needs to ensure that the endpoints of a session are present in the same location: arbitrary updates are safe as long as both endpoints are simultaneously updated with dual protocols. To relax our framework in this way, we would need to modify definitions for session matching (Definition 2.1) and interface ordering (Definition 3.2).

In future work, we plan to further validate the constructs in our framework by revisiting the model of *supervision trees* (a mechanism for fault-tolerance in Erlang) that we gave in [4]. Other interesting topics for further development include accounting for *asynchronous* communication (cf. Remark 3.7) and extending our event-based approach to choreographic protocols; the framework in [3] may provide a good starting point.

Table 5. Reduction semantics: Full set of rules. Above, α and β denote session types.

$\langle\text{R:Open}\rangle$ $C\{u(x:\alpha).P\} \mid D\{\overline{u}(y:\beta).Q\} \longrightarrow$
$$(\nu\kappa)(C\{P[\kappa^p/x] \mid \kappa^p\lfloor\alpha\rfloor\} \mid D\{Q[\kappa^{\overline{p}}/y] \mid \kappa^{\overline{p}}\lfloor\beta\rfloor\}) \quad (\alpha \perp_c \beta)$$

$\langle\text{R:Com}\rangle$ $C\{\overline{\kappa}^p(v).P \mid \kappa^p\lfloor!(T).\alpha\rfloor\} \mid D\{\kappa^{\overline{p}}(x).Q \mid \kappa^{\overline{p}}\lfloor?(T).\beta\rfloor\} \longrightarrow$
$$C\{P \mid \kappa^p\lfloor\alpha\rfloor\} \mid D\{Q[v/x] \mid \kappa^{\overline{p}}\lfloor\beta\rfloor\}$$

$\langle\text{R:Sel}\rangle$ $C\{\kappa^p \triangleright \{n_j:P_j\}_{j\in J} \mid \kappa^p\lfloor\&\{n_j:\alpha_j\}_{j\in J}\rfloor\} \mid D\{\kappa^{\overline{p}} \triangleleft n_i; Q \mid \kappa^{\overline{p}}\lfloor\oplus\{n_j:\beta_j\}_{j\in J}\rfloor\}$
$$\longrightarrow C\{P_i \mid \kappa^p\lfloor\alpha_i\rfloor\} \mid D\{Q \mid \kappa^{\overline{p}}\lfloor\beta_i\rfloor\} \quad (i \in J)$$

$\langle\text{R:Clo}\rangle$ $C\{\text{close}\,(\kappa^p).P \mid \kappa^p\lfloor\varepsilon\rfloor\} \mid D\{\text{close}\,(\kappa^{\overline{p}}).Q \mid \kappa^{\overline{p}}\lfloor\varepsilon\rfloor\} \longrightarrow C\{P\} \mid D\{Q\}$

$\langle\text{R:Eva}\rangle$ if $e \longrightarrow e'$ then $\mathsf{E}[e] \longrightarrow \mathsf{E}[e']$

$\langle\text{R:Par}\rangle$ if $P \longrightarrow P'$ then $P \mid Q \longrightarrow P' \mid Q$

$\langle\text{R:ResN}\rangle$ if $P \longrightarrow P'$ then $(\nu a)P \longrightarrow (\nu a)P'$

$\langle\text{R:ResC}\rangle$ if $P \longrightarrow P'$ then $(\nu\kappa)P \longrightarrow (\nu\kappa)P'$

$\langle\text{R:Str}\rangle$ if $P \equiv P'$, $P' \longrightarrow Q'$, and $Q' \equiv Q$ then $P \longrightarrow Q$

$\langle\text{R:Rec}\rangle$ $\text{rec}\,\mathcal{X}.P \longrightarrow P[\text{rec}\,\mathcal{X}.P/\mathcal{X}]$

$\langle\text{R:IfTrue}\rangle$ if true then P else $Q \longrightarrow P$

$\langle\text{R:IfFalse}\rangle$ if false then P else $Q \longrightarrow Q$

$\langle\text{R:UReq}\rangle$ $C\{\text{loc}\lfloor\tilde{r}_1\rfloor\} \mid D\{\overline{\text{loc}}(r)\} \longrightarrow C\{\text{loc}\lfloor\tilde{r}_1 \cdot r\rfloor\} \mid D\{\mathbf{0}\}$

$\langle\text{R:Arr1}\rangle$ $$\frac{\tilde{r} = r_1 \cdot \tilde{r}_0}{C\{\mathsf{E}[\text{arrive}(\text{loc}, r_1)]\} \mid D\{\text{loc}\lfloor\tilde{r}\rfloor\} \longrightarrow C\{\mathsf{E}[\text{true}]\} \mid D\{\text{loc}\lfloor\tilde{r}_0\rfloor\}}$$

$\langle\text{R:Arr2}\rangle$ $$\frac{(\tilde{r} = r_2 \cdot \tilde{r}_0 \wedge r_1 \neq r_2) \vee \tilde{r} = \epsilon}{C\{\mathsf{E}[\text{arrive}(\text{loc}, r_1)]\} \mid D\{\text{loc}\lfloor\tilde{r}\rfloor\} \longrightarrow C\{\mathsf{E}[\text{false}]\} \mid D\{\text{loc}\lfloor\tilde{r}\rfloor\}}$$

$\langle\text{R:Upd}\rangle$ $$\frac{\begin{array}{c}\text{fc}(P) = \{\kappa_1^p, \ldots, \kappa_m^p\} \quad \forall j \in [1,..,m].(\kappa_j^p\lfloor\alpha_j\rfloor \in P) \\ (V = P) \vee \exists l.(\text{match}_I(l, \{\alpha_1, \ldots, \alpha_m\}, \{\beta_1^i, \ldots, \beta_m^i\}_{i\in I}) \wedge \\ V = Q_l[\kappa_1^p, \ldots, \kappa_m^p/x_1, \ldots, x_m])\end{array}}{C\{\text{loc}[P]\} \mid D\Big\{\text{loc}\{\text{case}\,\tilde{x}\,\text{of}\,\{(x_1:\beta_1^i; \cdots ; x_m:\beta_m^i) : Q_i\}_{i\in I}\}\Big\} \longrightarrow \\ C\{\text{loc}[V]\} \mid D\{\mathbf{0}\}}$$

Acknowledgments. We are grateful to Ilaria Castellani, Mariangiola Dezani-Ciancaglini, and the anonymous reviewers for useful remarks. This research was partially supported by COST Action IC1201: Behavioural Types for Reliable Large-Scale Software Systems.

A   Reduction Semantics: Full Set of Rules

Table 5 gives the full set of reduction semantics rules.

Table 6. Additional typing rules.

$$\frac{}{\Gamma \vdash \texttt{true, false} \rhd \texttt{bool}} \langle \text{T.BOOL} \rangle \qquad \frac{}{\Gamma \vdash u \rhd \texttt{name}} \langle \text{T.NAME} \rangle$$

$$\frac{}{\Gamma, x : \texttt{bool} \vdash x \rhd \texttt{bool}} \langle \text{T.BVAR} \rangle \qquad \frac{}{\Gamma, x : \texttt{name} \vdash x \rhd \texttt{name}} \langle \text{T.NVAR} \rangle$$

$$\frac{d = u \vee d = \kappa^p \vee d = x}{\Gamma \vdash d = d \rhd \texttt{bool}} \langle \text{T.EQ} \rangle \qquad \frac{\alpha \perp_c \beta}{\Gamma, u : \langle \alpha_q, \beta_q \rangle \vdash u \rhd \langle \alpha_q, \beta_q \rangle} \langle \text{T.SER} \rangle$$

$$\frac{}{\Gamma ; \Theta \vdash \mathbf{0} \rhd \emptyset; \emptyset} \langle \text{T.NIL} \rangle$$

$$\frac{}{\Gamma; \Theta, \mathcal{X} : \Delta, \mathcal{I} \vdash \mathcal{X} : \Delta; \mathcal{I}} \langle \text{T.RVAR} \rangle \qquad \frac{\Gamma ; \Theta, \mathcal{X} : \Delta; \mathcal{I} \vdash P \rhd \Delta; \mathcal{I}}{\Gamma ; \Theta \vdash \mu \mathcal{X}.P \rhd \Delta; \mathcal{I}} \langle \text{T.REC} \rangle$$

$$\frac{\Gamma ; \Theta \vdash P \rhd \Delta, k : \beta; \mathcal{I}}{\Gamma ; \Theta \vdash \overline{k}(k').P \rhd \Delta, k : !(\alpha).\beta, k' : \alpha; \mathcal{I}} \langle \text{T.THR} \rangle \qquad \frac{\Gamma ; \Theta \vdash P \rhd \Delta, k : \beta, x : \alpha; \mathcal{I}}{\Gamma ; \Theta \vdash k(x).P \rhd \Delta, k : ?(\alpha).\beta; \mathcal{I}} \langle \text{T.CAT} \rangle$$

$$\frac{\Gamma, x : \tau ; \Theta \vdash P \rhd \Delta, k : \alpha; \mathcal{I}}{\Gamma ; \Theta \vdash k(x).P \rhd \Delta, k : ?(\tau).\alpha; \mathcal{I}} \langle \text{T.IN} \rangle \qquad \frac{\Gamma ; \Theta \vdash P \rhd \Delta, k : \alpha; \mathcal{I} \quad \Gamma \vdash e \rhd \tau}{\Gamma ; \Theta \vdash \overline{k}(e).P \rhd \Delta, k : !(\tau).\alpha; \mathcal{I}} \langle \text{T.OUT} \rangle$$

$$\frac{\Gamma ; \Theta \vdash P \rhd \Delta; \mathcal{I} \quad \kappa^+, \kappa^- \notin dom(\Delta)}{\Gamma ; \Theta \vdash (\nu \kappa)P \rhd \Delta; \mathcal{I}} \langle \text{T.WEAKC} \rangle \qquad \frac{\Gamma ; \Theta \vdash P \rhd \Delta; \mathcal{I} \quad u \notin dom(\mathcal{I})}{\Gamma ; \Theta \vdash (\nu u)P \rhd \Delta; \mathcal{I}} \langle \text{T.WEAKN} \rangle$$

$$\frac{\Gamma ; \Theta \vdash e \rhd \texttt{bool} \quad \Gamma ; \Theta \vdash P \rhd \Delta; \mathcal{I} \quad \Gamma ; \Theta \vdash Q \rhd \Delta; \mathcal{I}}{\Gamma ; \Theta \vdash \texttt{if } e \texttt{ then } P \texttt{ else } Q \rhd \Delta; \mathcal{I}} \langle \text{T.IF} \rangle$$

$$\frac{\Gamma ; \Theta \vdash P_1 \rhd \Delta, k : \alpha_1; \mathcal{I}_1 \quad \cdots \quad \Gamma ; \Theta \vdash P_m \rhd \Delta, k : \alpha_m; \mathcal{I}_m \quad \mathcal{I} = \mathcal{I}_1 \uplus ... \uplus \mathcal{I}_m}{\Gamma ; \Theta \vdash k \rhd \{n_1 : P_1 \parallel \cdots \parallel n_m : P_m\} \rhd \Delta, k : \&\{n_1 : \alpha_1, ..., n_m : \alpha_m\}; \mathcal{I}} \langle \text{T.BRA} \rangle$$

$$\frac{\Gamma ; \Theta \vdash P \rhd \Delta, k : \alpha_i; \mathcal{I} \quad 1 \leq i \leq m}{\Gamma ; \Theta \vdash k \triangleleft n_i; P \rhd \Delta, k : \oplus\{n_1 : \alpha_1, ..., n_m : \alpha_m\}; \mathcal{I}} \langle \text{T.SEL} \rangle$$

B Type System: Additional Typing Rules

Table 6 gives additional typing rules for the system in Sect. 3.

References

1. Anderson, G., Rathke, J.: Dynamic software update for message passing programs. In: Jhala, R., Igarashi, A. (eds.) APLAS 2012. LNCS, vol. 7705, pp. 207–222. Springer, Heidelberg (2012)
2. Bravetti, M., Di Giusto, C., Pérez, J.A., Zavattaro, G.: Adaptable processes. Logical Methods Comput. Sci. **8**(4:13), 1–71 (2012)
3. Coppo, M., Dezani-Ciancaglini, M., Venneri, B.: Self-adaptive monitors for multiparty sessions. In: PDP 2014, pp. 688–696. IEEE (2014)
4. Di Giusto, C., Pérez, J.A.: Session types with runtime adaptation: Overview and examples. In: PLACES. EPTCS, vol. 137, pp. 21–32 (2013)
5. Di Giusto, C., Perez, J.A.: An Event-Based Approach to Runtime Adaptation in Communication-Centric Systems. Research report, December 2014. https://hal.archives-ouvertes.fr/hal-01093090
6. Dumas, M., Rosa, M.L., Mendling, J., Reijers, H.A.: Fundamentals of Business Process Management. Springer, Berlin (2013)

7. Gay, S.J., Hole, M.: Subtyping for session types in the pi calculus. Acta Inf. **42**(2–3), 191–225 (2005)
8. Di Giusto, C., Pérez, J.A.: Disciplined structured communications with disciplined runtime adaptation. Sci. Comput. Program. **97**, 235–265 (2015)
9. Honda, K., Vasconcelos, V.T., Kubo, M.: Language primitives and type discipline for structured communication-based programming. In: Hankin, C. (ed.) ESOP 1998. LNCS, vol. 1381, pp. 122–138. Springer, Heidelberg (1998)
10. Hu, R., Kouzapas, D., Pernet, O., Yoshida, N., Honda, K.: Type-safe eventful sessions in Java. In: D'Hondt, T. (ed.) ECOOP 2010. LNCS, vol. 6183, pp. 329–353. Springer, Heidelberg (2010)
11. Kouzapas, D.: A Study of Bisimulation Theory for Session Types. Ph.D. thesis, Imperial College London (2012)
12. Kouzapas, D., Yoshida, N., Honda, K.: On asynchronous session semantics. In: Bruni, R., Dingel, J. (eds.) FORTE 2011 and FMOODS 2011. LNCS, vol. 6722, pp. 228–243. Springer, Heidelberg (2011)
13. Kouzapas, D., Yoshida, N., Hu, R., Honda, K.: On asynchronous eventful session semantics. Math. Struct. Comput. Sci. **26**(2), 303–364 (2016)
14. Costa Seco, J., Caires, L.: Types for dynamic reconfiguration. In: Sestoft, P. (ed.) ESOP 2006. LNCS, vol. 3924, pp. 214–229. Springer, Heidelberg (2006)

Designing Efficient XACML Policies
for RESTful Services

Marc Hüffmeyer[(✉)] and Ulf Schreier

Furtwangen University of Applied Sciences, Furtwangen im Schwarzwald, Germany
marc.hueffmeyer@hs-furtwangen.de

Abstract. The popularity of REST grows more and more and so does
the need for fine-grained access control for RESTful services. Attribute
Based Access Control (ABAC) is a very generic concept that generalizes
multiple different access control mechanisms. XACML is an implementation of ABAC based on XML and is established as a standard solution.
Its flexibility opens the opportunity to specify detailed security policies.
But on the other hand it has some drawbacks regarding maintenance
and performance when the complexity of security policies grows. Long
processing times for authorization requests are the consequence in environments that require fine-grained access control. We describe how to
design a security policy in a resource oriented environment so that its
drawbacks are minimized. The results are faster processing times for
access requests and a guideline to structure security policies for REST-
ful services easing their maintenance.

1 Introduction

Many of today's information systems and applications manage huge amounts of
users and data. Often users share their own content (e.g. photos, documents)
within these applications. A substantial need to control who may access this
content is the consequence. In an environment where a lot of users share a lot
of data and specify multiple access rights, a flexible, high-performance access
control mechanism is required. Because classic access control mechanisms like
Role Based Access Control (RBAC) or Access Control Lists (ACL) have been
developed for a different purpose, they do not fit the need for flexibility. For
example trying to protect the resources of a web application with RBAC may
lead to overengineering of roles, which means that too many roles must be
introduced. ACL is not suitable in dynamic environments, when access rights
depend on changing resource or subject state. Attribute Based Access Control
(ABAC) seems to be a suitable candidate that allows the creation of flexible
access rules [15]. The challenge that comes with ABAC is to create security
policies in a way that high performance can be guaranteed even in complex
environments. This work describes how to utilize the architecture of a RESTful
application to write attribute based access control policies. Also we assume that
the resources of this application require individual access rules.

© Springer International Publishing Switzerland 2016
T. Hildebrandt et al. (Eds.): WS-FM 2014/WS-FM 2015, LNCS 9421, pp. 86–100, 2016.
DOI: 10.1007/978-3-319-33612-1_6

2   Foundations

In this section we will introduce the eXtensible Access Control Markup Language [5] and an architectural style to build distributed services called REST [4].

2.1   XACML - eXtensible Access Control Markup Language

Attribute Based Access Control is a solution for flexible access control [15]. The main idea behind it is that any property of an entity can be used to determine authorization decisions. The eXtensible Access Control Markup Language (XACML) is a standard that describes how to implement ABAC. It consists of three parts: an **architecture** describes multiple components and their responsibilities in the authorization context, a **declaration language** can be used to specify access control policies based on XML and a **request language** to formulate access requests and responses.

This work focuses the declaration language. There are three core elements in the structure of a XACML document: **Rules** describe if an access request is permitted or denied. **Policies** group different rules together and **policy sets** group different policies together. Policy sets may also contain other policy sets enforcing a hierarchical composition. Each of those elements has a **target** that defines conditions which describe if the element can be applied to a request. Besides the condition, also a category is assigned to the target. A category can be interpreted as a type. Examples for categories are *Subject, Action* or *Resource*. An textual example for a target is *The subject must have the name "marc"*. Single access requests may be applicable to multiple policy sets, policies and rules with different **effects** (*Permit* or *Deny*) and a winning rule must be found. XACML uses **combining algorithms** for that purpose. An example for such an algorithm is *PermitOverrides*. It states that an applicable rule with the effect *Permit* will win against a rule with the effect *Deny*.

Figure 1 shows a schematic version of a XACML document. The policy contains two rules and is applicable to a *HTTP GET* request on a resource with

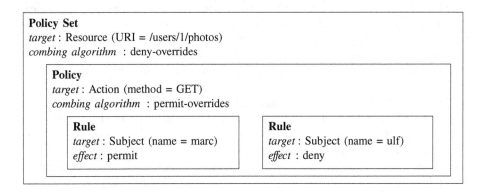

Fig. 1. A XACML policy regulating HTTP GET access to the photos of an user

the URI */users/1/photos*. The first rule grants access to a user with the name *marc* while the second rule prohibits access to a user with the name *ulf*.

2.2   REST - Representational State Transfer

The concept of Representational State Transfer (REST) describes an architectural style for distributed systems and services. Services that follow the architectural style are usually called *RESTful*. A RESTful service must follow four main principles. For efficient policy design the first two principles (**resource orientation and addressability** and an **uniform interface**) play a key role. For completeness we give a short overview over the two other principles, too.

The first concept is RESTful services is named **resource orientation and addressability**. Each resource is addressed with an URI that identifies the resource. A good URI design is important and might be a challenge for unexperienced software designers. URIs have a fixed composition and are built using the expression *scheme:authority:path:query*. An example for an URI is http://example.org/users/1/photos?date=20150101. The scheme is *http*, the authority is *example.org*, the path is */users/1/photos* and the query is *date=20150101*. While scheme and authority are usually unchanged in one application, the path has a big impact on the application structure and requires a good design. A proper design has a hierarchical nature forming a graph of resources and subresources. A query can be interpreted as a filter that selects a subset of resources. In the example only the photos of a specific date are requested.

Another important concept of RESTful services is a **uniform interface** to perform actions on resources. For each resource the same finite set of actions may be executed. Usually RESTful services are associated with the Hypertext Transfer Protocol HTTP [8]. Therefore the HTTP methods specify the methods of the interface. That means for each resource GET, POST, PUT, DELETE and other HTTP methods like OPTIONS or HEAD can be applied. That offers the opportunity to use standardized clients (e.g. browsers) to perform operations on a resource. The only required client capability is the support for the uniform interface.

The differentiation between **resources and representations** is the third concept of a RESTful service. A client requests a resource and a server returns a representation of that resource. For example the client may request a single user and the server responds with an identity card of that user which represents him. The client usually has the option to specify preferred representations of a resource.

The fourth concept is that **communication is stateless** in RESTful services. The client must hold any information about the state of the application because the server does not hold these information. The server only stores the state of the resource expressed as hypermedia and sends possible next states as part of the metadata of a resource to the client. Therefore the concept is often called *Hypermedia as the engine of application state (HATEOAS)*.

3   Efficient XACML for RESTful Services

An efficient security policy design should enable fast request processing and should be easy to maintain. The security policy described in XACML is a unidirectional graph without cycles. The nodes of that graph describe access conditions in terms of *targets*. Edges of the graph represent conjunctions of these *targets*.

Figure 2 introduces a graphical notation for *targets* of XACML policies that should help to understand the mathematical foundations of XACML. The graph is the *target* representation of the XACML document shown in Fig. 1. Each box illustrates a target in which categories (e.g. *Resource*) and corresponding access conditions (e.g. *URI = /users/1/photos*) are listed.

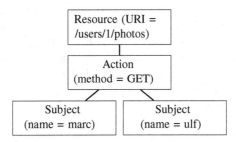

Fig. 2. A graphical notation for XACML policies targets

To enable fast request processing we need to consider the costs of processing an access request in a single node of that graph. We define the cost function as:

$$c : T \times Q \to \mathbb{Q} \tag{1}$$

with T being the set of *targets* of the XACML document, Q being the set of possible access requests and $\mathbb{Q}$ being the set of rational numbers.

To derive the cost function, we define p as the path between two targets. The path between two targets describes the conjunction of all access conditions between those two targets:

$$p : T \times T \to \mathcal{P}(T) \tag{2}$$

with $\mathcal{P}(T)$ being the power set of T. For example if we select the targets of the policy set and the first rule from Fig. 1 as arguments, then the path p is defined as the conjunction of all targets between the policy set and the first rule. This conjunction can be expressed as: *Resource (URI = /users/1/photos) ∧ Action (method = GET) ∧ Subject (name = marc)*.

Additionally we define the length of a path between two targets as the number of targets that are conjuncted. We note the length of a path as:

$$|p(t_1, t_2)| \tag{3}$$

The path mentioned in the previous example has a length of 3 because 3 targets are conjuncted. The set of child targets of a target t can be expressed as:

$$T'_t := \{t' \in T \mid |p(t, t')| = 2\} \qquad (4)$$

Let α_t be the combining algorithm of a policy set or policy with the target t and let A be the set of combining algorithms. Let ϵ be an effect within the set of effects E. Then one has the following proposition for XACML:

$$\forall \alpha_t \in A \; \exists \epsilon \in E : evaluate(t_i, q) = \epsilon \Rightarrow \alpha_t \; stops; \; t_i \in T'_t, q \in Q \qquad (5)$$

That means that for any given combining algorithm there are one or more effects that cause the algorithm to stop if one of the child targets computes to one of these effects. If none of these effects occurs, the algorithm stops after processing the last child target. For example the policy shown in Fig. 1 contains two rules and has the combining algorithm *PermitOverrides*. If the first rule computes to *Permit*, the result of the evaluation of the policy will also be *Permit* no matter what the result of the second rule may be. Therefore the combining algorithm might stop and should not process the second rule. We define a function γ for target t that describes this behavior:

$$\gamma_t(t_i, q) = \begin{cases} 1 & \text{if } \forall t' \in \{t_1, ..., t_{i-1}\} : \alpha_t \; does \; not \; stop \\ 0 & \text{if } \exists t' \in \{t_1, ..., t_{i-1}\} : \alpha_t \; does \; stop \end{cases} \qquad (6)$$

With $t_i \in T'_t$ and $q \in Q$. For the example mentioned above, the γ function of the target associated with the policy is equal to 1 for the target associated with the first rule and equal to 0 for the target associated with the second rule. The cost function c then can be expressed as:

$$c(t, q) = \tau(t, q) + \sum_{i=1}^{|T'_t|} \gamma_t(t_i, q) * c(t_i, q) \qquad (7)$$

The function $\tau(t, q)$ describes the cost for matching the attribute conditions of a target t against a request q. Therefore it is mainly dependent on how many attribute conditions are specified in the target. Hence, the costs for processing a target depends on the number of attribute conditions in the target, the sum of child targets and the combining algorithm resp. the order of the child targets. The following sections describe how to minimize the costs of processing access requests and decrease maintenance efforts for each of the listed factors. Maintenance of policies is important as for any software component due to error correction or adapting to new requirements.

3.1   Target Design (Minimize $\tau(t, q)$)

As one can see in formula (7) attributes should be added carefully to targets, to keep the target small and thus reduce the number of comparisons needed to be executed in the worst case. For example a security policy might address two pairs of conditions. Each pair specifies a subject condition (name = *userid*) and a resource condition (URI = /users/*userid*/photos). An intuitive way would be handling each pair of conditions in one target as indicated in Fig. 3(a). Both access conditions are combined in a single target of a rule.

Processing a request with a subject condition (name = Ulf) and a resource condition (URI = /users/3/photos) requires four attribute comparisons in the worst case because XACML does not specify an order in which attributes must be checked within a target. But if one splits a pair of conditions into multiple targets of rules, policies and policy sets as indicated in Fig. 3(b), a maximum of three comparisons is required. This optimization reduces the worst-case cost of processing targets that are not applicable to a request while the cost for processing a target that is applicable to a request remains unchanged. The optimization reduces variations of processing times down to a minimum but leaves the average processing time unchanged.

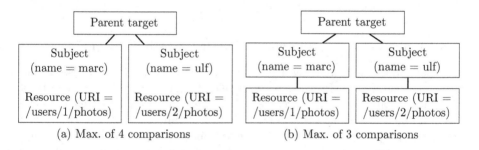

(a) Max. of 4 comparisons   (b) Max. of 3 comparisons

Fig. 3. Target design

In addition, there is a maintenance benefit, since it becomes easier to add new conditions that affect a resource with the attribute *name* and the value *marc* but not a resource with the attribute *URI* and the value */users/1/photos*. For example if one wants to add a target that is applicable to a subject condition (name = marc) and an action condition (method = GET), in Fig. 3(a) either a new target with both conditions must be added or the target on the left side must be divided into two parts. For the structure in Fig. 3(b) only a new branch below the top left condition is required.

3.2   Number of Child Targets (Minimize $\sum_{i=1}^{|T'_t|} c_{t_i}$)

From the sum in (7) one can derive that it is required to have as less targets as possible to optimize the processing time. Hence, wherever possible targets should be grouped together. That means an efficient policy design must have its branching points at the lowest possible position.

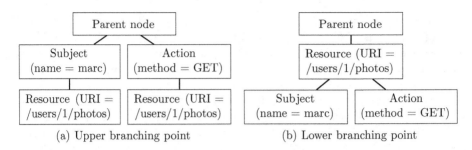

(a) Upper branching point   (b) Lower branching point

Fig. 4. Number of child targets

Besides the performance gain this optimization also has a maintenance benefit. Maintenance efforts for the resource with the attribute condition (URI = /users/1/photos) can be reduced because the target that handles the resource does not occur twice in the security policy. Figure 4 indicates how redundancy is prevented if targets are grouped together.

3.3   Combining Algorithm and Child Order (Minimize γ_k)

The selection of the combining algorithm and the child node order also has an effect on performance. Processing those rules first that override the effects of other rules, leads to shorter average processing times for access request. The reason for that is that no other rule needs to be evaluated if an overriding rule matches. And if there is no overriding rule that matches, the combining algorithm might stop after the first match of the non-overriding rules because those rules cannot be overridden anymore. This is the basic idea of so called normalization described in [10].

Figure 5 shows the effect of normalization. A given policy with the combining algorithm *DenyOverrides* and two rules as indicated in Fig. 4(a) is transformed so that it has a combing algorithm of *FirstApplicable* and a node order that gives performance improvements. In Fig. 4(a) both Rule A and Rule B must be processed to find a decision. But for the policy indicated in Fig. 4(b) it might be enough to process Rule B.

(a) Not normalized   (b) Normalized

Fig. 5. Normalization

3.4   Guidelines for Policy Design

As described in the previous sections, one core concept of REST is resource orientation. Therefore in our approach the security policy is also based on resources. This is a reasonable technique in a resource oriented architecture and offers the benefit of very fast identification of authorization rules that must be applied during the evaluation process. That means for efficient security policies, the targets of policy sets must only contain exactly one resource attribute: the URI. With this constraint it is not necessary to consider combining algorithms since multiple matches of different policy sets or policies are not possible because a dedicated URI is unique. That means that the combining algorithm *FirstApplicable* can be used in every policy set to improve performance as described in Sect. 3.3. In consequence, the processing time for access requests can be kept small even if new resource paths are added or the security policy is extended.

We also mentioned that RESTful service always have an uniform interface. Therefore we consider that the set of allowed methods is limited to the methods of that interface (the HTTP methods). In our approach these methods are used as possible actions in the security policy. For each action a dedicated policy should be used and this policy should be included as a child node of the policy set for the resource. Within these policies rules may be specified that describe under which circumstances the resource may be accessed. That means that all attributes except the URI and the HTTP method are handled in rules.

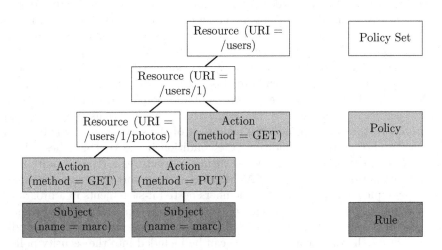

Fig. 6. An example of efficient XACML for RESTful services

Figure 6 shows an efficient security policy for a RESTful application that follows the optimizations described in the previous sections. The white boxes represent policy sets whose targets only address URIs of corresponding resources. The lighter gray boxes represent policies whose targets address the methods of the uniform interface of the RESTful service. Finally, the darker gray boxes indicate rules that may contain multiple access conditions within their targets. Our example in Fig. 6 has only one condition about the subject name, but this could be extended with other predicates on any category. Hence, an access control designer applying these guideline has still flexibility to write her own rules.

Architects, developers and consumers of the RESTful service can easily navigate through the security policy because it has the same structure as the service itself. This is a great maintenance benefit because the identification of possible failures becomes very easy and changes to the security policy can be implemented very fast.

3.5   Grouping of Child Targets

Extensibility is an important characteristic for RESTful services. With a growing number of resources also the number of entries in the security policy increases. If resources are of the same type, their corresponding entries in the security policy are on the same level and share the same parent target. Imagine a new user resource is created in the security policy shown in Fig. 6. The policy set for this user will be placed under the *users* resource and on the same level like the other user resources. If the number of users grows, also the average processing time for a request grows.

To keep the gain of processing time in an acceptable range, it is a good advice to utilize tree structures because they enable faster search algorithms than flat structures. Let $O(f)$ be the order of a function f in terms of complexity. As it is well known (see for instance [2]) a search operation on a binary tree with n nodes runs in $O(log_2 n)$ worst-case time. While on the other side the same operation runs in $O(n)$ worst-case time for a linear chain of nodes. We can adapt this idea to increase the performance of processing security policies described in the previous sections by transforming the structure of policy sets into a more efficient form.

With XACML in general the utilization of additional tree structures is not a simple task because the security policy may be built on various types of access conditions. But in our approach the main part of the security policy is built on just one type of attribute condition (the condition if the URI matches). That means we can easily utilize additional tree-like structures for this condition to increase the performance. While XACML does not support data structures and has only simple control logic that remembers nested if-statements in a programming language (but with additional control by policy combination algorithms), it is possible to simulate a tree structure by nesting policies with target conditions. Figure 7 shows how a binary tree can be included into the security policy to increase the performance during the evaluation of an access request. The target tree for a security policy of a RESTful service shown in Fig. 7 might handle 8 users (resp. user accounts/profiles addressed by a corresponding URI). The first step to create a tree of policy sets is splitting the total amount of users into two intervals. For each interval a policy set must be created that handles access to the user resources. This step is then repeated multiple times until the intervals only contains one user resource. We use brackets in our target tree figures to indicate intervals.

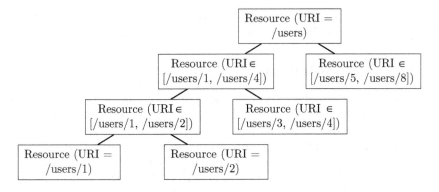

Fig. 7. Using tree structure to increase performance

While the utilization of trees allows faster processing times, the security policy becomes far more complex because more policy sets are added. This is a drawback for maintenance. Therefore a tradeoff between performance and maintenance efforts is required. The tradeoff could be eliminated if the tree structure could be utilized internally in an implementation of the access control model. In this case well-known algorithms [2] for trees with dynamic size could be used. But that is not possible with XACML implementations due to the generic design of XACML.

Depending on the computation capabilities of the device that handles the access request and the amount of resources of the same type, the structure of the tree can be varied. A binary tree might cause larger maintenance efforts than a tree based on more intervals (more child nodes) for each node. As one can see in Fig. 9 of the *Validation* section, processing times still are acceptable for about 100 nodes arranged in a chain. That means instead of using binary trees one could think about using trees with 100 child nodes per node. That decreases maintenance efforts because a smaller tree depth is required to handle the same amount of resources.

4 Validation

We performed multiple tests on different security policies designed to protect a RESTful service. In a first set of tests we analyzed the effect of the optimizations described in Sects. 3.1 to 3.4. In a second set of tests we analyzed the impact of additional tree structures as described in Sect. 3.5. We created synthetic policies to perform the validation. Real world policies should show similar results because the architectural foundations of a RESTful application remain the same. The only variable that differs is the amount of resources at a dedicated level. To be able to handle different amounts we introduced grouping of child targets.

All sets of tests have been executed using *Balana*[1] which is an open source implementation of XACML. The measurement was executed on a dual core

---

[1] https://github.com/wso2/balana.

system (Intel i7-3250M, 2,90GHz) with 8GB working memory reserved for the
tests. Each set of tests has been executed at least 20 times.

4.1   Effect of Optimizations

To measure the effect of the optimizations described in Sects. 3.1 to 3.4, we
created three test suites with four complete security policies in each suite. Generally, the test policies are on the lines of the examples in the previous sections.
The security policies of the first suite contain 10 access conditions on the URI
attribute of 10 resources (one condition for each resource). A single condition for
each of the main HTTP methods (GET, POST, PUT and DELETE) is assigned
to the resources. Finally, for each of those conditions a single rule is assigned
again with an additional condition about a subject, resulting in 40 rules per security policy. In the second suite we added 10 subresources to each resource having
a total number of 110 resources), resulting in 440 rules. In the third suite we
added again 10 subresources to each resource having 1110 resources and 4440
rules. Each test suite contains four security policies: a non-optimized security
policy (flat condition structure and all conditions in the rules following the pattern of Fig. 3(a)), a normalized security policy with the optimizations described
in Sect. 3.3 (pattern of Fig. 5(b)), a structure-optimized security policy moving
conditions from rules to policy/policy set targets containing the optimizations
described in Sects. 3.1 and 3.2 (pattern of Figs. 3(b) and 4(b)) and finally a
security policy with all of the optimizations described in Sects. 3.1 to 3.3 which

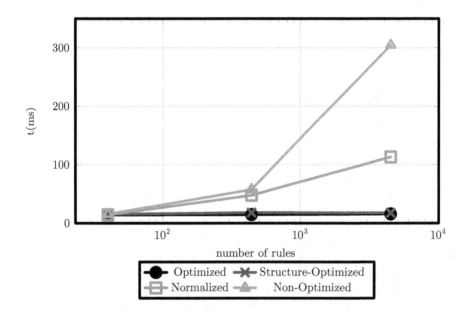

Fig. 8. Average processing time

follows the guidelines described in Sect. 3.4. All security policies within a test suite are functionally equal and produce the same access decisions.

Figure 8 shows the average processing time for an access request. As one can see the processing times for the set with the smallest policies only differ insignificantly. But with growing policy complexity the difference becomes considerably. While the average processing time for the optimized policy remains approximately constant at about 15 ms, the average processing time for the non-optimized policies increases up to 304 ms.

The main contribution to the performance benefit of the optimized security policy is delivered by the structure changes indicated in Fig. 4. Normalization only has a significant impact for larger policies with many rules and without an optimized structure. Also normalization causes great variations in processing time of up to nearly 200 % of the average processing time, while the non-optimized policies has a variation in processing time of about 50 % and the optimized policies resp. structure-optimized policies show a variation of about 25 %. The normalized policy has a worst-case processing time of 316 ms.

4.2 Impact of Grouping Child Targets

As described is the previous sections the average processing time grows with an increasing number of resources of the same type. If the number of resources becomes too large, also the optimizations described in Sects. 3.1 to 3.4 cannot prevent that the processing time increases up to a not suitable value. This is because resources of the same type form a flat structure which can only be scanned for matching targets with larger efforts. For large numbers of resources of the same type, it is important to group child targets together to keep the average processing time small.

To test the impact of grouping child targets together, we created different security policies with 10, 100, 1.000 and 10.000 resources. We then compared the average processing time for an access request of a security policy without grouping with the processing time of a security policy with grouping based on URIs. We selected a group size of 10 for each policy set which means each policy set has again 10 policy sets as children. That means the additional trees that are included in the security policies due to grouping of targets, have a depth of 1 (100 resources), 2 (1.000 resources) and 3 (10.000 resources).

Figure 9 shows the average processing time for different amounts of resources. Without grouping the processing time grows linear with the number of resources. If grouping is used, the processing time grows in a logarithmic order. For the policies that do not utilize grouping of targets, the processing time increases from 14 ms for 10 resources to 689 ms for 10.000 resources. On the other hand the growth for the policies that do utilize grouping of targets is less than 2 ms and therefore not mentionable due to the fact that an initialization overhead of about 14 ms related to the XACML implementation is the most significant effort for the calculation of an access decision. The processing time only increases from 14.1 ms for 10 resources to 15.7 ms for 10.000 resources.

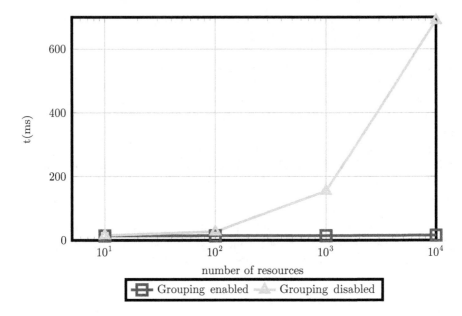

Fig. 9. Growing number of resources

5   Related Work

XACML computes access decisions at runtime and must evaluate multiple attributes of different categories to find a decision. Therefore the average computation time for an access request increases with growing policy complexity. The problem of computation at runtime is related to the architecture resp. the general concept of XACML. A graph based approach described in [14] tries to address performance issues by changing the processing algorithms. Two different trees are used to evaluate an access request. The first tree identifies applicable rules. The second tree holds the original structure of the security policy and identifies the winning rule. Another approach uses numericalization and normalization to optimize performance [9,10]. Numericalization converts every attribute to an integer value. Normalization converts every combining algorithm into FirstApplicable. In [12] processing time is optimized by reordering policy sets and policies based on statistics of past results. A similar approach to ours also reorders policies based on cost functions but focuses on categories rather than attributes [13]. Also they assume that a rule always is a 4-tuple of a subject, an action, a resource and an effect. Other categories and combinations are not allowed.

Another aim of our transformation rules for XACML is the readability of policy definitions by introducing a lucid hierarchical structure of policy sets. Changes should be possible in an easy way. XACML does not define how to handle changes to a security policy. The most common way is manually inserting new policy sets, policies and rules supported by a graphical user interface like in [11]. But manually modifying complex policies is very error prone because multiple changes in different branches of the structure may be required. A lot of works exists that addresses the manipulation of XML documents [3,18]. The key aspect is on fast detection of differences, not on impact analysis of policy changes.

Declarative authorization for RESTful services is handled in [6]. Attributes are not considered in this approach. Another approach that targets authorization for RESTful Services is described in [1]. But this work is focused on RBAC. In [19] an architecture is described to secure web services (SOAP) based on attributes. Another approach that targets authorization for RESTful Services is described in [1]. But this work is focused on RBAC which is way simpler than ABAC. In [19] an architecture is described to secure web services (SOAP) based on attributes. Another approach that is focused on SOAP is described in [16]. The detection of access control vulnerabilities in web applications is discussed in [17]. This work covers web applications that use RBAC as access mechanism.

6   Conclusions

We have shown two major steps to write efficient XACML policies for RESTful services. The first step uses transformation rules that are derived from a cost function for an access request. We have developed a guideline how attribute based access control policies should be built for RESTful services leading to a clearly laid out structure that opens the opportunity to reduce maintenance efforts. We restrict the design of policy sets and single policies in XACML by aligning it to principles of RESTful service design, but keep flexibility at rule level. In a second step, we simulate a tree data structure inside of XACML without actually extending the language that allows faster access of rules, but with drawbacks on policy maintenance. We have validated our work in multiple rounds of tests that showed improved performance for larger amounts of resources.

A problem that we have not addressed is XACML's restrictiveness. With every target on a path to a rule, access conditions become more restrictive. This can be a problem for RESTful services. A service might have a resource user list */users* and access to this resource is granted only to some administrators but not to single users. But a resource */users/1* might be accessed by administrators and user 1. Since user 1 is a subresource of the user list, the policy set that handles access to this subresource should be placed below the policy set that handles access to the user list. In XACML you cannot extend a condition at sub policy level. In consequence the same condition must be repeated multiple times which causes the policy complexity to grow unnecessarily and increases the maintenance efforts.

To handle the performance and maintenance problems described in the previous sections and the restriction problems mentioned above, we are developing an alternative language which is inspired by XACML. The language targets RESTful services and should guarantee that the optimizations described in Sect. 3 are respected. We introduce a first language version in [7]. A draft version already exists and a prototype is implemented. First results show slightly improved performance even to optimized XACML policies.

References

1. Brachmann, E., Dittmann, G., Schubert, K.: Simplified authentication and authorization for RESTful services in trusted environments. In: Proceedings of the First European Conference on Service-Oriented and Cloud Computing, ESOCC 2012 (2012)
2. Cormen, T., Leiserson, C., Rivest, R., Stein, C.: Introduction to Algorithms. MIT Press, Cambridge (2001)
3. Cubera, D., Epstein, A.: Fast difference and update of XML documents. In: XTech 1999 (1999)
4. Fielding, T.R.: Architectural Styles and the Design of Network-based Software Architectures. University of California, Irvine (2000)
5. Organization for the Advancement of Structured Information Standard. eXtensible Access Control Markup Language (XACML) Version 3.0. OASIS Standard (2013)
6. Graf, S., Zholudev, V., Lewandowski, L., Waldvogel, M.: Hecate, managing authorization with RESTful XML. In: WS-REST 2011 (2011)
7. Hüffmeyer, M., Schreier, U.: An attribute based access control model for RESTful services. In: SummerSOC 2015 (2015)
8. Internet Engineering Task Force. Hypertext Transfer Protocol - HTTP/1.1. RFC 2616 (1999)
9. Liu, A., Chen, F., Hwang, J., Xie, T.: Xengine: a fast and scalable XACML policy evaluation engines. In: SIGMETRICS 2008 (2008)
10. Liu, A., Chen, F., Hwang, J., Xie, T.: Designing fast and scalable XACML policy evaluation engines. IEEE Trans. Comput. **60**, 1802–1817 (2011)
11. Lorch, M., Kafura, D., Shah, S.: An XACML-based policy management and authorization service for globus resources. In: GRID 2003 (2003)
12. Marouf, F., Shehab, M., Squicciarini, A., Sundareswaran, S.: Adaptive reordering and clustering-based framework for efficient XACML policy evaluation. IEEE Trans. Serv. Comput. **4**, 300–313 (2010)
13. Miseldine, P.: Automated XACML policy reconfiguration for evaluation optimisation. In: SESS 2008 (2008)
14. Ros, S., Lischka, M., Marmol, F.: Graph-based XACML evaluation. In: SACMAT 2012 (2012)
15. Sandhu, D.: The authorization leap from rights to attributes: maturation or chaos? In: SACMAT 2012 (2012)
16. Shen, H., Hong, F.: An attribute based access control model for web services. In: Parallel and Distributed Computing, Applications and Technologies, PDCAT 2006 (2006)
17. Sun, F., Xu, L., Su, Z.: Static detection of access control vulnerabilities in web applications. In: Proceedings of the 20th USENIX Conference on Security, SEC 2011 (2011)
18. Wang, Y., DeWitt, D., Cai, J.: X-diff: an effective change detection algorithm for XML documents. In: ICDE 2003 (2003)
19. Yuan, E., Tong, J.: Attributed based access control (ABAC) for web services. In: IEEE International Conference on Web Services, ICWS 2005 (2005)

Behavioral Types

Type Inference for Session Types
in the π-calculus

Eva Fajstrup Graversen, Jacob Buchreitz Harbo, Hans Hüttel[(✉)],
Mathias Ormstrup Bjerregaard, Niels Sonnich Poulsen, and Sebastian Wahl

Department of Computer Science, Aalborg University,
Selma Lagerløfs Vej 300, 9220 Aalborg Ø, Denmark
{egrave11,jharbo11,mobj11,nspo11,swahl11}@student.aau.dk,
hans@cs.aau.dk

Abstract. In this paper we present a direct algorithm for session type inference for the π-calculus. Type inference for session types has previously been achieved by either imposing limitations and restriction on the π-calculus, or by reducing the type inference problem to that for linear types. Our approach is based on constraint generation and solving. We generate constraints for a process based on its syntactical components, and afterwards solve the generated constraints in a predetermined order. We prove the soundness, completeness, and termination of this approach.

1 Introduction

From small concurrent applications, to web applications and services, to large distributed systems, communication between processes is a central aspect of concurrent systems and networking protocols. Properties of such concurrent computations can be formally modelled and analysed with process calculi such as the π-calculus, in which interprocess communication is described as *message* passing along named *channels*.

To further formalise and structure interactions between communicating processes, behavioural type systems can be applied. One such approach is *binary session types* [6] using a dialect of the π-calculus with types. Session types describe the protocol used on a communication channel, but do not restrict the channel to a single *type* of message. Instead, a session type describes a sequence of message types, and may even include *choices* between a number of messages; a channel's session type is thus the *communication protocol* of the channel.

In this paper we consider a type system based on that of [4], though without subtyping and describe a type inference algorithm for binary session types that allow us to automatically deduce the types of the session channels. We show that the procedure will deduce a typing for a process P if and only if P can be well-typed.

Linear types is a seemingly simple type discipline; in a linear type system for the π-calculus, each channel type is associated with a multiplicity and a polarity which indicate how many times, and for what purpose, a channel may

© Springer International Publishing Switzerland 2016
T. Hildebrandt et al. (Eds.): WS-FM 2014/WS-FM 2015, LNCS 9421, pp. 103–121, 2016.
DOI: 10.1007/978-3-319-33612-1_7

be used [8]. In [7] Kobayashi outlines how binary session types can be encoded as linear types, and this encoding is investigated and proved correct by Dardha et al. [3].

The existence of this encoding has two consequences; Firstly that session types are no more expressive than linear types, and secondly that many of the results from linear types can also be applied to session types. Thus a possible indirect approach to type inference for session types is to first convert the input to linear types, and then use a type inference algorithm for linear types. Such an algorithm is presented by Padovani in [11].

However, it is not generally the case that one can use this translational approach, as it depends on the existence of a correspondence. In this paper we provide a *direct approach* to session type inference for a full session-based version of the π-calculus by means of constraint solving. The constraints that are to be solved are ones that will appear in other systems for binary session types, so the methodology developed will have a wider applicability to other language settings.

A direct approach to type inference for session types is outlined by Tasistro et al. in [12], but this work imposes severe restrictions to the π-calculus in terms of syntax; in particular the notions of branching and selection are not dealt with. In another paper, Mezzina [10] describes type inference for a binary session type system for a finitary process calculus for service-oriented computations; there are notions of branching and selection presented but they do not involve named sessions, and neither does the notion of communication involve named session channels. Moreover, the type rules for branching and selection due to Mezzina are nondeterministic, so it becomes necessary to first establish an equivalent and algorithmically tractable set of rules.

In our presentation we are able to avoid these complications. The account of type inference is inspired by the approach by Lhoussaine in [9] which describes constraint generation and solution by means of a set of small-step reduction rules. This facilitates the proof of the correctness of our algorithm.

Our paper is organised as follows: In Sect. 2 we formally introduce the π-calculus and session types. In Sect. 3 we introduce rules for constructing and solving constraints, and, by doing so, inferring the type of a process (assuming the process can be typed).

2   Preliminaries

In this section we introduce the π-calculus and session types in Sects. 2.1 and 2.2 respectively. We do this in order to eliminate any confusion as to which version of the π-calculus and session type system we consider.

2.1   The π-calculus

The π-calculus that we consider is similar to the ones introduced in [2,3,13]. Its syntax of the π-calculus can be seen in Table 1. We assume a countably infinite set of names Names and a countably infinite set of labels Labels.

The *subject* of an action is given by $\mathrm{subj}(x!y) = \{x\}$, $\mathrm{subj}(x?y) = \{x\}$ and $\mathrm{subj}(\tau) = \emptyset$. The set of free names in a process P is denoted $\mathrm{fn}(P)$.

In what follows, we write $(\nu x_1 \ldots x_m)P$ for $(\nu x_1) \ldots (\nu x_m)P$ and omit trailing 0 processes where appropriate.

The reduction semantics is given in Table 3. It assumes a standard notion of structural congruence, defined in Table 2.

Table 1. Syntax of the π-calculus

$P, Q, R ::=$	processes	x, y	names
$(\nu x)P$	restriction	ℓ	labels
$P \mid Q$	composition	$\alpha ::=$	actions
$x \triangleleft \ell.P$	selection	$x!y$	send output on x
$x \triangleright \{\ell_i : P_i\}_{i \in I}$	branching	$x?y$	receive input on x
$\alpha.P$	action		
0	inactivity		

Table 2. Structural congruence of the π-calculus

[Sref] $P \equiv P$	[Sparcom] $P \mid Q \equiv Q \mid P$
[Ssym] $P \equiv Q \Rightarrow Q \equiv P$	[Sparas] $(P \mid Q) \mid R \equiv P \mid (Q \mid R)$
[Stran] $P \equiv Q, Q \equiv R \Rightarrow P \equiv R$	[Sresres] $(\nu x)(\nu y)P \equiv (\nu y)(\nu x)P$
[Sres] $P \equiv Q \Rightarrow (\nu x)P \equiv (\nu x)Q$	[Srespar] $(\nu x)(P \mid Q) \equiv P \mid (\nu x)Q$ if $x \notin \mathrm{fn}(P)$
[Spar] $P \equiv Q \Rightarrow P \mid R \equiv Q \mid R$	[Sparnil] $P \mid 0 \equiv P$
[Sact] $P \equiv Q \Rightarrow \alpha.P \equiv \alpha.Q$	[Ssubnam] $(\nu x)P \equiv (\nu y)P[yx]$ if $y \notin \mathrm{fn}(P)$
[Sinp] $x?y.P \equiv x?z.Pz/y$ if $z \notin \mathrm{fn}(P)$	

Table 3. Semantics of the π-calculus

[Ract] $\qquad \alpha.P \xrightarrow{\alpha} P$

[Rcom] $\dfrac{P \xrightarrow{x?y} P' \quad Q \xrightarrow{x!z} Q'}{P \mid Q \xrightarrow{\tau} P'\{z/y\} \mid Q'}$

[Rpar] $\dfrac{P \xrightarrow{\alpha} P'}{P \mid Q \xrightarrow{\alpha} P' \mid Q}$

[Rstr] $\dfrac{P \equiv Q, Q \xrightarrow{\alpha} Q', Q' \equiv P'}{P \xrightarrow{\alpha} P'}$

[Rcho] $\dfrac{\ell_j \in I}{x \triangleleft l_j.P \mid x \triangleright \{l_i : Q_i\}_{i \in I} \xrightarrow{\tau} P \mid Q_j}$

[Rres] $\dfrac{P \xrightarrow{\alpha} P'}{(\nu x)P \xrightarrow{\alpha} (\nu x)P'} \qquad x \neq \mathrm{subj}(\alpha)$

2.2 Binary Session Types

Our type system for binary session types is close to that of [3]. The syntax of types is described in Table 4.

We let Type denote the set of types. As usual, a binary session type describes the protocol followed by a channel in the form of the sequence of types sent along the channel A channel outputting a datum of type T is written $!T$ and a channel receiving something of type T is written $?T$.

Table 4. Syntax of session types

$S, T ::=$	Session type
end	termination
$?T.S$	input
$!T.S$	output
$\&\{\ell_i : S_i\}_{i \in I}$	branching
$\oplus\{\ell_i : S_i\}_{i \in I}$	selection

Duality is formally defined as seen in Definition 1. The definition is as expected and is similar to the definition from [2,13].

Definition 1. *If S is a session type, then the dual of S, denoted $\overline{S}$, is defined by*

$$\overline{?T.S} = !T.\overline{S} \qquad\qquad \overline{!T.S} = ?T.\overline{S}$$

$$\overline{\&\{\ell_i : S_i\}_{i \in I}} = \oplus\{\ell_i : \overline{S_i}\}_{i \in I} \qquad \overline{\oplus\{\ell_i : S_i\}_{i \in I}} = \&\{\ell_i : \overline{S_i}\}_{i \in I}$$

$$\overline{\text{end}} = \text{end}$$

In addition we will make use of the concept of *polarity* to the describe the ends of a channel as introduced by [4]. The two ends of a channel named x can are denoted x^+ and x^-, respectively. The set of polarized names is denoted by PNames and we let p range over the polarities $\{+, -\}$.

A type environment is now a function with finite support that assigns types to polarized names.

Definition 2. *A type environment Γ is a function $\Gamma : \text{PNames} \rightharpoonup \text{Type}$.*

We use Environment to denote the set of environments.

Definition 3 (Balanced and complete environments [4]). *Let Γ be a type environment. We say that Γ is completed, written Γ comp, if every session type in Γ is end. Γ is balanced if for every $x^+, x^- \in \text{dom}(\Gamma)$ we have $\Gamma(x^+) = T \iff \Gamma(x^-) = \overline{T}$.*

Definition 4 (Type environment extension [4]). *Addition of a typed name to an environment is defined by*

$$\Gamma + x^+ : S = \Gamma, x^+ : S \text{ if } x^+ \notin \text{dom}(\Gamma) \text{ and } x \notin \text{dom}(\Gamma)$$
$$\Gamma + x^- : S = \Gamma, x^- : S \text{ if } x^- \notin \text{dom}(\Gamma) \text{ and } x \notin \text{dom}(\Gamma)$$

This definition extends in an iterative fashion to environments as follows: if $\Gamma_2 = x_1 : T_1 + \cdots + x_k : T_k$ (for $k \geq 0$) we have $\Gamma_1 + \Gamma_2 = ((\Gamma_1 + x_1 : T_1) + \cdots + x_k : T_k)$.

The typing rules for the session types are presented in Table 5 and correspond to the typing rules introduced by [4].

Table 5. Typing rules for session types

$$[\text{T} - \text{NIL}] \quad \frac{\Gamma \text{ comp}}{\Gamma \vdash 0} \qquad\qquad [\text{T} - \text{PAR}] \quad \frac{\Gamma_1 \vdash P \quad \Gamma_2 \vdash Q}{\Gamma_1 + \Gamma_2 \vdash P \mid Q}$$

$$[\text{T} - \text{IN}] \quad \frac{\Gamma, x^p : S, y : U \vdash P}{\Gamma, x^p : ?U.S \vdash x^p?y.P} \qquad [\text{T} - \text{OUT}] \quad \frac{\Gamma, x^p : S \vdash P}{(\Gamma, x^p : !U.S) + y^q : U \vdash x^p!y^q.P}$$

$$[\text{T} - \text{CHO}] \quad \frac{l = l_j \in \{l_i\}_{i \in I} \quad \Gamma, x^p : S_j \vdash P}{\Gamma, x^p : \oplus\{l_i : S_i\}_{i \in I} \vdash x^p \triangleleft l.P} \qquad [\text{T} - \text{NEW}] \quad \frac{\Gamma, x^+ : S, x^- : S' \vdash P \quad S = \overline{S'}}{\Gamma \vdash (\nu x)P}$$

$$[\text{T} - \text{BRA}] \quad \frac{\forall i \in I : \ \Gamma, x^p : S_i \vdash P_i}{\Gamma, x^p : \&\{l_i : S_i\}_{i \in I} \vdash x^p \triangleright \{l_i : P_i\}_{i \in I}}$$

Let us say that a process P is *well-balanced* if $\Gamma \vdash P$ where Γ is balanced. The type system guarantees that a well-balanced process will always stay well-balanced after a reduction. This property is proved in [4].

Theorem 5. *If $\Gamma \vdash P$ and Γ is balanced and $P \xrightarrow{\tau} P'$ then $\Gamma' \vdash P'$ where Γ' is balanced.*

3   Type Inference

In this section we describe an algorithm that performs type inference by means of constraint generation and solving. We will modify the typing rules from Table 5 to generate constraints in Sect. 3.1 and present an algorithm to solve this constraint satisfaction problem by creating a substitution solution in Sect. 3.2.

3.1   Constraint Generation for Type Inference

The constraints that will be generated belong to the constraint language seen in Table 6.

In our constraints we use type and environment variables, for which we use τ and γ respectively. We use TVar and EVar to denote the sets of type variables and environment variables.

The constraints are of the following three main kinds; most of them correspond directly to the conditions encountered in the rules of the type system.

– Constraints that describe properties for types:

$$C_T :: = \tau_1 = \tau_2 \mid \tau_1 \xrightarrow{!\tau_2} \tau_3 \mid \tau_1 \xrightarrow{?\tau_2} \tau_3 \mid \tau_1 \xrightarrow{\triangleright\ell} \tau_2 \mid \tau_1 \xrightarrow{\triangleleft\ell} \tau_2 \mid \tau_1 \perp \tau_2$$

The meaning of the constraints are as follows: $\tau_1 \xrightarrow{!\tau_2} \tau_3$ means $\tau_1 = !\tau_2.\tau_3$, $\tau_1 \xrightarrow{?\tau_2} \tau_3$ means $\tau_1 = ?\tau_2.\tau_3$, $\tau_1 \xrightarrow{\triangleleft\ell} \tau_2$ means $\tau_1 = \oplus\{\ldots, \ell : \tau_2, \ldots\}$, $\tau_1 \xrightarrow{\triangleright\ell} \tau_2$ means $\tau_1 = \&\{\ldots, \ell : \tau_2, \ldots\}$, $\tau_1 \perp \tau_2$ means $\tau_1 = \overline{\tau_2}$

– Constraints for relationships/properties of environments:

$$C_E :: = \gamma_1 = \gamma_2 + x : \tau \mid \gamma_1 \supseteq \gamma_2 + \gamma_3 \mid \gamma_1 \subseteq \gamma_2 + \gamma_3 \mid \gamma \text{ comp}$$

Here γ comp means that γ is completed as described in Definition 3, and addition of environments is done according to Definition 4.

– Constraints for other requirements:

$$C_O :: = \mathscr{L}(\tau) = L \mid x \notin \text{dom}(\gamma)$$

The labelling constraint $\mathscr{L}(\tau) = L$ denotes that the labels for branching/section are those of L. This constraint makes use of the function $\mathscr{L}$ defined in Definition 6.

The formation rules are found in Table 6.

Table 6. Constraint language

$$C ::= C_T \mid C_E \mid C_O$$
$$C_T ::= \tau_1 = \tau_2 \mid \tau_1 \xrightarrow{!\tau_2} \tau_3 \mid \tau_1 \xrightarrow{?\tau_2} \tau_3 \mid \tau_1 \xrightarrow{\triangleright\ell} \tau_2 \mid \tau_1 \xrightarrow{\triangleleft\ell} \tau_2 \mid \tau_1 \perp \tau_2$$
$$C_E ::= \gamma_1 = \gamma_2 + x : \tau \mid \gamma_1 \supseteq \gamma_2 + \gamma_3 \mid \gamma_1 \subseteq \gamma_2 + \gamma_3 \mid \gamma \text{ comp}$$
$$C_O ::= \mathscr{L}(\tau) = L \mid x \notin \text{dom}(\gamma)$$

Definition 6 (Label function $\mathscr{L}$). $\mathscr{L} : \text{Type} \to 2^{\text{Label}}$ *is a function such that*

$$\mathscr{L}(\&\{\ell_i : T_i\}_{i \in I}) = \{\ell_i \mid i \in I\}$$
$$\mathscr{L}(\oplus\{\ell_i : T_i\}_{i \in I}) = \{\ell_i \mid i \in I\}$$

We present constraint generation in the form of a reduction relation, inspired by Lhoussaine [9]. The reductions are all of the form

$$P \rightsquigarrow \gamma, \mathscr{C}$$

where P is a process, γ is an environment variable, and $\mathscr{C}$ is a set of constraints. A reduction of this form should be read as stating that for process P to be well-typed the constraints in $\mathscr{C}$ must be satisfied and the type environment γ must be used.

The reduction rules defining constraint generation rules are found in Table 7. The rules are syntax-directed and thus correspond to the typing rules presented in Table 5. In addition we assume that each new variable introduced in each rule is fresh i.e. the variable is not used in any of the previous constraints. The idea behind each rule is to collect constraints that describe the side conditions that must be satisfied in order for the corresponding type rule to be applicable.

As an example, consider the constraint generation rule $[C - IN]$. The typing rule $[T - IN]$ describes for an input process $x?y.P$ to be typable in environment Γ, the name x must be a channel of type $?U.S$ on which an input of a name of type U can be performed. The continuation P must then be typable in an environment where x now has type U and an assumption about the type of y is added. This is an example of a rule that mentions multiple environment variables in one rule; here we get the environment constraints $\{\gamma = \gamma_1 + x : \tau_1,\ \gamma_2 = \gamma_1 + x : \tau_2,\ \gamma_2 = \gamma_3 + y : \tau_3\}$ where γ corresponds to the environment Γ of $[T - IN]$ and the two other constraints together denote the modified environment of the premise in the typing rule.

As another example, consider the rule $[C - BRA]$. This rule corresponds to the typing rule $[T - BRA]$ and again the environment constraints describe how the type environments are updated in the premises of $[T - BRA]$ and that the selections must be possible. In the last constraint mentioned we use the label function defined in Definition 6 to collect the labels available in the branching.

Note also that in the rule $[C - PAR]$ we create two constraints, $\gamma \supseteq \gamma_1 + \gamma_2$ and $\gamma \subseteq \gamma_1 + \gamma_2$, instead of one $\gamma_3 = \gamma_1 + \gamma_2$. Both of these choices were made since this makes the constraints easier to solve in (see Sect. 3.2).

It is important that constraint generation is correct in the sense that a solution to the generated constraints for a process P must provide us with a type environment Γ such that P becomes well-typed under the assumptions in Γ. If on the other hand the process P cannot be well typed for any choice of Γ, the constraints generated must not be solvable. That this is actually the case is captured by Theorem 7.

Theorem 7 (Correctness of constraint generation). *There exists a Γ such that $\Gamma \vdash P$ if and only if $P \rightsquigarrow \gamma; \mathscr{C}$ and there exists a substitution $\sigma :$ TVar $\cup$ EVar $\rightarrow$ Type $\cup$ Environment such that every constraint in $\sigma(\mathscr{C})$ is satisfied and $\sigma(\gamma) = \Gamma$.*

3.2   Constraint Solving

Now that we have generated the constraints required for the type inference, we want to solve the constraints by finding a substitution which assigns a type to each type variable and assigns an environment to each environment variable. From now on we assume an extended version of the language of types in which type variables can appear.

In our treatment of branching and selection we introduce a new kind of variable, called a *pair variable*, denoted by λ. Pair variables are used to represent a set of pairs of labels and types in branching and selection types. We will refer to the set of pair variables as PVar.

Constraints must be solved in a particular order; we describe this by first defining a stratification of our constraints. This ordering can be seen in Table 8. The strategy employed is that for any $1 \leq i < 8$. Constraints in stratum i must be solved before constraints in stratum $i + 1$ are solved.

In the rest of this paper, we will only discuss solutions found by solving constraints in the correct order given by the stratification.

Again we follow Lhoussaine [9] by presenting constraint solution in the form of a reduction relation. Reductions of the form

$$\langle \mathscr{C}_u, \mathscr{C}_s, \sigma \rangle \rightsquigarrow \langle \mathscr{C}'_u, \mathscr{C}'_s, \sigma' \rangle$$

Table 7. Constraint generation rules

$[\text{C} - \text{NIL}]$ $\quad 0 \rightsquigarrow \gamma; \{\gamma \text{ comp}\}$

$[\text{C} - \text{NEW}]$ $\quad \dfrac{P \rightsquigarrow \gamma; \mathscr{C}}{(\nu x)P \rightsquigarrow \gamma_2; \mathscr{C} \cup \left\{ \begin{array}{l} \gamma = \gamma_1 + x^+ : \tau_1, \\ \gamma_1 = \gamma_2 + x^- : \tau_2, \\ \tau_1 \perp \tau_2 \end{array} \right\}}$

$[\text{C} - \text{CHO}]$ $\quad \dfrac{P \rightsquigarrow \gamma; \mathscr{C}}{x \triangleleft l.P \rightsquigarrow \gamma_2; \mathscr{C} \cup \{\gamma = \gamma_1 + x : \tau_1, \gamma_2 = \gamma_1 + x : \tau_2, \tau_2 \xrightarrow{\triangleleft l} \tau_1\}}$

$[\text{C} - \text{IN}]$ $\quad \dfrac{P \rightsquigarrow \gamma; \mathscr{C}}{x?y.P \rightsquigarrow \gamma_3; \mathscr{C} \cup \left\{ \begin{array}{l} \gamma = \gamma_1 + x : \tau_1, \\ \gamma_2 = \gamma_1 + x : \tau_2, \tau_2 \xrightarrow{?\tau_3} \tau_1, \\ \gamma_2 = \gamma_3 + y : \tau_3, \end{array} \right\}}$

$[\text{C} - \text{OUT}]$ $\quad \dfrac{P \rightsquigarrow \gamma; \mathscr{C}}{x!y.P \rightsquigarrow \gamma_3; \mathscr{C} \cup \left\{ \begin{array}{l} \gamma = \gamma_1 + x : \tau_1, \tau_1 \xrightarrow{!\tau_3} \tau_1, \\ \gamma_2 = \gamma_1 + x : \tau_2, \\ \gamma_3 = \gamma_2 + y : \tau_3 \end{array} \right\}}$

$[\text{C} - \text{BRA}]$ $\quad \dfrac{\forall i \in I : P_i \rightsquigarrow \gamma_i; \mathscr{C}_i}{x \triangleright \{l_i : P_i\}_{i \in I} \rightsquigarrow \gamma'; \bigcup\limits_{i \in I} \mathscr{C}_i \cup \left\{ \begin{array}{l} \gamma_i = \gamma_{1i} + x : \tau_i \\ \gamma' = \gamma_{1i} + x : \tau, \tau \xrightarrow{\triangleright l_i} \tau_i \end{array} \right\} \atop \cup \{\mathscr{L}(\tau) = \{l_i \mid i \in I\}\}}$

$[\text{C} - \text{PAR}]$ $\quad \dfrac{P_1 \rightsquigarrow \gamma_1; \mathscr{C}_1 \quad P_2 \rightsquigarrow \gamma_2; \mathscr{C}_2}{P_1 \mid P_2 \rightsquigarrow \gamma; \mathscr{C}_1 \cup \mathscr{C}_2 \cup \{\gamma \supseteq \gamma_1 + \gamma_2, \gamma \subseteq \gamma_1 + \gamma_2\}}$

Table 8. Constraint ordering

Stratum	Constraint type	Condition
1	$\gamma_1 = \gamma_2 + x : \tau$	
2	$\gamma_1 \supseteq \gamma_2 + \gamma_3$	
3	$\gamma_1 \subseteq \gamma_2 + \gamma_3$	
4	γ comp	
5	$\tau_1 \xrightarrow{?\tau_2} \tau_3$ $\tau_1 \xrightarrow{!\tau_2} \tau_3$ $\tau_1 \xrightarrow{\vartriangleleft \ell} \tau_2$ $\tau_1 \xrightarrow{\vartriangleright \ell} \tau_2$	
6	$\tau_1 = \tau_2$ $\tau_1 \perp \tau_2$	$\sigma^*(\tau_1)$ or $\sigma^*(\tau_2)$ is not a type variable, **end**, $\&\lambda$, or $\oplus\lambda$
7	$\tau_1 \perp \tau_2$	$\sigma^*(\tau_1)$ and $\sigma^*(\tau_2)$ are both a type variable, **end**, $\&\lambda$, or $\oplus\lambda$
8	$x \notin \mathsf{dom}(\gamma)$ $\mathscr{L}(\tau) = L$	

where $\mathscr{C}_u$ and $\mathscr{C}'_u$ are sets of unsolved constraints, $\mathscr{C}_s$ and $\mathscr{C}'_s$ are sets of solved constraints, and σ and σ' are substitutions on environment-, pair-, and type variables.

The rules defining the reduction relation for solving constraints are presented in Table 9.

We use the identity function as the initial substitution, and refer to it as σ_{start}. We also define the notation σ^* in Definition 8 as the function that keeps substituting type- and environment variables in a type or type variable expression α, until the point where $\sigma(\alpha) = \alpha$, i.e. until the application of the substitution has no further effect.

Definition 8 (σ^*). *Let* $\sigma : \mathsf{EVar} \cup \mathsf{Tvar} \cup \mathsf{PVar} \rightarrow \mathsf{Environment} \cup \mathsf{Type} \cup \{\ell : \tau \mid \ell \in \mathsf{Label} \text{ and } \tau \in \mathsf{TVar}\}$ *be a substitution function. Then*

$$\sigma^1 = \sigma$$
$$\sigma^{k+1} = \sigma \circ \sigma^k$$
$$\sigma^* = \sigma^n \text{ where } n \in \mathbb{N} \text{ is the smallest value such that } \sigma^n = \sigma^{n+1}$$

The rules for substitution are rather intuitive and do not require an extensive explanation. We define $\Gamma_1 \setminus \Gamma_2$ to mean $\{x : T \mid \Gamma_1(x) = T \text{ and } x \notin \mathsf{dom}(\Gamma_2)\}$. In addition we use $\emptyset$ to denote the empty environment. When all type constraints have been solved, we can set any unassigned λ to $\emptyset$ and any unassigned type to end. When discussing satisfiability, we use $\sigma(\mathscr{C})$ to denote $\sigma\left(\bigwedge_{c \in \mathscr{C}} c\right)$.

In order to show that our rules for substitution do indeed provide a solution to the constraints we put forth Theorems 9, 10 and 13. In the proof of Theorem 13 we make use of Lemmas 11 and 12.

Our first theorem states that a terminating reduction will indeed provide us with a solution.

Theorem 9 (Soundness of constraint solving). *Let $\mathscr{C}$ be a set of constraints. If $\langle \mathscr{C}, \emptyset, \sigma_{start}\rangle \rightsquigarrow^* \langle \emptyset, \mathscr{C}', \sigma\rangle$ then $\sigma^*(\mathscr{C}')$ is satisfied*

Proof. (Sketch) We prove Theorem 9, by proving the contraposition i.e. "If $\sigma(\mathscr{C}')$ is not satisfied, then $\langle \mathscr{C}, \emptyset, \sigma_{start}\rangle \not\rightsquigarrow^* \langle, \emptyset\mathscr{C}', \sigma\rangle$". We prove the contraposition by contradiction, assuming that $\sigma(\mathscr{C}')$ is not satisfied and that $\langle \mathscr{C}, \emptyset, \sigma_{start}\rangle \rightsquigarrow^* \langle \emptyset, \mathscr{C}', \sigma\rangle$.

Note that in the above we have $\mathscr{C} \subseteq \mathscr{C}'$, so the σ^* found will also solve the original constraints in $\mathscr{C}$.

Theorem 10 (Termination of the constraint solving). *For any set of constraints $\mathscr{C}_u$, there exists some finite reduction sequence such that $\langle \mathscr{C}_u, \emptyset, \sigma_{start}\rangle \rightsquigarrow^* \langle \mathscr{C}'_u, \mathscr{C}_s, \sigma\rangle$ and no $\langle \mathscr{C}''_u, \mathscr{C}'_s, \sigma'\rangle$ exists such that $\langle \mathscr{C}'_u, \mathscr{C}_s, \sigma\rangle \rightsquigarrow \langle \mathscr{C}''_u, \mathscr{C}'_s, \sigma'\rangle$.*

Proof. (Sketch) We prove termination by a case analysis of the reduction rules. By assigning a tuple, (n_1, n_2, n_3, n_4), to each step, $\langle \mathscr{C}_u, \mathscr{C}_s, \sigma\rangle$, in the reduction and showing that the tuples assigned to each step are in a strict decreasing lexicographical order i.e. if $\langle \mathscr{C}_u, \mathscr{C}_s, \sigma\rangle \rightsquigarrow \langle \mathscr{C}'_u, \mathscr{C}'_s, \sigma'\rangle \rightsquigarrow \ldots$ then $(n_1, n_2, n_3, n_4) > (n'_1, n'_2, n'_3, n'_4) > \ldots$. We define the tuples (n_1, n_2, n_3, n_4) for each $\langle \mathscr{C}_u, \mathscr{C}_s, \sigma\rangle$ such that

- n_1 is the number of environment constraints in $\mathscr{C}_u$,
- n_2 is the number of constraints that are not environment constraints and not of the form $\tau_1 = \tau_2$ or $\tau_1 \perp \tau_2$ in $\mathscr{C}_u$,
- n_3 is the number of remaining necessary unifications for the minimal solution, and
- n_4 is the cardinality of the range of σ^*.

In the proof of completeness, the following two results are crucial. Firstly, it is crucial that if the constraint set is satisfiable, then the new constraint set that results from applying a reduction will also be satisfiable.

Lemma 11 (Preservation of constraint satisfiability). *If $P \rightsquigarrow \gamma, \mathscr{C}_u$, $\mathscr{C}_u$ is satisfiable, and $\langle \mathscr{C}_u, \emptyset, \sigma_{start}\rangle \rightsquigarrow^* \langle \mathscr{C}'_u, \mathscr{C}_s, \sigma\rangle$ then $\sigma^*(\mathscr{C}'_u)$ is satisfiable.*

Secondly, we need a lemma that expresses that constraints can be solved in accordance with the stratification. We say that a rule is applicable for stratum x on $\langle \mathscr{C}_u, \mathscr{C}_s, \sigma\rangle$ if there exists a constraint in $\mathscr{C}_u$ belonging to stratum x and the reduction step involves this particular constraint.

Table 9. Reduction rules for constraint solving

Constraint/substitution configuration	New constrain/substitution configuration	Side conditions
$\langle\{\gamma_1 = \gamma_2 + x : \tau\} \cup \mathscr{C}_u, \mathscr{C}_s, \sigma\rangle$	$\langle\{x \notin \mathrm{dom}(\gamma_2)\} \cup \mathscr{C}_u, \{\gamma_1 = \gamma_2 + x : \tau\} \cup \mathscr{C}_s, \sigma[\gamma_1 \mapsto \gamma_2, x : \tau]\rangle$	if $\sigma(\gamma_1) = \gamma_1$
	$\left\langle \bigcup_{(\tau_1,\tau_2)\in S} \{\tau_1 = \tau_2\} \cup \{x \notin \mathrm{dom}(\gamma_2)\} \cup \mathscr{C}_u, \; \{\gamma_1 = \gamma_2 + x : \tau\} \cup \mathscr{C}_s, \; \sigma\begin{bmatrix}\gamma_1' \mapsto \gamma_3, (\Gamma_2 \setminus \Gamma_1), x : \tau \\ \gamma_2' \mapsto \gamma_3, (\Gamma_1 \setminus \Gamma_2)\end{bmatrix}\right\rangle$	if $\sigma^*(\gamma_1) = \gamma_1', \Gamma_1$, $\sigma^*(\gamma_2) = \gamma_2', \Gamma_2$, $x \notin \mathrm{dom}(\Gamma_1)$, and $S = \{(\tau_1, \tau_2) \mid \exists x \text{ s.t. } \Gamma_1(x) = \tau_1 \text{ and } \Gamma_2(x) = \tau_2\}$
	$\left\langle \bigcup_{(\tau_1,\tau_2)\in S} \{\tau_1 = \tau_2\} \cup \{x \notin \mathrm{dom}(\gamma_2)\} \cup \mathscr{C}_u, \; \{\gamma_1 = \gamma_2 + x : \tau\} \cup \mathscr{C}_s, \; \sigma\begin{bmatrix}\gamma_1' \mapsto \gamma_3, (\Gamma_2 \setminus (\Gamma_1, \Gamma_1')) \\ \gamma_2' \mapsto \gamma_3, ((\Gamma_1, \Gamma_1') \setminus \Gamma_2)\end{bmatrix}\right\rangle$	if $\sigma^*(\gamma_1) = \gamma_1', \Gamma_1, x : \tau, \Gamma_1'$, $\sigma^*(\gamma_2) = \gamma_2', \Gamma_2$, and $S = \{(\tau_1, \tau_2) \mid \exists x \text{ s.t. } \Gamma_1, \Gamma_1'(x) = \tau_1 \text{ and } \Gamma_2(x) = \tau_2\}$
	$\left\langle \bigcup_{(\tau_1,\tau_2)\in S} \{\tau_1 = \tau_2\} \cup \{x \notin \mathrm{dom}(\gamma_2)\} \cup \{\tau = \tau'\} \cup \mathscr{C}_u, \; \{\gamma_1 = \gamma_2 + x : \tau\} \cup \mathscr{C}_s, \; \sigma\begin{bmatrix}\gamma_1' \mapsto \gamma_3, (\Gamma_2 \setminus (\Gamma_1, \Gamma_1')) \\ \gamma_2' \mapsto \gamma_3, ((\Gamma_1, \Gamma_1') \setminus \Gamma_2)\end{bmatrix}\right\rangle$	if $\sigma^*(\gamma_1) = \gamma_1', \Gamma_1, x : \tau', \Gamma_1'$ and $\sigma^*(\gamma_2) = \gamma_2', \Gamma_2$, and $S = \{(\tau_1, \tau_2) \mid \exists x \text{ s.t. } \Gamma_1, \Gamma_1'(x) = \tau_1 \text{ and } \Gamma_2(x) = \tau_2\}$

(continued)

Table 9. (*Continued*)

$$\langle \{\gamma_3 \supseteq \gamma_1 + \gamma_2\} \cup \mathscr{C}_u, \mathscr{C}_s, \sigma \rangle$$

$$\left\langle \bigcup_{x \in D} \{x \notin \mathsf{dom}(\gamma_3)\} \cup \mathscr{C}_u, \{\gamma_3 \supseteq \gamma_1 + \gamma_2\} \cup \mathscr{C}_s, \sigma[\gamma_4 \mapsto \gamma'_4, \Gamma] \right\rangle$$

if $\sigma^*(\gamma_3) = \gamma_4$,
$\sigma^*(\gamma_1) = \gamma'_1, \Gamma_1$,
$\sigma^*(\gamma_2) = \gamma'_2, \Gamma_2, \Gamma = \Gamma_1 + \Gamma_2$,
$D = \{x \mid \exists \Gamma', \Gamma'' \text{ s.t. } \{\text{``}x \notin$
$\mathsf{dom}(\gamma'_1, \Gamma')\text{''}, \text{``}x \notin$
$\mathsf{dom}(\gamma'_2, \Gamma'')\text{''}\} \subseteq \sigma^* \mathscr{C}_u \wedge x \notin$
$\mathsf{dom}(\Gamma_4)\}$, $\nexists c \in$
$\mathscr{C}_u, \Gamma', \gamma_5, \gamma_6, \gamma_7 : c = \text{``}\gamma_7 \supseteq$
$\gamma_5 + \gamma_6\text{''} \wedge \sigma^*(\gamma_7) = \gamma'_1, \Gamma'$,
and
$\nexists c \in \mathscr{C}_u, \Gamma', \gamma_5, \gamma_6, \gamma_7 : c =$
$\text{``}\gamma_7 \supseteq \gamma_5 + \gamma_6\text{''} \wedge \sigma^*(\gamma_7) = \gamma'_2, \Gamma'$

$$\left\langle \bigcup_{(\tau_1, \tau_2) \in S} \{\tau_1 = \tau_2\} \bigcup_{x \in D} \{x \notin \mathsf{dom}(\gamma_3)\} \cup \mathscr{C}_u, \{\gamma_3 \supseteq \gamma_1 + \gamma_2\} \cup \mathscr{C}_s, \sigma[\gamma'_3 \mapsto \gamma''_3, (\Gamma_4 \setminus \Gamma_3)] \right\rangle$$

if $\sigma^*(\gamma_1) = \gamma'_1, \Gamma_1$,
$\sigma^*(\gamma_2) = \gamma'_2, \Gamma_2$,
$\sigma^*(\gamma_3) = \gamma'_3, \Gamma_3, \Gamma_4 = \Gamma_1 + \Gamma_2$,
$S = \{(\tau_1, \tau_2) \mid \exists x \text{ s.t. } \Gamma_4(x) =$
$\tau_1 \text{ and } \Gamma_3(x) = \tau_2\}$,
$D = \{x \mid \exists \Gamma', \Gamma'' \text{ s.t. } \{\text{``}x \notin$
$\mathsf{dom}(\gamma'_1, \Gamma')\text{''}, \text{``}x \notin$
$\mathsf{dom}(\gamma'_2, \Gamma'')\text{''}\} \subseteq \sigma^* \mathscr{C}_u \wedge x \notin$
$\mathsf{dom}(\Gamma_4)\}$, $\nexists c \in$
$\mathscr{C}_u, \Gamma', \gamma_5, \gamma_6, \gamma_7 : c = \text{``}\gamma_7 \supseteq$
$\gamma_5 + \gamma_6\text{''} \wedge \sigma^*(\gamma_7) = \gamma'_1, \Gamma'$,
and
$\nexists c \in \mathscr{C}_u, \Gamma', \gamma_5, \gamma_6, \gamma_7 : c =$
$\text{``}\gamma_7 \supseteq \gamma_5 + \gamma_6\text{''} \wedge \sigma^*(\gamma_7) = \gamma'_2, \Gamma'$

(*continued*)

Table 9. (*Continued*)

$\langle \{\gamma_3 \sqsubseteq \gamma_1 + \gamma_2\} \cup \mathscr{C}_u, \mathscr{C}_s, \sigma \rangle$	$\langle \mathscr{C}_u, \{\gamma_3 \sqsubseteq \gamma_1 + \gamma_2\} \cup \mathscr{C}_s, \sigma[\gamma_4 \mapsto \emptyset] \rangle$	if $\sigma^*(\gamma_3) = \gamma_4,$ $\sigma^*(\gamma_1) = \gamma_1', \Gamma_1,$ $\sigma^*(\gamma_2) = \gamma_2', \Gamma_2, \Gamma = \Gamma_1 + \Gamma_2,$ $\nexists c \in \mathscr{C}_u, \Gamma', \gamma_5, \gamma_6, \gamma_7 : c =$ "$\gamma_7 \sqsubseteq \gamma_5 + \gamma_6$" $\wedge \sigma^*(\gamma_5) =$ $\gamma_4, \Gamma',$ and $\nexists c \in \mathscr{C}_u, \Gamma', \gamma_5, \gamma_6, \gamma_7 : c =$ "$\gamma_7 \sqsubseteq \gamma_5 + \gamma_6$" $\wedge \sigma^*(\gamma_6) = \gamma_4, \Gamma'$
	$\left\langle \begin{array}{l} \bigcup_{(\tau_1, \tau_2) \in S} \{\tau_1 = \tau_2\} \cup \mathscr{C}_u, \{\gamma_3 \sqsubseteq \gamma_1 + \gamma_2\} \cup \mathscr{C}_s, \\ \sigma[\gamma_3' \mapsto \emptyset][\gamma_1 \mapsto \gamma_1'', B_1][\gamma_2' \mapsto \gamma_2'', B_2] \end{array} \right\rangle$	if $\sigma^*(\gamma_1) = \gamma_1', \Gamma_1,$ $\sigma^*(\gamma_2) = \gamma_2', \Gamma_2,$ $\sigma^*(\gamma_3) = \gamma_3', \Gamma_3, \Gamma_4 = \Gamma_1 + \Gamma_2,$ $B_1 = \{x : \Gamma_3(x) \mid x \in$ $\mathbf{dom}(\Gamma_3 \setminus \Gamma_4) \wedge \nexists \Gamma' : "x \notin$ $\mathbf{dom}(\gamma_1, \Gamma')" \in \sigma^*(\mathscr{C}_u)\},$ $B_2 = \{x : \Gamma_3(x) \mid x \in$ $\mathbf{dom}(\Gamma_3 \setminus \Gamma_4) \wedge \nexists \Gamma' : "x \notin$ $\mathbf{dom}(\gamma_1, \Gamma')" \in \sigma^*(\mathscr{C}_u)\},$ $S = \{(\tau_1, \tau_2) \mid \exists x \text{ s.t. } \Gamma_4(x) =$ $\tau_1 \text{ and } \Gamma_3(x) = \tau_2\}, \nexists c \in$ $\mathscr{C}_u, \Gamma', \gamma_5, \gamma_6, \gamma_7 : c = "\gamma_7 \sqsubseteq$ $\gamma_5 + \gamma_6" \wedge \sigma^*(\gamma_5) = \gamma_3', \Gamma',$ and $\nexists c \in \mathscr{C}_u, \Gamma', \gamma_5, \gamma_6, \gamma_7 : c =$ "$\gamma_7 \sqsubseteq \gamma_5 + \gamma_6" \wedge \sigma^*(\gamma_6) = \gamma_3', \Gamma'$
$\langle \{\gamma \text{ comp}\} \cup \mathscr{C}_u, \mathscr{C}_s, \sigma \rangle$	$\left\langle \mathscr{C}_u, \{\gamma \text{ comp}\} \cup \mathscr{C}_s, \sigma \left[\forall x \in (X \cap \mathsf{TVar}) : x \mapsto \mathsf{end} \right] \right\rangle$	if $\sigma^*(\gamma) = \Gamma, X$ is the range of Γ, and $X \subseteq \{\mathsf{end}\} \cup \mathsf{TVar}$
	$\left\langle \mathscr{C}_u, \{\gamma \text{ comp}\} \cup \mathscr{C}_s, \sigma \cap \left[\forall x \in (X \cup \mathsf{TVar}) \ni x \mapsto \mathsf{end} \right] \right\rangle$	if $\sigma^*(\gamma) = \gamma', \Gamma, X$ is the range of Γ, and $X \subseteq \{\mathsf{end}\} \cup \mathsf{TVar}$

(*continued*)

Table 9. (*Continued*)

Configuration	Result	Condition
$\langle\{\tau_1 \xrightarrow{!\tau_2} \tau_3\} \cup \mathscr{C}_u, \mathscr{C}_s, \sigma\rangle$	$\langle\mathscr{C}_u, \{\tau_1 \xrightarrow{!\tau_2} \tau_3\} \cup \mathscr{C}_s, \sigma[\tau_4 \mapsto !\tau_2.\tau_3]\rangle$	if $\sigma^*(\tau_1) = \tau_4$
	$\mathscr{C}_u \cup \{\tau_2 = \tau_4, \tau_3 = \tau_5\}, \{\tau_1 \xrightarrow{!\tau_2} \tau_3\} \cup \mathscr{C}_s, \sigma[\tau_4 \mapsto T_4][\tau_5 \mapsto T_5]\rangle$	if $\sigma^*(\tau_1) = !T_4.T_5$
$\langle\{\tau_1 \xrightarrow{?\tau_2} \tau_3\} \cup \mathscr{C}_u, \mathscr{C}_s, \sigma\rangle$	$\langle\mathscr{C}_u, \{\tau_1 \xrightarrow{?\tau_2} \tau_3\} \cup \mathscr{C}_s, \sigma[\tau_4 \mapsto ?\tau_2.\tau_3]\rangle$	if $\sigma^*(\tau_1) = \tau_4$
	$\mathscr{C}_u \cup \{\tau_2 = \tau_4, \tau_3 = \tau_5\}, \{\tau_1 \xrightarrow{?\tau_2} \tau_3\} \cup \mathscr{C}_s, \sigma[\tau_4 \mapsto T_4][\tau_5 \mapsto T_5]\rangle$	if $\sigma^*(\tau_1) = ?T_4.T_5$
$\langle\{\tau_1 \xleftarrow{\triangleleft\ell} \tau_2\} \cap \mathscr{C}_u, \mathscr{C}_s, \sigma\rangle$	$\langle\mathscr{C}_u, \{\tau_1 \xleftarrow{\triangleleft\ell} \tau_2\} \cap \mathscr{C}_s, \sigma[\lambda] \cup \{\ell : \tau_2\} \cup \lambda'\rangle$	if $\sigma^*(\tau_1) = \oplus\{\ell_i : T_i\}_{i\in I} \cup \lambda$ and $I \ni i\,\ell : \ell \neq \ell_i$
	$\{\tau_2 = \tau_4\} \cup \mathscr{C}_u, \{\tau_1 \xrightarrow{\triangleleft\ell} \tau_2\} \cup \mathscr{C}_s, \sigma[\tau_4 \mapsto T_i]\rangle$	if $\sigma^*(\tau_1) = \oplus\{\ell_i : T_i\}_{i\in I} \cup \lambda$ and $i \,\exists\, I : \ell = \ell_i$
$\langle\{\tau_1 \xleftarrow{\triangleleft\ell} \tau_2\} \cup \mathscr{C}_u, \mathscr{C}_s, \sigma\rangle$	$\langle\mathscr{C}_u, \{\tau_1 \xleftarrow{\triangleleft\ell} \tau_2\} \cup \mathscr{C}_s, \sigma[\tau_3 \mapsto \oplus\{\ell : \tau_2\} \cup \lambda]\rangle$	if $\sigma^*(\tau_1) = \tau_3$
$\langle\{\tau_1 \xleftarrow{\triangleq\ell} \tau_2\} \cup \mathscr{C}_u, \mathscr{C}_s, \sigma\rangle$	$\langle\mathscr{C}_u, \{\tau_1 \xrightarrow{\triangleq\ell} \tau_2\} \cap \mathscr{C}_s, \sigma[\lambda] \cup \{\ell : \tau_2\} \cup \lambda'\rangle$	if $\sigma^*(\tau_1) = \&\{\ell_i : T_i\}_{i\in I} \cup \lambda$ and $I \ni i\,\ell : \ell \neq \ell_i$
	$\langle\mathscr{C}_u, \{\tau_1 \xrightarrow{\triangleq\ell} \tau_2\} \cup \mathscr{C}_u, \sigma[\tau_3 \mapsto \&\{\ell : \tau_2\} \cup \lambda]\rangle$	if $\sigma^*(\tau_1) = \tau_3$
$\langle\{\tau_1 = \tau_2\} \cup \mathscr{C}_u, \mathscr{C}_s, \sigma\rangle$	$\langle\mathscr{C}_u, \{\tau_1 = \tau_2\} \cup \mathscr{C}_s, \sigma[\tau_3 \mapsto \tau_2]\rangle$	if $\sigma^*(\tau_1) = \tau_3$ and $\sigma^*(\tau_2) \neq \tau_3$
	$\langle\mathscr{C}_s, \{\tau_1 = \tau_2\} \cup \mathscr{C}_s, \sigma\rangle$	if $\sigma^*(\tau_1) = \sigma^*(\tau_2)$
	$\langle\mathscr{C}_u, \{\tau_1 = \tau_2\} \cup \mathscr{C}_s, \sigma[\tau_3 \mapsto \tau_1]\rangle$	if $\sigma^*(\tau_1) \not\equiv \text{Tvar}$ and $\sigma^*(\tau_2) = \tau_3$
	$\{\tau_3 = \tau_4, \tau_5 = \tau_6\} \cup \mathscr{C}_u, \{\tau_1 = \tau_2\} \cup \mathscr{C}_s,$ $\sigma[\tau_3 \mapsto T_3][\tau_4 \mapsto T_4][\tau_5 \mapsto T_5][\tau_6 \mapsto T_6]\rangle$	if $\sigma^*(\tau_1) = ?T_3.T_5$ and $\sigma^*(\tau_2) = ?T_4.T_6$

(*continued*)

Table 9. (*Continued*)

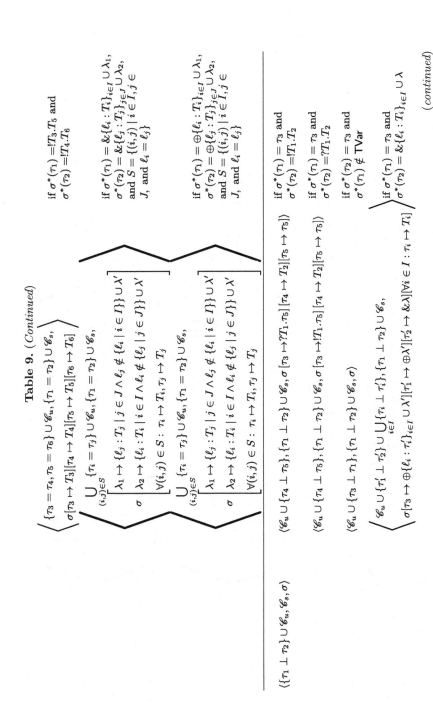

(*continued*)

Table 9. (*Continued*)

$$\mathscr{C}_u \cup \{\tau_1' \perp \tau_2'\} \cup \bigcup_{i\in I}\{\tau_i \perp \tau_i'\}, \{\tau_1 \perp \tau_2\} \cup \mathscr{C}_s,$$
$$\sigma[\tau_3 \mapsto \&\{\ell_i : \tau_i'\}_{i\in I} \cup \lambda][\tau_1' \mapsto \&\lambda'][\tau_2' \mapsto \oplus\lambda][\forall i \in I : \tau_i \mapsto T_i]$$
if $\sigma^*(\tau_1) = \tau_3$ and
$\sigma^*(\tau_2) = \oplus\{\ell_i : T_i\}_{i\in I} \cup \lambda$

$$\mathscr{C}_u \cup \{\tau_4 \perp \tau_6, \tau_3 = \tau_5\}, \{\tau_1 \perp \tau_2\} \cup \mathscr{C}_s,$$
$$\sigma[\tau_3 \mapsto T_3][\tau_4 \mapsto T_4][\tau_5 \mapsto T_5][\tau_6 \mapsto T_6]$$
if $\sigma^*(\tau_1) = !T_3.T_4$ and
$\sigma^*(\tau_2) = ?T_5.T_6$

$$\mathscr{C}_u \cup \{\tau_4 \perp \tau_6, \tau_3 = \tau_5\}, \{\tau_1 \perp \tau_2\} \cup \mathscr{C}_s,$$
$$\sigma[\tau_3 \mapsto T_3][\tau_4 \mapsto T_4][\tau_5 \mapsto T_5][\tau_6 \mapsto T_6]$$
if $\sigma^*(\tau_1) = ?T_3.T_4$ and
$\sigma^*(\tau_2) = !T_5.T_6$

$$\{\tau_1' \perp \tau_2'\} \cup \bigcup_{(i,j)\in S}\{\tau_i \perp \tau_j'\} \cup \bigcup_{j\in J, \ell_j \notin \{\ell_i \mid i\in I\}}\{\tau_j' \perp \tau_j\}$$
$$\{\tau_i' \perp \tau_{i}\} \cup \mathscr{C}_u, \{\tau_1 \perp \tau_2\} \cup \mathscr{C}_s,$$
$$\sigma\begin{bmatrix}\lambda_1 \mapsto \{\ell_j : \tau_j' \mid j \in J \wedge \ell_j \notin \{\ell_i \mid i\in I\}\} \cup \lambda_1' \\ \lambda_2 \mapsto \{\ell_i : \tau_i' \mid i \in I \wedge \ell_i \notin \{\ell_j \mid j\in J\}\} \cup \lambda_2' \\ \forall i \in I : \tau_i \mapsto T_i \\ \tau_1' \mapsto \&\lambda_1' \qquad\qquad \tau_2' \mapsto \oplus\lambda_2'\end{bmatrix}$$
$$\forall j \in J : \tau_j' \mapsto T_j$$
if $\sigma^*(\tau_1) = \&\{\ell_i : T_i\}_{i\in I} \cup \lambda_1,$
$\sigma^*(\tau_2) = \oplus\{\ell_j : T_j\}_{j\in J} \cup \lambda_2,$
$S = \{(i,j) \mid i \in I, j \in$
$J,$ and $\ell_i = \ell_j\},$ and $I \cup J \neq \emptyset$

$$\{\tau_1' \perp \tau_2'\} \cup \bigcup_{(i,j)\in S}\{\tau_i \perp \tau_j'\} \cup \bigcup_{j\in J, \ell_j \notin \{\ell_i \mid i\in I\}}\{\tau_j' \perp \tau_j\}$$
$$\{\tau_i' \perp \tau_{i}\} \cup \mathscr{C}_u, \{\tau_1 \perp \tau_2\} \cup \mathscr{C}_s,$$
$$\sigma\begin{bmatrix}\lambda_1 \mapsto \{\ell_j : \tau_j' \mid j \in J \wedge \ell_j \notin \{\ell_i \mid i\in I\}\} \cup \lambda_1' \\ \lambda_2 \mapsto \{\ell_i : \tau_i' \mid i \in I \wedge \ell_i \notin \{\ell_j \mid j\in J\}\} \cup \lambda_2' \\ \forall i \in I : \tau_i \mapsto T_i \\ \tau_1' \mapsto \oplus\lambda_1' \qquad\qquad \tau_2' \mapsto \&\lambda_2'\end{bmatrix}$$
$$\forall j \in J : \tau_j' \mapsto T_j$$
if $\sigma^*(\tau_1) = \oplus\{\ell_i : T_i\}_{i\in I} \cup \lambda_1,$
$\sigma^*(\tau_2) = \&\{\ell_j : T_j\}_{j\in J} \cup \lambda_2,$
$S = \{(i,j) \mid i \in I, j \in$
$J,$ and $\ell_i = \ell_j\},$ and $I \cup J \neq \emptyset$

(*continued*)

Table 9. (*Continued*)

	$\langle \mathscr{C}_u, \{\tau_1 \perp \tau_2\} \cup \mathscr{C}_s, \sigma \rangle$	if $\sigma^*(\tau_1) = \sigma^*(\tau_2) = \mathbf{end}$
	$\langle \mathscr{C}_u, \{\tau_1 \perp \tau_2\} \cup \mathscr{C}_s, \sigma \rangle$	if $\sigma^*(\tau_1) = \tau_3$ and $\sigma^*(\tau_2) = \mathbf{end}$
	$\langle \mathscr{C}_u, \{\tau_1 \perp \tau_2\} \cup \mathscr{C}_s, \sigma \rangle$	if $\sigma^*(\tau_1) = \tau_3$ and $\sigma^*(\tau_2) = \tau_4$
	$\langle \mathscr{C}_u, \{\tau_1 \perp \tau_2\} \cup \mathscr{C}_s, \sigma \rangle$	if $\sigma^*(\tau_1) = \oplus\lambda_1$ and $\sigma^*(\tau_2) = \&\lambda_2$
	$\langle \mathscr{C}_u, \{\tau_1 \perp \tau_2\} \cup \mathscr{C}_s, \sigma \rangle$	if $\sigma^*(\tau_1) = \&\lambda_1$ and $\sigma^*(\tau_2) = \oplus\lambda_2$
$\langle \mathscr{C}_u, \mathscr{C}_s, \sigma \rangle$	$\langle \mathscr{C}_u, \mathscr{C}_s, \sigma[\exists\lambda \text{ s.t. } \sigma(\lambda) = \lambda : \lambda \mapsto \emptyset]\rangle$	if $\exists\lambda$ such that $\sigma(\lambda) = \lambda$
$\langle \mathscr{C}_u, \mathscr{C}_s, \sigma \rangle$	$\langle \mathscr{C}_u, \mathscr{C}_s, \sigma[\forall\tau \text{ s.t } \sigma(\tau) = \tau : \tau \mapsto \mathbf{end}]\rangle$	if $\exists\tau$ such that $\sigma(\tau) = \tau$
$\langle \{x \notin \mathrm{dom}(\gamma)\} \cup \mathscr{C}_u, \mathscr{C}_s, \sigma \rangle$	$\langle \mathscr{C}_u, \{x \notin \mathrm{dom}(\gamma)\} \cup \mathscr{C}_s, \sigma \rangle$	if $x \notin \mathrm{dom}(\sigma^*(\gamma))$
$\langle \{\mathscr{L}(\tau) = L\} \cup \mathscr{C}_u, \mathscr{C}_s, \sigma \rangle$	$\langle \mathscr{C}_u, \{\mathscr{L}(\tau) = L\} \cup \mathscr{C}_s, \sigma \rangle$	if $\mathscr{L}(\sigma^*(\tau)) = L$

Lemma 12 (Step order). *For any $1 \leq x \leq 8$ and $\mathscr{C}_u$, if no rules for strata less than x are applicable on $\langle \mathscr{C}_u, \mathscr{C}_s, \sigma \rangle$ and $\langle \mathscr{C}_u, \mathscr{C}_s, \sigma \rangle \rightsquigarrow \langle \mathscr{C}'_u, \mathscr{C}'_s, \sigma' \rangle$, then no rules for strata less than x are applicable on $\langle \mathscr{C}'_u, \mathscr{C}'_s, \sigma' \rangle$.*

Theorem 13 (Completeness of the constraint solving). *For any set of constraints $\mathscr{C}_u$, generated by using the rules from Table 7, if there exists a substitution σ such that $\forall c \in \mathscr{C}_u : \sigma(c) = \mathsf{true}$ then $\langle \mathscr{C}_u, \emptyset, \sigma_{start} \rangle \rightsquigarrow^* \langle \emptyset, \mathscr{C}_s, \sigma \rangle$.*

Proof. (Sketch) We prove Theorem 13 by showing that if $\mathscr{C}_u$ was generated from the constraint generation rules and $\langle \mathscr{C}_u, \emptyset, \sigma_{start} \rangle \rightsquigarrow^* \langle \mathscr{C}'_u, \mathscr{C}_s, \sigma \rangle$, then $\langle \mathscr{C}'_u, \mathscr{C}_s, \sigma \rangle \rightsquigarrow \langle \mathscr{C}''_u, \mathscr{C}'_s, \sigma' \rangle$, or $\mathscr{C}_u$ is unsatisfiable. By Lemma 11 we have that if $\langle \mathscr{C}_u, \emptyset, \sigma_{start} \rangle \rightsquigarrow^* \langle \mathscr{C}'_u, \mathscr{C}_s, \sigma \rangle$ and there exists a $c' \in \mathscr{C}'_u$ such that $\sigma^*(c')$ is unsatisfiable then $\mathscr{C}_u$ is unsatisfiable, and therefore, to prove that $\mathscr{C}_u$ is unsatisfiable, we only need to prove the existence of such a c'. We do this by a case analysis of the composition of $\mathscr{C}'_u$.

In the case analysis we make use of two observations: firstly, by Lemma 11, we know that all generated constraints are satisfiable if the original constraint is satisfiable, and it is thus enough to consider the parent constraint; secondly we know, by Lemma 12, that we never encounter a situation where we have to consider constraints of an order already solved.

4   Conclusion

In this paper we have defined a method for direct session type inference by creating a constraint language, converting the typing rules for session types [4] into constraint generation rules for session types, and created rules for solving the resulting constraint satisfaction problem. We have also proven the soundness, completeness, and termination of the constraint solving process.

While the approach described in this paper handles standard binary session types, a desired extension would be to include session types with recursion and subtyping. We believe that one can extend our approach to include type inference for both recursive types and subtyping. In the case of recursion one could consider the type system due to Giunti and Vasconcelos [5] and adopt its notion of linear and unlimited types. The constraint generation and solving will then have to be adapted to including new kinds of constraints. In particular, one will need constraints of the forms un τ and lin τ for describing that a type τ is respectively unrestricted or linear.

A more subtle modification would be one of efficiency, namely to investigate how the definition of the reduction rules for constraint solution can be simplied without affecting the soundness, completeness, and termination of our approach. A particular cause for concern is the rules for constraint generation for parallel composition, since this involves the splitting of a type environment. A possible simplification would involve the notion of simultaneous restriction $(\nu\, xy)P$ introduced by Vasconcelos in which the two endpoints of a session channel are distinct co-variables x and y [13].

Subtyping is discussed in [4], on which we have based our type system, and the addition of subtypes seems quite feasible, although the constraint language together with both the generation and solution rules will now have to be modified to include constraints for subtyping and reduction rules for solving subtype constraints that make use of the coinductive definition of subtyping given in [4]. Another interesting direction to consider is that of studying type inference in the presence of the various definitions of type duality studied by Bernardi et al. [1].

References

1. Bernardi, G., Dardha, O., Gay, S.J., Kouzapas, D.: On duality relations for session types. In: Maffei, M., Tuosto, E. (eds.) TGC 2014. LNCS, vol. 8902, pp. 51–66. Springer, Heidelberg (2014)
2. Dardha, O.: Recursive session types revisited. In: Carbone, M. (ed.) Proceedings of the Third Workshop on Behavioural Types, BEAT 2014. EPTCS, vol. 162, Rome, Italy, 1st, pp. 27–34, September 2014
3. Dardha, O., Giachino, E., Sangiorgi, D.: Session types revisited. In: Proceedings of the 14th Symposium on Principles and Practice of Declarative Programming, pp. 139–150. ACM (2012)
4. Gay, S., Hole, M.: Subtyping for session types in the pi calculus. Acta Informatica **42**(2–3), 191–225 (2005)
5. Giunti, M., Vasconcelos, V.T.: Linearity, session types and the pi calculus. Mathematical Structures in Computer Science, 1–32 (2013)
6. Honda, K., Vasconcelos, V.T., Kubo, M.: Language primitives, type discipline for structured communication-based programming. In: Hankin, C. (ed.) Programming Languages and Systems. LNCS, vol. 1381, pp. 122–138. Springer, Heidelberg (1998). Observation of strains. Infect. Dis. Ther. 3(1), 35–43 (2011)
7. Kobayashi, N.: Type systems for concurrent programs. In: Aichernig, B.K. (ed.) Formal Methods at the Crossroads. From Panacea to Foundational Support. LNCS, vol. 2757, pp. 439–453. Springer, Heidelberg (2003)
8. Kobayashi, N., Pierce, B.C., Turner, D.N.: Linearity, the pi-calculus. ACM Trans. Program. Lang. Syst. (TOPLAS) **21**(5), 914–947 (1999)
9. Lhoussaine, C.: Type inference for a distributed π-calculus. In: Degano, P. (ed.) ESOP 2003. LNCS, vol. 2618, pp. 253–268. Springer, Heidelberg (2003)
10. Mezzina, L.G.: How to infer finite session types in a calculus of services and sessions. In: Lea, D., Zavattaro, G. (eds.) COORDINATION 2008. LNCS, vol. 5052, pp. 216–231. Springer, Heidelberg (2008)
11. Padovani, L.: Type reconstruction for the linear π-calculus with composite and equi-recursive types. In: Muscholl, A. (ed.) FOSSACS 2014. LNCS, vol. 8412, pp. 88–102. Springer, Heidelberg (2014)
12. Tasistro, A., Copello, E., Szasz, N.: Principal type scheme for session types. Int. J. Logic Comput. **3**(1), 34–43 (2012)
13. Vasconcelos, V.T.: Fundamentals of session types. In: Bernardo, M., Padovani, L., Zavattaro, G. (eds.) SFM 2009. LNCS, vol. 5569, pp. 158–186. Springer, Heidelberg (2009)

Type Checking Purpose-Based Privacy Policies in the π-Calculus

Eleni Kokkinofta and Anna Philippou[(✉)]

Department of Computer Science, University of Cyprus, Nicosia, Cyprus
{ekokki01,annap}@cs.ucy.ac.cy

Abstract. In this paper we propose a formal framework for studying privacy preserving policies based on the notion of purpose. Our framework employs the π-calculus with groups accompanied by a type system for capturing privacy requirements. It also incorporates a privacy policy language which captures how different entities within a system, which are distinguished by their roles, may access sensitive information and the purposes for which they are allowed to process the data. We show that a system respects a policy if the typing of the system is compatible with the policy. We illustrate our methodology via analysis of privacy-aware services of a health-care system.

1 Introduction

Privacy is considered to be a key issue in information technology and, as a result, a great deal of multi-disciplinary work is concentrating on understanding the types of practices and policies which are appropriate for preserving the privacy rights of individuals in the context of technological advancements, e.g. [28,31]. One strand of such works concentrates on the development of formal privacy policy languages, models and enforcement technologies [5,16,25]. In these works, the notion of a *purpose* appears as a central concept which considers the data user's intended use as a key factor in making access control decisions. In particular, policy languages have been developed that allow to specify the purposes for which private information may be used by a data holder while laws and customer demand motivate organizations towards this practice.

The motivation of this paper is derived from the need of developing methodologies for reasoning and enforcing purpose-based privacy requirements. More precisely, in this work we have isolated the objective of developing a static method for ensuring that a purpose-based, role-involved privacy policy is satisfied by an information system. The computational framework which we employ is the well-established theory of the π-calculus. In particular, we extend [23] with the notion of a purpose in order to check purposed-based privacy policies via type checking. While the proposed methodology may in fact be embedded in the framework of [23], the extension allows us to reason directly about the notion of a purpose both at the level of privacy policies as well as the level of systems, as common in standard privacy policy frameworks.

© Springer International Publishing Switzerland 2016
T. Hildebrandt et al. (Eds.): WS-FM 2014/WS-FM 2015, LNCS 9421, pp. 122–142, 2016.
DOI: 10.1007/978-3-319-33612-1_8

1.1 Motivating Example

As an example consider a medical system obligated to protect patient data. Inside the system a nurse may disseminate medical files to doctors for the purpose of treatment and to the accounting department for the purpose of billing. Doctors are able to process the data and disseminate it to specialized doctors if a specialist opinion is required for the diagnosis of the patient's condition. Thus, we distinguish three purposes for handling patient data, namely, *treat*, *diagnosis* and *bill*. We may capture this hierarchy of entities as the tree illustrated in Fig. 1 with the allowed purposes for each entity associated with the respective nodes of the tree.

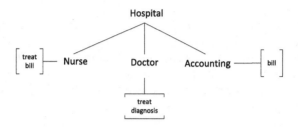

Fig. 1. The hospital group hierarchy and purposes assignment

In our framework we formalize the policy as follows:

$$\mathsf{t} \gg \mathsf{Hospital} : [\ \mathsf{Nurse} : \{treat, bill\},$$
$$\mathsf{Doctor} : \{treat, diagnosis\},$$
$$\mathsf{Accounting} : \{bill\}]$$

where t is the type of the patient's data. The policy describes the existence of the Hospital entity at the higher level of the hierarchy and, within this structure, there exist nurses who may handle patient files for the purposes of *treat* and *bill*, doctors who may handle files for the purposes of *treat* and *diagnosis* and the accounting office, members of which may handle the data for *billing*.

At this stage we observe that different entities of the system working towards a common purpose may have different permission rights to the same data. For instance, while a doctor will be allowed to write medical files while performing treatment, a nurse might not be allowed to do so. We capture this role-dependant assignment of permissions to purposes via a function as follows:

$$\pi(u, G) = \begin{cases} \{\mathsf{disclose\ Hospital}\} & \text{if } G = \mathsf{Nurse\ and\ } u \in \{treat, bill\} \\ \{\mathsf{read, write, access, disclose\ Doctor}\} & \text{if } G = \mathsf{Doctor\ and\ } u = treat \\ \{\mathsf{read, access}\} & \text{if } G = \mathsf{Doctor\ and\ } u = diagnosis \\ \{\mathsf{read, access}\} & \text{if } G = \mathsf{Accounting\ and\ } u = bill \end{cases}$$

According to this, a nurse may disseminate patient files within the hospital (but is not allowed to read or write these files) for both the purposes of billing and treatment. Similarly a doctor may be given access to a patient file and read it (permissions access and read) for the purposes of treatment and diagnosis and may additionally write and disseminate patient files to other doctors for the purpose of treatment (permissions write and disclose Doctor). Finally, members of the accounting office may gain access and read patient files for the purpose of billing.

Moving on to the framework underlying our study, we employ the π-calculus with groups [11] as adapted in [23]. This calculus extends the π-calculus with the notion of *groups* and an associated type system in a way that controls how data is being disseminated inside a system. It turns out that groups give a natural abstraction for the representation of entities in a system. Thus, in [23] the group memberships of processes are used to distinguish their roles within systems. Information processing issues can be analysed through the use of names of the calculus in input, output and object position to identify when a channel is reading or writing private data or when links to private data are being communicated between groups. Additionally, in the present work, we include the notion of a purpose. At the process level, entities state the intended purpose of their execution. Then satisfaction of a policy is carried out at two levels. Firstly, it is necessary to ensure that an entity is allowed to work towards the intended purpose specified and, secondly, it is ensured that the data handling performed by the entity conforms to the permissions allowed to the entity while working towards the specified purpose.

An implementation of a segment of the hospital scenario in the π-calculus with groups would be

$$\text{System} = (\nu\ \text{Hospital})[\ (\nu\ \text{Nurse})\ N\langle treat \rangle$$
$$|\ (\nu\ \text{Doctor})\ D_1\langle treat \rangle$$
$$|\ (\nu\ \text{Doctor})\ D_2\langle diagnosis \rangle\ ]$$
$$N = \overline{a}\langle l \rangle.\mathbf{0}$$
$$D_1 = a(x).x(y).\overline{b}\langle x \rangle.c(z).\overline{x}\langle d \rangle.\mathbf{0}$$
$$D_2 = b(x).\overline{c}\langle z \rangle.\mathbf{0}$$

In this system, one nurse and two doctors are nested within the hospital environment, where the nurse and one of the doctors are working towards treating a patient and a second doctor is called to aid with the diagnosis. The group memberships of the three processes and their associated purposes characterize their nature while reflecting the entity and purpose hierarchy expressed in the privacy policy defined above.

The types of the names in the above process are defined as $y : \mathsf{t}, d : \mathsf{t}$, that is y and d are values of sensitive data, while $l : \mathsf{Hospital}[\mathsf{t}]$ signifies that l is a channel that can be used only by processes which belong to group Hospital to carry data of type t. Further, $a : \mathsf{Hospital}[\mathsf{Hospital}[\mathsf{t}]]$ states that a is a channel that can be used by members of group Hospital, to carry objects of type $\mathsf{Hospital}[\mathsf{t}]$, and, similarly, $b : \mathsf{Doctor}[\mathsf{Hospital}[\mathsf{t}]]$. Let us assume that $z : T$ and $c : \mathsf{Doctor}[T]$, for some T other than t, are names used for communication between the specialist doctor D_2 and the responsible doctor D_1.

Intuitively, we may see that this system conforms to the defined policy, both in terms of the group structure as well as the purposes and the permissions exercised by the processes to achieve their goal. Instead, if doctor D_2 were able to engage in a $\bar{l}\langle d \rangle$ action then the defined policy would be violated since doctor D_2 is operating for the purpose of diagnosis and is not permitted to write any medical files. This would also be the case if the type of b was defined as b : Hospital[Hospital[t]] since a doctor is only allowed to disclose information to other doctors.

Using these building blocks, our methodology is applied as follows: Given a system and a typing, we perform type checking to confirm that the system is well-typed while we infer a permission interface. To check that the system complies with a privacy policy we provide a correspondence between policies and permission interfaces the intention being that: a permission interface satisfies a policy if and only if all the components engage in allowed purposes and for each purpose they exercise no more than the permissions associated with the purpose. With this machinery at hand, we state and prove a safety theorem according to which, if a system S type-checks and produces an interface Θ, and Θ satisfies a privacy policy $\mathscr{P}$, then S respects $\mathscr{P}$.

1.2   Related Work

There exists a large body of literature concerned with reasoning about privacy. To begin with, a number of languages have been proposed to express privacy policies [4,12,15,19,25–27]. Some of these languages are associated with formal semantics and can be used to verify the consistency of policies or to check whether a system complies with a certain policy. These verifications may be performed *a priori* via static techniques such as model checking [2,22,25], on-the-fly using monitoring, e.g. [6,29], or *a posteriori*, e.g. through audit procedures [5,16,17].

The notion of a purpose has been recognized as a central concept for privacy and it has been studied in a number of privacy protecting access control models [3,9,13,30,32]. In these works it is advocated that privacy protection cannot be easily achieved by traditional access control models due to the fact that privacy policies concentrate mostly on which data object is used for which purpose(s). Furthermore, works such as [9,13,32] consider how to enforce purpose-based privacy policies in database management systems at run-time. Finally, we mention the work of [30] which considers the semantics of purpose restrictions and proposes a methodology based on planning to determine whether an action is *for* a purpose or not. Our work is inspired by these papers, our aim being to propose a formal framework for reasoning about purpose-based privacy policies and an enforcement technique based on type checking.

Also related to our work is the research line on typed-based security in process calculi. Among these works, numerous studies have focused on access control. For instance the work on the Dπ calculus has introduced sophisticated type systems for controlling the access to distributed resources [20,21]. Furthermore, discretionary access control has been considered in [8] which similarly to our work employs the π-calculus with groups, while role-based access control

(RBAC) has been considered in [7,14,18]. In addition, multiparty session type systems enriched with security levels for access control and secure information flow have been considered in e.g. [10,24]. While adopting a similar approach, our work departs from these works in the following respects: To begin with we note that role-based access control is insufficient for reasoning about certain privacy violations. While in RBAC it is possible to express that a doctor may read patient's data and send emails, it is not possible to detect the privacy violation breach executed when the doctor sends an email with the sensitive patient data. In our framework, we may control such information dissemination by distinguishing between different types of data and how these can be manipulated. Furthermore, our work considers checking policy compliance of privacy policies by systems. Thus we propose a policy language which allows to express hierarchical arrangements of systems into disclosure zones while allowing the inheritance of permissions and purposes between groups within a hierarchy. Finally, our work considers the notion of a purpose which has not been studied in the above-mentioned frameworks.

2   The Calculus

Our calculus is based on the calculus of [23], where the π-calculus with groups by Cardelli et al. [11] is adopted to reason about privacy requirements. Specifically, we extend the calculus of [23] to allow reasoning about the notion of a purpose.

We assume the existence of three basic entities: $\mathscr{G}$, ranged over by $G, G_1, \ldots$ is the set of groups, $\mathscr{N}$, ranged over by $a, b, x, y, \ldots$, is the set of names and $\mathscr{U}$, ranged over by $u, u_1, \ldots$, is the set of purposes. Furthermore, we assume a set of basic types D, ranged over by t, which refer to the basic data of our calculus on which privacy requirements should be enforced. Specifically, we assign each name in $\mathscr{N}$ a type such that a name may either be of some base type t or of type $G[T]$, where G is the group of the name and T the type of value that can be carried on the name. The intuition behind the notion of group G in $G[T]$ is that a name $x : G[T]$ may only be communicated between processes that "belong" to group G. Given the above, a type is constructed via the following BNF.

$$T \ ::= \ \mathsf{t} \ \mid \ G[T]$$

Then the syntax of the calculus is defined at two levels. At the process level, P, we have the standard π-calculus syntax. At the system level, S, we include the purpose construct $P\langle u \rangle$ which assigns a purpose to a process P and the group construct, $(\nu\,G)$, applied both at the level of purpose-bearing processes $(\nu\,G)P\langle u \rangle$, and at the level of systems, $(\nu\,G)S$. Associating a process P with a purpose u is intended to capture the goal towards which the process is being executed, whereas associating a process/system with a group captures the groups memberships of the process/system. At the system level we also include the name restriction construct as well as parallel composition.

$$P \ ::= \ x(y{:}T).P \ \mid \ \overline{x}\langle z \rangle.P \ \mid \ (\nu\,a{:}T)P \ \mid \ P_1 \mid P_2 \ \mid \ !P \ \mid \ \mathbf{0}$$
$$S \ ::= \ (\nu\,G)P\langle u \rangle \ \mid \ (\nu\,G)S \ \mid \ (\nu\,a{:}T)S \ \mid \ S_1 \mid S_2 \ \mid \ \mathbf{0}$$

In $(\nu\ a{:}T)P$ and $(\nu\ a{:}T)S$, name a is bound in P and S, respectively, and in process $x(y{:}T).P$, name y is bound in P. In $(\nu\ G)P\langle u\rangle$ and $(\nu\ G)S$, the group G is bound in P and S. We write $\mathtt{fn}(P)$ and $\mathtt{fn}(S)$ for the sets of names free in a process P and a system S, and $\mathtt{fg}(S)$ and $\mathtt{fg}(T)$, for the free groups in a system S and a type T, respectively. Note that free occurrences of groups occur within the types T of a process/system.

We now turn to defining a labelled transition semantics for the calculus. We first define a set of labels:

$$\ell\ ::=\ \tau\ \mid\ x(y)\ \mid\ \overline{x}\langle y\rangle\ \mid\ (\nu\ y)\overline{x}\langle y\rangle$$

Label τ is the internal action whereas labels $x(y)$ and $\overline{x}\langle y\rangle$ are the input and output actions, respectively. Label $(\nu\ y)\overline{x}\langle y\rangle$ is the restricted output where the object y of the action is restricted. Functions $\mathtt{fn}(\ell)$ and $\mathtt{bn}(\ell)$ return the set of the free and bound names of ℓ, respectively. We also define the relation $\mathsf{dual}(\ell,\ell')$ which relates dual actions as

$$\mathsf{dual}(\ell,\ell')\ \text{if and only if}\ \{\ell,\ell'\} = \{x(y),\overline{x}\langle y\rangle\}\ \text{or}\ \{\ell,\ell'\} = \{x(y),(\nu\ y)\overline{x}\langle y\rangle\}.$$

We use the meta-notation $(F\ ::=\ P\ \mid\ S)$ to define the labelled transition semantics (Fig. 2).

$$x(y:T).P \xrightarrow{x(z)} P\{z/y\}\ \text{(In)} \qquad\qquad \overline{x}\langle z\rangle.P \xrightarrow{\overline{x}\langle z\rangle} P\ \text{(Out)}$$

$$\frac{F_1 \xrightarrow{\ell} F_1'\quad \mathtt{bn}(\ell)\cap\mathtt{fn}(F_2)=\emptyset}{F_1 \mid F_2 \xrightarrow{\ell} F_1' \mid F_2}\ \text{(ParL)} \qquad \frac{F_2 \xrightarrow{\ell} F_2'\quad \mathtt{bn}(\ell)\cap\mathtt{fn}(F_1)=\emptyset}{F_1 \mid F_2 \xrightarrow{\ell} F_1 \mid F_2'}\ \text{(ParR)}$$

$$\frac{F \xrightarrow{\ell} F'\quad x\notin\mathtt{fn}(\ell)}{(\nu\,x:T)F \xrightarrow{\ell} (\nu\,x:T)F'}\ \text{(ResN)} \qquad \frac{F \xrightarrow{\overline{x}\langle y\rangle} F'}{(\nu\,y:T)F \xrightarrow{(\nu\,y)\overline{x}\langle y\rangle} F'}\ \text{(Scope)}$$

$$\frac{S \xrightarrow{\ell} S'}{(\nu\,G)S \xrightarrow{\ell} (\nu\,G)S'}\ \text{(ResGS)} \qquad \frac{P \xrightarrow{\ell} P'}{(\nu\,G)P\langle u\rangle \xrightarrow{\ell} (\nu\,G)P'\langle u\rangle}\ \text{(ResGP)}$$

$$\frac{P \xrightarrow{\ell} P'}{!P \xrightarrow{\ell} P' \mid !P}\ \text{(Repl)} \qquad \frac{F_1 \xrightarrow{\ell_1} F_1'\quad F_2 \xrightarrow{\ell_2} F_2'\quad \mathsf{dual}(\ell_1,\ell_2)}{F_1 \mid F_2 \xrightarrow{\tau} (\nu\,\mathtt{bn}(\ell_1)\cup\mathtt{bn}(\ell_2))(F_1' \mid F_2')}\ \text{(Com)}$$

$$\frac{F \equiv_\alpha F''\quad F'' \xrightarrow{\ell} F'}{F \xrightarrow{\ell} F'}\ \text{(Alpha)}$$

Fig. 2. The labelled transition system

The labelled transition semantics follows along the lines of standard π-calculus semantics where $\equiv_\alpha$ denotes α-equivalence.

3   Policies

A privacy policy is a set of statements with legal status which set rules and requirements for the collection, processing and disclosure of sensitive data. A system that
handles personal information defines requirements for the protection of this data
through its privacy policy and it is responsible to ensure that these requirements
are satisfied through all operations performed within the system.

A typical privacy policy restricts the use of sensitive information to an explicit
list of purposes. These restrictions enunciate that certain information may *not* be
used *for* certain purposes or that it may used *only for* certain purposes. In both
cases, restrictions refer to access on *data attributes* which are types of sensitive
data within a system such as *medical records* and, in particular, how the various
agents, who are referred to by their *roles*, may/may not handle this data.

The notions of an attribute and a role are reflected in our framework via
the notions of base types and groups, respectively. Thus, our policy language is
defined in such a way as to specify the purposes for which an entity/role is allowed
to process different types of sensitive data. Policies express restrictions of the
"*only for*" kind, as discussed above, thus, the absence of a purpose assignment
for a data type to a role signifies that entities of the role are not allowed to
process the data for the specific purpose. While in [9] the model of purposes
is organized according to the hierarchical relationships between purposes, for
simplicity we opt to work with a flat purpose structure. Nonetheless, our results
can be easily extended to more complex purpose hierarchies.

In order to express policies as explained above we employ the following entities:

(Permissions)	Perm	$::=$	read	$\mid$	write	$\mid$	access	$\mid$	disclose G
(Hierarchies)	H	$::=$	ε	$\mid$	$G : \widetilde{u}[H_j]_{j \in J}$				
(Policies)	$\mathscr{P}$	$::=$	$\mathsf{t} \gg \langle H, \pi \rangle$	$\mid$	$\mathscr{P}; \mathscr{P}$				

A policy is based on the set of *policy permissions* Perm: they express that
data may be read (read) and written (write) and that links to data may be
accessed (access) or disclosed within some group G (disclose G).

In turn, the components H_i, which we refer to as *permission hierarchies*,
specify the group-purpose associations for each base type. Specifically, a permission hierarchy captures the hierarchy in place between the different roles in a
system and assigns a set of purposes at each level of the hierarchy. The intention
is that roles at a lower level within a hierarchy inherit permissions from higher
levels of the hierarchy. More precisely, a permission hierarchy H has the form
$G{:}\widetilde{u}[H_1, \ldots, H_m]$, and expresses that an entity belonging to group G may use
the data in question for purposes $\widetilde{u}$ and, if additionally it is a member of some
group G_i where $H_i = G_i{:}\widetilde{u}_i [\ldots]$, then it is also entitled to work towards purposes $\widetilde{u}_i$, and so on. Note that the precise permissions an entity is allowed to
perform is determined by the function π as we discuss below.

Finally, a policy has the form $\mathsf{t}_1 \gg \langle H_1, \pi_1 \rangle; \ldots; \mathsf{t}_n \gg \langle H_n, \pi_n \rangle$ associating
each type of sensitive data t_i with a permission hierarchy H_i and a function π_i.
The π_i components are functions of type $\pi : \mathscr{U} \times \mathscr{G} \longrightarrow 2^{\mathsf{Perm}}$ that associate each
pair (u, G), where u is a purpose and G a group, with the set of permissions $\widetilde{p}$

allowed to members of group G for manipulating the sensitive data in question while acting towards purpose u. Note that, π records a set of permissions as opposed to a specific sequence of actions/permissions, the intuition being that a policy does not dictate a fixed sequence of actions for achieving a purpose but simply the type of actions that can be performed towards this goal. For example, in a medical system a doctor may be given access to medical data for both reading and writing for the purpose of treating the patient (where the two operations may take place freely and in any order) but only for reading if the data is to be used in the context of a research study.

We define the auxiliary function $\mathsf{groups}(H)$ so as to gather the set of groups inside a hierarchy structure:

$$
\mathsf{groups}(H) = \begin{cases} \{G\} \cup (\bigcup_{j\in J} \mathsf{groups}(H_j)) & \text{if } H = G : \widetilde{u}[H_j]_{j\in J} \\ \emptyset & \text{if } H = \varepsilon \end{cases}
$$

We say that a policy $\mathscr{P} = \mathsf{t}_1 \gg \langle H_1, \pi_1 \rangle; \ldots; \mathsf{t}_n \gg \langle H_n, \pi_n \rangle$ is *well formed*, written $\mathscr{P} : \diamond$, if it satisfies the following:

1. The t_i are distinct.
2. If $H = G : \widetilde{u}[H_j]_{j\in J}$ occurs within some H_i then $G \notin \mathsf{groups}(H_j)$ for all $j \in J$, that is, the group hierarchy is acyclic.

Hereafter, we assume that policies are well-formed policies. As a shorthand, we write $G : \widetilde{u}$ for $G : \widetilde{u}[\varepsilon]$ and we abbreviate G for $G : \emptyset$.

Example 1. We will now present an example adopted from [9]. Suppose that a company has established the following privacy policy pertaining to the practices associated with the use of sensitive client information:

1. Personal information of customers is used for purchasing purposes (purposes *purchase* and *shipping* below) and to inform customers of services that may better meet their needs (purpose *direct* below).
2. Personal information of customers may be disclosed to co-operating companies (third parties) if the customer gives their consent (purpose *thirdparty* below).
3. Personal information of customers under the age of thirteen is only used for purchasing purposes (purposes *purchase* and *shipping* below).

To implement the above policy we note that personal data is subdivided into three different types: personal data of persons under the age of 13, personal data of persons who have given consent for third-party marketing and personal data of persons who have not given consent for third-party marketing. We assign to these data the base types pd^{13}, pd^+ and pd^-, respectively. (For simplicity we do not distinguish between the subcategories of personal information.)

Assuming a role hierarchy within the company consisting of an administration department, a marketing department and an order-processing department, further subdivided into a purchase-management department and a shipping department, a graphical view of the policy hierarchies, can be viewed in Fig. 3 where

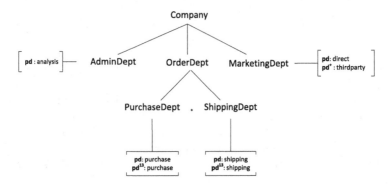

Fig. 3. The company purpose hierarchy and purposes assignment

we have condensed the role-purpose associations of all three base types and we write pd when an association is present for both the pd^+ and the pd^- base types. So, in this figure we may observe the hierarchical structure of the roles within the company as well as the purposes that can be used by entities at each level of the role hierarchy and for each data type. For instance, employees at the Marketing Department may access personal data of all persons over the age of 13 for the purpose of direct marketing (pd : *direct*), but only data of persons who have given their consent for the purpose of third-party marketing (pd : *thirdparty*). However, they may *not* access personal data of persons under 13 as there is no stated purpose allowing such an access. Formally, the policy can be written as

$$\mathscr{P} = pd^{13} \gg \langle H_1, \pi_1 \rangle \; ; \; pd^+ \gg \langle H_2, \pi_2 \rangle \; ; \; pd^- \gg \langle H_3, \pi_3 \rangle$$

where

$$
\begin{aligned}
H_1 \; &= \; \text{Company:[OrderDept[PurchaseDept} : \{purchase\}, \\
&\qquad\qquad\qquad \text{ShippingDept} : \{shipping\}] \\
H_2 \; &= \; \text{Company:[AdminDept} : \{analysis\}, \\
&\qquad\qquad \text{OrderDept[PurchaseDept} : \{purchase\}, \\
&\qquad\qquad\qquad\quad \text{ShippingDept} : \{shipping\}], \\
&\qquad\quad \text{MarketingDept} : \{direct, thirdparty\}] \\
H_3 \; &= \; \text{Company:[AdminDept} : \{analysis\}, \\
&\qquad\qquad \text{OrderDept[PurchaseDept} : \{purchase\}, \\
&\qquad\qquad\qquad\quad \text{ShippingDept} : \{shipping\}], \\
&\qquad\quad \text{MarketingDept} : \{direct\}]
\end{aligned}
$$

We encode the permissions assigned to each role-purpose pair by the functions that follow. In the case of type pd^{13} only the purchase and shipping department may access information, where the purchase department may disclose the shipping department information relevant to the shipping purpose.

$$
\pi_1(u, G) = \begin{cases}
\{\text{read, disclose OrderDept}\} & \text{if } u = purchase, G = \text{PurchaseDept} \\
\{\text{read, access}\} & \text{if } u = shipping, G = \text{ShippingDept} \\
\emptyset & \text{otherwise}
\end{cases}
$$

Additionally, for type pd^+, the administration department may both read, and write personal information for analysis purposes and the marketing department may read and write personal information for direct marketing purposes and additionally it may access and disseminate such information to associated companies (group ThirdParty).

$$\pi_2(u, G) = \begin{cases} \{\text{read}, \text{write}, \text{access}\} & \text{if } u = analysis, G = \text{AdminDept} \\ \{\text{read}, \text{write}, \text{disclose OrderDept}\} & \text{if } u = purchase, G = \text{PurchaseDept} \\ \{\text{read}, \text{access}\} & \text{if } u = shipping, G = \text{ShippingDept} \\ \{\text{read}, \text{write}\} & \text{if } u = direct, G = \text{MarketingDept} \\ \{\text{access}, \text{disclose ThirdParty}\} & \text{if } u = thirdparty, G = \text{MarketingDept} \end{cases}$$

For type pd^- the permission assignment is similar to the one for pd^+ with the exception of the *thirdparty* purpose.

$$\pi_3(u, G) = \begin{cases} \{\text{read}, \text{write}, \text{access}\} & \text{if } u = analysis, G = \text{AdminDept} \\ \{\text{read}, \text{write}, \text{disclose OrderDept}\} & \text{if } u = purchase, G = \text{PurchaseDept} \\ \{\text{read}, \text{access}\} & \text{if } u = shipping, G = \text{ShippingDept} \\ \{\text{read}, \text{write}\} & \text{if } u = direct, G = \text{MarketingDept} \\ \emptyset & \text{otherwise} \end{cases}$$

4   The Type System

In this section we present a typing system for the calculus which is essentially the type system of [23] with small extensions to reason about purposes. As with [23], the aim of the type system is on the one hand to verify that the system conforms to its typing and on the other hand to produce an interface which captures the permissions exercised by the different components of a system, in the name of which purposes and under which roles for each of the base types.

Typing Judgements. The environment on which type checking is carried out consists of the component Γ. During type checking we infer the two additional structures of Δ-environments and Θ-interfaces as follows

$$\Gamma ::= \emptyset \quad | \quad \Gamma \cdot x : T \quad | \quad \Gamma \cdot G$$
$$\Delta ::= \emptyset \quad | \quad \mathsf{t} : \widetilde{p} \cdot \Delta$$
$$\Theta ::= \emptyset \quad | \quad \mathsf{t} \gg \langle H^\downarrow, \widetilde{p} \rangle; \Theta$$

with $H^\downarrow ::= G[H^\downarrow] \quad | \quad G[\widetilde{u}]$. Note that $H^\downarrow$ captures hierarchies where the nesting of groups is linear. We refer to $H^\downarrow$ as *interface hierarchies*. The domain of environment Γ, $\mathsf{dom}(\Gamma)$, contains all groups and names recorded in Γ. Environment Δ has the form $\mathsf{t}_1 : \widetilde{p}_1 \cdot \ldots \cdot \mathsf{t}_n : \widetilde{p}_n$ and it assigns permissions $\widetilde{p}_i \subseteq \mathsf{Perm}$ to sensitive data types t. When associated with a base type t, permissions read and write express that it is possible to read/write data of type t along channels of type $G[\mathsf{t}]$ for any group G. Permission access, when associated with a type t, expresses that it is possible to receive a channel of type $G[\mathsf{t}]$ for any G and, finally, if permission disclose G is associated with t then it is possible to send channels of type $G[\mathsf{t}]$. Thus, while permissions read and write are related to manipulating sensitive data directly, permissions access and disclose are related to manipulating links to sensitive data. Finally, interface Θ associates base types with a set of permissions and a linear hierarchy of groups referring to a set of purposes, namely, an entity of the form $G_1[G_2[\ldots G_n[\widetilde{u}]\ldots]]$. Intuitively, $\mathsf{t} \gg \langle G_1[G_2[\ldots G_n[\widetilde{u}]\ldots]], \widetilde{p}\rangle$ captures that there exists an entity in our system that belongs to groups $G_1,\ldots,G_n$, works towards purposes $\widetilde{u}$ and exercises permissions $\widetilde{p}$ on data of type t.

We define three typing judgements: $\Gamma \vdash x \triangleright T$, $\Gamma \vdash P \triangleright \Delta$ and $\Gamma \vdash S \triangleright \Theta$. Judgement $\Gamma \vdash x \triangleright T$ says that under typing environment Γ, name x has type T. Judgement $\Gamma \vdash P \triangleright \Delta$ stipulates that process P is well typed under the environment Γ and produces a permission environment Δ. In this judgement, Γ records the types of the names of P and Δ records the permissions exercised by the names in P for each base type. Finally, judgement $\Gamma \vdash S \triangleright \Theta$ defines that system S is well typed under the environment Γ and produces interface Θ which records the group memberships of all components of S as well as the permissions exercised by each component and the purposes in which the components were engaged.

Typing System. We now move on to our typing system. We begin with some useful notation. We write:

$$\Delta_T^r = \begin{cases} \mathsf{t} : \mathsf{read} & \text{if } T = \mathsf{t} \\ \mathsf{t} : \mathsf{access} & \text{if } T = G[\mathsf{t}] \\ \emptyset & \text{otherwise} \end{cases} \qquad \Delta_T^w = \begin{cases} \mathsf{t} : \mathsf{write} & \text{if } T = \mathsf{t} \\ \mathsf{t} : \mathsf{disclose}\, G & \text{if } T = G[\mathsf{t}] \\ \emptyset & \text{otherwise} \end{cases}$$

Furthermore, we define the $\oplus$ operator as:

$$G[u] \oplus (\mathsf{t}_1 : \widetilde{p}_1, \ldots, \mathsf{t}_m : \widetilde{p}_m) = \mathsf{t}_1 \gg \langle G[u], \widetilde{p}_1\rangle; \ldots; \mathsf{t}_m \gg \langle G[u], \widetilde{p}_m\rangle$$
$$G \oplus (\mathsf{t}_1 \gg \langle H_1^\downarrow, \widetilde{p}_1\rangle; \ldots; \mathsf{t}_m \gg \langle H_m^\downarrow, \widetilde{p}_m\rangle) = \mathsf{t}_1 \gg \langle G[H_1^\downarrow], \widetilde{p}_1\rangle; \ldots; \mathsf{t}_m \gg \langle G[H_m^\downarrow], \widetilde{p}_m\rangle$$

Thus, operator $\oplus$ when applied to a group G, a purpose u and an interface Δ produces a Θ interface, whereas, when applied to a group G and an interface Θ, it attaches group G to all interface hierarchies of Θ. Finally, we define $\Delta_1 \uplus \Delta_2 = \{\mathsf{t} : \widetilde{p}_1 \cup \widetilde{p}_2 \mid \mathsf{t} : \widetilde{p}_1 \in \Delta_1, \mathsf{t} : \widetilde{p}_2 \in \Delta_2\}$, where we assume that $\mathsf{t} : \emptyset \in \Delta$ if $\mathsf{t} : \widetilde{p} \notin \Delta$.

The typing system is defined in Fig. 4. Rule (Name) is used to type names: in name typing we require that all group names of the type are present in Γ. Process $\mathbf{0}$ can be typed under any typing environment (axiom (Nil)) to infer the empty Δ-interface.

Rule (In) types the input-prefixed process. If environment Γ extended with the type of y produces Δ as an interface of P, we conclude that the process $x(y).P$ produces an interface where the type of T is extended with the permissions Δ_T^r, where (i) if T is base type t then Δ is extended by $\mathsf{t} : \mathsf{read}$ since the process is reading an object of type t, (ii) if $T = T'[\mathsf{t}]$ then Δ is extended by $\mathsf{t} : \mathsf{access}$, since the process has obtained access to a link for base type t and (iii) Δ remains unaffected otherwise.

(Name) $\dfrac{\mathbf{fg}(T) \subseteq \Gamma}{\Gamma \cdot x : T \vdash x \triangleright T}$

(Nil) $\quad \Gamma \vdash \mathbf{0} \triangleright \emptyset$

(In) $\dfrac{\Gamma \cdot y : T \vdash P \triangleright \Delta \quad \Gamma \vdash x \triangleright G[T]}{\Gamma \vdash x(y : T).P \triangleright \Delta \uplus \Delta_T^r}$

(Out) $\dfrac{\Gamma \vdash P \triangleright \Delta \quad \Gamma \vdash x \triangleright G[T] \quad \Gamma \vdash y \triangleright T}{\Gamma \vdash \overline{x}\langle y \rangle.P \triangleright \Delta \uplus \Delta_T^w}$

(ParP) $\dfrac{\Gamma \vdash P_1 \triangleright \Delta_1 \quad \Gamma \vdash P_2 \triangleright \Delta_2}{\Gamma \vdash P_1 \mid P_2 \triangleright \Delta_1 \uplus \Delta_2}$

(ParS) $\dfrac{\Gamma \vdash S_1 \triangleright \Theta_1 \quad \Gamma \vdash S_2 \triangleright \Theta_2}{\Gamma \vdash S_1 \mid S_2 \triangleright \Theta_1 ; \Theta_2}$

(ResNP) $\dfrac{\Gamma \cdot x : T \vdash P \triangleright \Delta}{\Gamma \vdash (\nu\, x : T)P \triangleright \Delta}$

(ResNS) $\dfrac{\Gamma \cdot x : T \vdash S \triangleright \Theta}{\Gamma \vdash (\nu\, x : T)S \triangleright \Theta}$

(ResGP) $\dfrac{\Gamma \cdot G \vdash P \triangleright \Delta}{\Gamma \vdash (\nu\, G)P\langle u \rangle \triangleright G[u] \oplus \Delta}$

(ResGS) $\dfrac{\Gamma \cdot G \vdash S \triangleright \Theta}{\Gamma \vdash (\nu\, G)S \triangleright G \oplus \Theta}$

(Rep) $\dfrac{\Gamma \vdash P \triangleright \Delta}{\Gamma \vdash !P \triangleright \Delta^!}$

Fig. 4. The Typing System

Rule (Out) is similar: If y is of type T, x of type $G[T]$ and Δ is the permission interface for P, then, $\overline{x}\langle y \rangle.P$ produces an interface which extends Δ with permissions Δ_T^w. These permissions are (i) $\{\mathsf{t} : \mathsf{write}\}$ if $T = \mathsf{t}$ since the process is writing data of type t, (ii) $\{\mathsf{t} : \mathsf{disclose}G\}$ if $T = G[\mathsf{t}]$, since the process is disclosing a link to private data via a channel of group G, and (iii) the empty set of permissions otherwise.

Rule (ParP) uses the $\uplus$ operator to compose the process interfaces of P_1 and P_2. Parallel composition of systems, rule (ParS), concatenates the system interfaces of S_1 and S_2. For name restriction, (ResNP) specifies that if P type checks within an environment $\Gamma \cdot x : T$, then $(\nu x)P$ type checks in environment Γ. (ResNS) is defined similarly. Moving on to group creation, for rule (ResGP) we have that, if P produces a typing Δ, then system $(\nu\, G)P\langle u \rangle$ produces the Θ-interface $G[u] \oplus \Delta$ whereas for rule (ResGS), we have that if S produces a typing interface Θ then process $(\nu\, G)S$ produces interface $G \oplus \Theta$. Finally, for replication, axiom (Rep) states that if P produces an interface Δ then $!P$ also produces the interface Δ.

Example 2. As an example consider a possible component of the company in Example 1, where an entity of the marketing department reads private data of a customer and emails the customer with service suggestions, while another entity of the same department receives a link to customer data for forwarding to a co-operating company:

$$S = (\nu\ \mathsf{Company})((\nu\ \mathsf{MarketingDept})DM\langle \mathit{direct} \rangle$$
$$\mid (\nu\ \mathsf{MarketingDept})TP\langle \mathit{thirdparty} \rangle)$$
$$DM = read(x : \mathsf{pd}^+).\overline{email}\langle y \rangle.\mathbf{0}$$
$$TP = dissem(link : T_{data}).\overline{send}\langle link \rangle.\mathbf{0}$$

We consider the following typing environment: Let us write $T_{data} = \text{Company}[\text{pd}^+]$, $T_{link} = \text{Company}[T_{data}]$ and $T_{out} = \text{ThirdParty}[T_{data}]$. Then for $\Gamma = read : T_{data} \cdot y : \text{pd}^+ \cdot email : T_{data} \cdot dissem : T_{link} \cdot send : T_{out}$ we obtain:

$\Gamma \vdash \mathbf{0} \triangleright \emptyset$ by (Nil)

$\Gamma \vdash \overline{email}\langle y\rangle.\mathbf{0} \triangleright \text{pd}^+ : \{\text{write}\}$ by (Out)

$\Gamma \vdash read(x).\overline{email}\langle y\rangle.\mathbf{0} \triangleright \text{pd}^+ : \{\text{read}, \text{write}\}$ by (In)

$\Gamma \vdash (\nu\, \text{MarketingDept})DM\langle direct\rangle \triangleright$
    $\text{pd}^+ \gg \langle \text{MarketingDept}[direct], \{\text{read}, \text{write}\}\rangle$ by (ResGP)

$\Gamma \vdash \overline{send}\langle link\rangle.\mathbf{0} \triangleright \text{pd}^+ : \{\text{disclose ThirdParty}\}$ by (Out)

$\Gamma \vdash dissem(link).\overline{send}\langle link\rangle.\mathbf{0} \triangleright \text{pd}^+ : \{\text{access}, \text{disclose ThirdParty}\}$ by (In)

$\Gamma \vdash (\nu\, \text{MarketingDept})TP\langle thirdparty\rangle \triangleright$
    $\text{pd}^+ \gg \langle \text{MarketingDept}[thirdparty], \{\text{access}, \text{disclose ThirdParty}\}\rangle$ by (ResGP)

$\Gamma \vdash (\nu\, \text{MarketingDept})DM\langle direct\rangle \mid (\nu\, \text{MarketingDept})TP\langle thirdparty\rangle \triangleright$
    $\text{pd}^+ \gg \langle \text{MarketingDept}[direct], \{\text{read}, \text{write}\}\rangle;$
    $\text{pd}^+ \gg \langle \text{MarketingDept}[thirdparty], \{\text{access}, \text{disclose ThirdParty}\}\rangle$ by (ParS)

$\Gamma \vdash S \triangleright \text{pd}^+ \gg \langle \text{Company}[\text{MarketingDept}[direct]], \{\text{read}, \text{write}\}\rangle;$
    $\text{pd}^+ \gg \langle \text{Company}[\text{MarketingDept}[thirdparty]], \{\text{access}, \text{disclose ThirdParty}\}\rangle$
     by (ResGS)

We observe that the process of type checking has yielded an interface of the system capturing the permissions exercised by the two components of the system and the purposes towards which each entity was engaged in.

5   Soundness and Safety

Our framework enjoys soundness and safety results inherited by [23]. We begin with a definition that captures an order on permission interfaces. Relation $\preceq$, defined in [23], captures the changes on the interface environment when a process executes an action. Intuitively, during action execution names maintain or lose their interface capabilities that are expressed through their typing.

Definition 1 ($\Theta_1 \preceq \Theta_2$)

1. $\widetilde{p}_1 \preceq \widetilde{p}_2$ if $\widetilde{p}_1 \subseteq \widetilde{p}_2$.
2. $\Delta_1 \preceq \Delta_2$ if for all t such that $t : \widetilde{p}_1 \in \Delta_1$ we have that $t : \widetilde{p}_2 \in \Delta_2$ and $\widetilde{p}_1 \preceq \widetilde{p}_2$.
3. $\Theta_1 \preceq \Theta_2$ if (i) $\text{dom}(\Theta_1) = \text{dom}(\Theta_2)$, and (ii) for all t, such that $t \gg \langle H, \widetilde{p}_1\rangle \in \Theta_1$ we have that $t \gg \langle H, \widetilde{p}_2\rangle \in \Theta_2$ and $\widetilde{p}_1 \preceq \widetilde{p}_2$.

Theorem 1 (Type Preservation)

1. Let $\Gamma \vdash P \triangleright \Delta$ and $P \xrightarrow{\ell} P'$ then $\Gamma \vdash P' \triangleright \Delta'$ and $\Delta' \preceq \Delta$.
2. Let $\Gamma \vdash S \triangleright \Theta$ and $S \xrightarrow{\ell} S'$ then $\Gamma \vdash S' \triangleright \Theta'$ and $\Theta' \preceq \Theta$.

According to the theorem when a well-typed process/system executes an action it reduces to a well-type process/system. The associated Δ or Θ interface is reduced according to relation $\preceq$.

We are now ready to define the notion of *satisfaction* of a policy $\mathscr{P}$ by a permission interface Θ thus connecting our type system with policy compliance.

Definition 2

1. Consider a policy hierarchy H, a purpose-to-permission assignment π, an interface hierarchy $H^{\downarrow} = G_1[G_2[\cdots G_n[u] \cdots]]$ and a set of permissions $\widetilde{p}$. We write $\langle H, \pi \rangle \Vdash \langle H^{\downarrow}, \widetilde{p} \rangle$, if $\widetilde{p} \subseteq \mathsf{perms}_\pi(H, \langle G_1, \dots, G_n \rangle, u)$, where

$$
\mathsf{perms}_\pi(H, \widetilde{G}, u) = \begin{cases} \pi(u, G) \cup (\bigcup_{j \in J} \mathsf{perms}_\pi(H_j, \widetilde{G} - G, u)) \\ \qquad \text{if } H = G : \widetilde{u}[H_j]_{j \in J}, u \in \widetilde{u}, G \in \widetilde{G} \\ \bigcup_{j \in J} \mathsf{perms}_\pi(H_j, \widetilde{G} - G) \text{ if } H = G : \widetilde{u}[H_j]_{j \in J}, u \notin \widetilde{u}, G \in \widetilde{G} \\ \emptyset \qquad \text{if } \widetilde{G} = \varepsilon \\ \bot \qquad \text{if } H = G : \widetilde{u}[H_j]_{j \in J}, G \notin \widetilde{G}, \widetilde{G} \neq \varepsilon \end{cases}
$$

2. Consider a policy $\mathscr{P}$ and an interface Θ. Θ *satisfies* $\mathscr{P}$, written $\mathscr{P} \Vdash \Theta$, if:

$$
\frac{\langle H, \pi \rangle \Vdash \langle H^{\downarrow}, \widetilde{p} \rangle \quad \mathscr{P} \Vdash \Theta}{\mathsf{t} \gg \langle H, \pi \rangle; \mathscr{P} \Vdash \mathsf{t} \gg \langle H^{\downarrow}, \widetilde{p} \rangle; \Theta} \qquad \mathscr{P} \Vdash \emptyset
$$

According to the definition, $\langle H, \pi \rangle \Vdash \langle H^{\downarrow}, \widetilde{p} \rangle$, for $H^{\downarrow} = G_1[G_2[\dots G_n[u] \dots]]$, if the permissions $\widetilde{p}$ are a subset of the permissions endowed to groups $G_1, \dots, G_n$, for purpose u by $\langle H, \pi \rangle$. This set of permissions is defined inductively via function perms_u where we point out that while computing the permissions allowed by the policy, we simultaneously check that the groups $G_1, \dots, G_n$, of the $H^{\downarrow}$-hierarchy are compatible with the policy hierarchy; the function becomes undefined if at any point the root of the policy hierarchy is absent from the groups of the $H^{\downarrow}$-interface. In clause (2) of the definition, we specify that a Θ-interface satisfies a policy $\mathscr{P}$, $\mathscr{P} \Vdash \Theta$, if for each component $\mathsf{t} \gg \langle H^{\downarrow}, \widetilde{p} \rangle$ of Θ, there exists a component $\mathsf{t} \gg \langle H, \pi \rangle$ of $\mathscr{P}$ such that $\langle H, \pi \rangle \Vdash \langle H^{\downarrow}, \widetilde{p} \rangle$.

We may now define the notion of the *error process* which clarifies the satisfiability relation between the policies and processes.

Definition 3 (Error Process). Consider a policy $\mathscr{P}$, an environment Γ and a system

$$
S \equiv (\nu\, G_1)(\nu\, \widetilde{x}_1 : \widetilde{T}_1)(\dots ((\nu\, G_n)(\nu\, \widetilde{x}_n : \widetilde{T}_n) P \langle u \rangle \mid Q \langle u' \rangle \mid S_n) \dots \mid S_1)
$$

System S is an *error process* with respect to $\mathscr{P}$ and Γ, if there exists t such that $\mathscr{P} = \mathsf{t} \gg \langle H, \pi \rangle; \mathscr{P}'$ and at least one of the following holds, where $\widetilde{G} = \langle G_1, \dots, G_n \rangle$:

1. $\mathsf{read} \notin \bigcup_{G \in \widetilde{G}} \pi(u, G)$ and $\exists x$ such that $\Gamma \vdash x \triangleright G[\mathsf{t}]$ and $P = x(y).P'$.
2. $\mathsf{write} \notin \bigcup_{G \in \widetilde{G}} \pi(u, G)$ and $\exists x$ such that $\Gamma \vdash x \triangleright G[\mathsf{t}]$ and $P = \overline{x}\langle y \rangle.P'$.
3. $\mathsf{access} \notin \bigcup_{G \in \widetilde{G}} \pi(u, G)$ and $\exists x$ such that $\Gamma \vdash x \triangleright G[\mathsf{t}]$ and $P = y(x).P'$.
4. $\mathsf{disclose}\, G' \notin \bigcup_{G \in \widetilde{G}} \pi(u, G)$ and $\exists x, y$ such that $\Gamma \vdash x \triangleright G[\mathsf{t}]$, $\Gamma \vdash y \triangleright G'[G[\mathsf{t}]]$ and $P = \overline{y}\langle x \rangle.P'$.

The first two error processes expect that a process with no read or write permissions on a certain level of the hierarchy should not have, respectively, a prefix receiving or sending an object typed with the private data. Similarly an error process with no access permission on a certain level of the hierarchy should not have an input-prefixed subject with object a link to private data. An output-prefixed process that send links through a channel of sort G' is an error process if it is found in a specific group hierarchy with no discloseG' permission.

As expected, if a process is an error with respect to a policy $\mathscr{P}$ and an environment Γ its Θ-interface does not satisfy $\mathscr{P}$:

Lemma 1. *Let system S be an error process with respect to well formed policy $\mathscr{P}$ and sort Γ. If $\Gamma \vdash S \triangleright \Theta$ then $\mathscr{P} \not\Vdash \Theta$.*

By Lemma 1 we conclude with our safety theorem which verifies that the satisfiability of a policy by a typed process is preserved by the semantics.

Theorem 2 (Safety). *If $\Gamma \vdash S \triangleright \Theta$, $\mathscr{P} \Vdash \Theta$ and $S \xrightarrow{\ell}{}^{*} S'$ then S' is not an error with respect to policy $\mathscr{P}$.*

The above results may be proved by noting that our framework may be embedded into the one of [23] by associating every group-purpose pair in a system of the present framework to a new group of the framework of [23]. Thus by appropriate translations of systems and policies, the proofs of the results can be obtained. The details are omitted.

Example 3. Let us consider the policy of Example 1 and the system of Example 2. To confirm that system S of Example 2 satisfies policy $\mathscr{P}$ of Example 1, by Theorem 2 above, we should establish that $\mathscr{P} \Vdash \Theta$, where Θ is the interface obtained by type checking in Example 2. We have that for $\widetilde{G} = \langle \mathsf{Company}, \mathsf{MarketingDept} \rangle$

$$\mathsf{perms}_{\pi_2}(H_2, \widetilde{G}, direct) = \{\mathsf{read}, \mathsf{write}\}$$
$$\mathsf{perms}_{\pi_2}(H_2, \widetilde{G}, thirdparty) = \{\mathsf{access}, \mathsf{disclose\,ThirdParty}\}$$

Since $\Gamma \vdash S \triangleright \Theta$ where

$$\Theta = \mathsf{pd}^+ \gg \langle \mathsf{Company}[\mathsf{MarketingDept}[direct]], \{\mathsf{read}, \mathsf{write}\} \rangle$$
$$\mathsf{pd}^+ \gg \langle \mathsf{Company}[\mathsf{MarketingDept}[thirdparty]], \{\mathsf{access}, \mathsf{disclose\,ThirdParty}\} \rangle$$

the exercised permissions for each purpose for type pd^+ coincide with the allowed permissions and, we obtain $\mathscr{P} \Vdash \Theta$. Thus the system satisfies the policy.

However, if we consider Example 2 but with type pd^+ substituted by pd^-, type checking would yield $\Gamma \vdash S' \triangleright \Theta'$ where:

$$\Theta' = \mathsf{pd}^- \gg \langle \mathsf{Company}[\mathsf{MarketingDept}[direct]], \{\mathsf{read}, \mathsf{write}\} \rangle$$
$$\mathsf{pd}^- \gg \langle \mathsf{Company}[\mathsf{MarketingDept}[thirdparty]], \{\mathsf{access}, \mathsf{disclose\,ThirdParty}\} \rangle$$

Since

$$\mathsf{perms}_{\pi_3}(H_3, \langle \mathsf{Company}, \mathsf{MarketingDept} \rangle, direct) = \{\mathsf{read}, \mathsf{write}\}$$
$$\mathsf{perms}_{\pi_3}(H_3, \langle \mathsf{Company}, \mathsf{MarketingDept} \rangle, thirdparty) = \emptyset$$

we conclude that $\mathscr{P} \not\Vdash \Theta'$, and clearly the system violates the policy as it attempts to market private data of non-consenting customers to third-party entities.

6   Example

In this section, we illustrate our methodology to reason about privacy requirements as these might arise in a healthcare patient system. Our example is inspired from the MyHealth@Vanderbilt patient portal [1], a secure electronic health record system developed by Vanderbilt University Medical Center to provide patients the possibility to interact with their doctors and other healthcare professionals through a web-based messaging system. In the first example we show how the process of a patient sending a question to a doctor using the secretary as a proxy can be modelled in our framework and how we might verify that the defined procedure satisfies an associated privacy policy. In the second example we consider a process where a patient's medical records are forwarded by a healthcare provider to an external associate for specialized diagnosis. The process is constructed so as to satisfy the HIPAA privacy rule.

6.1   Submission of a Question

We consider the process whereby a patient submits a question to the system which is received by the secretary who is then responsible to forward it to the doctor. To preserve the privacy of the patient we must ensure that the secretary will be able to forward a *link* of the question to the doctor but unable to read the actual question.

In the $G\pi$-calculus we may model the system with the aid of four groups: HCS corresponds to the entirety of the healthcare system, Patient refers to the patient, HCP refers to the health care providers which are the Secretary and the Doctor subgroups.

Moreover, we assume the existence of three base types: hQuestion refers to a patient's question, hAnswer refers to a doctor's answer and medData refers to protected health records. We write $T_q = \mathsf{HCS}[\mathsf{hQuestion}]$, $T_{q*} = \mathsf{HCS}[T_q]$, $T_a = \mathsf{HCS}[\mathsf{hAnswer}]$, $T_{a*} = \mathsf{HCS}[T_a]$, $T_{mD} = \mathsf{HCP}[medData]$.

$$P = !(\nu \ query : T_q)\overline{query}\langle q \rangle.\overline{tosec}\langle query \rangle.$$
$$fromsec(answer : T_a).answer(a : \mathsf{hAnswer}).0$$
$$S = !tosec(q : T_q).\overline{todoc}\langle q \rangle.fromdoc(x : T_a).\overline{fromsec}\langle x \rangle.0$$
$$D = !todoc(question : T_q).question(q : \mathsf{hQuestion}).readD(d : \mathsf{medData}).$$
$$(\nu \ answer : T_a)(\nu \ a : \mathsf{hAnswer})\overline{answer}\langle a \rangle.\overline{fromdoc}\langle answer \rangle.0$$
$$\mathsf{System} = (\nu \ \mathsf{HCS})(\nu \ tosec : T_{q*})(\nu \ fromsec : T_{a*})(\nu \ todoc : T_{q*})(\nu \ fromdoc : T_{a*})$$
$$[\ (\nu \ \mathsf{HCP})((\nu \ \mathsf{Doctor}) \ D\langle question \rangle \ | \ (\nu \ \mathsf{Secretary}) \ S\langle question \rangle)$$
$$| \ (\nu \ \mathsf{Patient}) \ P\langle question \rangle \ ]$$

In the above model, we have three components representing the three participants of the procedure. The patient P, of group Patient, may communicate with the secretary S, of group Secretary, via names *tosec* and *fromsec*. The name *tosec* has type T_{q*} which can be used within the HCS system in order to communicate links (names of type T_q) to questions of type hQuestion. On receiving such a link, the secretary forwards it to the doctor D, of group Doctor, which uses the received link in order to read the contents of the question and, once obtaining the medical data of the patient, through channel *readD*, it produces an answer (of type hAnswer) and sends a link to the answer (of type T_a) to the secretary who continues to forward it to the patient.

A possible privacy policy for this system might be one that assigns the purpose *question* to every group defined in the system, and associates specific permissions to each group for every base type as follows:

$$\mathscr{P}_q = \mathsf{medData} \gg \langle H, \pi_{mD} \rangle; \mathsf{hQuestion} \gg \langle H, \pi_q \rangle; \mathsf{hAnswer} \gg \langle H, \pi_a \rangle$$

where $H = \mathsf{HCS} : \{question\}[\mathsf{Patient}, \mathsf{HCP}[\mathsf{Doctor}, \mathsf{Secretary}]]$ and

$$\pi_q(question, G) = \begin{cases} \{\mathsf{read}, \mathsf{write}, \mathsf{disclose\,HCS}\} & \text{if } G = \mathsf{Patient} \\ \{\mathsf{access}, \mathsf{disclose\,HCP}\} & \text{if } G = \mathsf{Secretary} \\ \{\mathsf{access}, \mathsf{read}\} & \text{if } G = \mathsf{Doctor} \end{cases}$$

$$\pi_a(question, G) = \begin{cases} \{\mathsf{read}, \mathsf{access}\} & \text{if } G = \mathsf{Patient} \\ \{\mathsf{access}, \mathsf{disclose\,HCS}\} & \text{if } G = \mathsf{Secretary} \\ \{\mathsf{read}, \mathsf{write}, \mathsf{disclose\,HCS}\} & \text{if } G = \mathsf{Doctor} \end{cases}$$

$$\pi_{mD}(question, G) = \begin{cases} \{\mathsf{read}\} & \text{if } G = \mathsf{Doctor} \\ \emptyset & \text{otherwise} \end{cases}$$

By applying the rules of the type system we may show that $\Gamma \vdash \mathsf{System} \triangleright \Theta$ where $\Gamma = \emptyset$ and

$$\begin{aligned} \Theta = \; & \mathsf{hQuestion} \gg \langle \mathsf{HCS}[\mathsf{Patient}[question]], \{\mathsf{write}, \mathsf{disclose\,HCS}\} \rangle; \\ & \mathsf{hQuestion} \gg \langle \mathsf{HCS}[\mathsf{HCP}[\mathsf{Secretary}[question]]], \{\mathsf{access}, \mathsf{disclose\,HCS}\} \rangle; \\ & \mathsf{hQuestion} \gg \langle \mathsf{HCS}[\mathsf{HCP}[\mathsf{Doctor}[question]]], \{\mathsf{access}, \mathsf{read}\} \rangle; \\ & \mathsf{hAnswer} \gg \langle \mathsf{HCS}[\mathsf{Patient}[question]], \{\mathsf{access}, \mathsf{read}\} \rangle; \\ & \mathsf{hAnswer} \gg \langle \mathsf{HCS}[\mathsf{HCP}[\mathsf{Secretary}[question]]], \{\mathsf{access}, \mathsf{disclose\,HCS}\} \rangle; \\ & \mathsf{hAnswer} \gg \langle \mathsf{HCS}[\mathsf{HCP}[\mathsf{Doctor}[question]]], \{\mathsf{write}, \mathsf{disclose\,HCP}\} \rangle; \\ & \mathsf{medData} \gg \langle \mathsf{HCS}[\mathsf{HCP}[\mathsf{Doctor}[question]]], \{\mathsf{read}\} \rangle; \end{aligned}$$

We may see that $\mathscr{P} \Vdash \Theta$ which implies that $\mathscr{P} \vdash S$, that is, the system S satisfies the policy as required.

6.2 Referral to External Associate

Consider the process where a doctor sends medical data of a patient to a medical lab for analysis relevant to the patient's treatment, and the lab responds with the results of the analysis as well as the payment details, according to the health care services provided to the patient, which are then forwarded to the patient by the doctor. This is an external process to the main healthcare provider as it involves the communication between a patient, a hospital and a medical lab, and, in particular, it involves the dissemination of the patient's data outside the hospital environment. In this case, the medical lab is considered to be a business associate of the healthcare provider and, as such, the workflow should follow the policies enunciated by the HIPAA Privacy Rule.

In the $G\pi$-calculus we may model the system with the aid of 6 groups: MedicalWorld corresponds to the complete environment of the system. The MedicalWorld is divided into group HCS for the healthcare system, and to the group MedicalLab for the medical lab. HCS is divided into three groups: Patient for patients, HCP for the health care providers within the system and its sub-group Doctor for doctors.

We assume the existence of two base types: medData referring to the protected health records of the patient and bill referring to the payment details. We write $T_b = $ MedicalWorld[bill], $T_{b*} = $ MedicalWorld[T_b], $T_{mD} = $ MedicalWorld[medData], $T_{mD*} = $ MedicalWorld[T_{mD}]. We may model the system as follows:

$$P = fromD(medBill : T_b).\overline{medBill}(b : bill).0$$
$$D_t = \overline{toLab}\langle mData\rangle.0$$
$$D_b = fromLab(bill : T_b).\overline{fromD}\langle bill\rangle.0$$
$$Lab_t = toLab(d : T_{mD}).d(data : medData).0$$
$$Lab_b = (\nu\ medicalBill : T_b)(\nu\ b : bill)\overline{medicalBill}\langle b\rangle.\overline{fromLab}\langle medicalBill\rangle.0$$
$$\text{System} = (\nu\ \text{MedicalWorld})[\ (\nu\ fromLab : T_{b*})(\nu\ toLab : T_{mD*})(\nu\ fromD : T_{b*})$$
$$(\nu\ HCS)((\nu\ HCP)((\nu\ \text{Doctor})D_t\langle treat\rangle\ \mid\ (\nu\ \text{Doctor})D_b\langle bill\rangle)$$
$$\mid\ (\nu\ \text{Patient})P\langle bill\rangle)$$
$$\mid\ (\nu\ \text{MedicalLab})Lab_t\langle treat\rangle\ \mid\ (\nu\ \text{MedicalLab})Lab_b\langle bill\rangle]$$

In the above model we have five entities working towards the purposes of *treat* and *bill*. In particular, the doctor may engage in process D_t via which it forwards the medical lab (process Lab_t) medical records of the patient in order for the lab to perform some special tests to aid the diagnosis and treatment of the patient. At the same time, processes Lab_b, D_b and P may communicate in order for a bill to be delivered to the patient for the purpose of billing. A possible privacy policy for this system is $\mathscr{P}_q = $ medData $\gg \langle H, \pi_{mD}\rangle;$ bill $\gg \langle H, \pi_b\rangle$ where

$$H = \text{MedicalWorld}: \{bill\}[\text{HCS}[\text{Patient}, \text{HCP}[\text{Doctor} : \{treat\}]], \text{MedicalLab}:\{treat\}]$$

and

$$\pi_{mD}(treat, G) = \begin{cases} \{access, read\} & \text{if } G = \text{MedicalLab} \\ \{read, write, disclose\ \text{MedicalWorld}\} & \text{if } G = \text{Doctor} \\ \emptyset & \text{otherwise} \end{cases}$$

$$\pi_b(bill, G) = \begin{cases} \{\text{read, write, disclose MedicalWorld}\} & \text{if } G = \text{MedicalLab} \\ \{\text{access, disclose MedicalWorld}\} & \text{if } G = \text{Doctor} \\ \{\text{access, read}\} & \text{if } G = \text{Patient} \end{cases}$$

By applying the rules of the type system we may show that $\Gamma \vdash \text{System} \triangleright \Theta$ where $\mathscr{P} \Vdash \Theta$ which implies that $\mathscr{P} \vdash S$, that is, the system S satisfies the policy as required.

Note that if the medical lab attempted to write the analysis results in the medical files of the patient (e.g. by executing an action $\overline{d}\langle data' \rangle$), this would result in a privacy violation: the type system would yield an interface where medData $\gg \langle \text{MedicalWorld}[\text{MedicalLab}[treat]]\{\text{access, read, write}\}\rangle$, which is not compatible with the defined policy. This would lead the analyst to adopt measures by either reconsidering the defined privacy restriction or by introducing a new data type for lab results where the medical laboratory would possess write-permissions.

7   Conclusions

In this paper we have presented a formal framework based on the π-calculus with groups for studying purpose-based, role-aware privacy policies. The framework has been implemented in a prototype tool for checking policy satisfaction by π-calculus processes.

Our framework, similarly to related literature on purpose-based access control, makes a distinction between intended purposes, which are the purposes for which sensitive data is intended to be used, as specified by a policy, and access purposes, which are the actual purposes for which data is requested in a system. Enforcement of a policy should ensure that access purposes are compliant with intended purposes. Simultaneously, it is crucial to ensure that when an entity claims access to sensitive data for a certain purpose, then the processing carried out on the data is consistent with the claimed purpose. In our framework we capture intended purposes via a policy language and we extract access purposes via type checking. Furthermore, to control the data processing carried in the name of a purpose, we introduce the concept of intended and access permissions: At the level of a policy, for each type of sensitive data, we assign to each role within the system a set of permissions (e.g. reading, writing, or disclosing the data) that may be exercised when engaging in a purpose. At the system level, we use type checking to deduce the actual usage exercised by a system. As before, the actual permissions exercised every time sensitive data is accessed or processed should be compliant with the intended permissions as enunciated by the policy. Thus, we may establish sufficient conditions for a system to satisfy a policy statically via type checking and by checking the compatibility between the policy and the output of the type inference.

Our methodology is based on [23] where the main concepts and machinery applied in this paper were developed in order to provide a semantical framework for reasoning about privacy and privacy violations relating to information collection, information processing and information dissemination. The contribution of this paper in comparison to [23] is that it fine-tunes the methodology of [23] to reason about purpose-based requirements. In this way, our policy language allows us to directly express privacy requirements that involve the notion of a purpose as is common in standard privacy policy languages. Furthermore, it opens the path for a fundamental study of the notion of a purpose and its relation to privacy violations.

As future work we intend to explore more complex policy languages relating to purpose-based privacy enforcement such as *conditional* roles as e.g. considered in [9], and the concept of *obligation* as employed in P-RBAC. Furthermore, it would be interesting to explore more dynamic settings where the roles evolve over time. As a long-term goal we would like to work towards providing foundations for the notion of privacy in the general context. Possible extensions of our work in this direction could involve adding semantics both at the level of our metatheory as well as our policy language to capture *identification*-related privacy violations such as *distortion* and *insecurity* violations or providing foundations to formally define aggregation of data and to distinguish when an adversary has achieved data aggregation over a data subject.

References

1. Vanderbilt University Medical Center, My Health at Vanderbilt (2015). http://www.vanderbilthealth.com/main/guide
2. Accorsi, R., Lehmann, A., Lohmann, N.: Information leak detection in business process models: theory, application, and tool support. Inf. Syst. **47**, 244–257 (2015)
3. Agrawal, R., Kiernan, J., Srikant, R., Xu, Y.: Hippocratic databases. In: Proceedings of VLDB 2002, pp. 143–154. Morgan Kaufmann (2002)
4. Backes, M., Pfitzmann, B., Schunter, M.: A toolkit for managing enterprise privacy policies. In: Snekkenes, E., Gollmann, D. (eds.) ESORICS 2003. LNCS, vol. 2808, pp. 162–180. Springer, Heidelberg (2003)
5. Barth, A., Datta, A., Mitchell, J.C., Nissenbaum, H.: Privacy, contextual integrity: framework and applications. In: Proceedings of S&P 2006, pp. 184–198 (2006)
6. Basin, D., Klaedtke, F., Müller, S.: Policy monitoring in first-order temporal logic. In: Touili, T., Cook, B., Jackson, P. (eds.) CAV 2010. LNCS, vol. 6174, pp. 1–18. Springer, Heidelberg (2010)
7. Braghin, C., Gorla, D., Sassone, V.: Role-based access control for a distributed calculus. J. Comput. Secur. **14**(2), 113–155 (2006)
8. Bugliesi, M., Colazzo, D., Crafa, S., Macedonio, D.: A type system for discretionary access control. Math. Struct. Comput. Sci. **19**(4), 839–875 (2009)
9. Byun, J., Bertino, E., Li, N.: Purpose based access control of complex data for privacy protection. In: Proceedings of SACMAT 2005, pp. 102–110. ACM (2005)
10. Capecchi, S., Castellani, I., Dezani-Ciancaglini, M.: Typing access control and secure information flow in sessions. Inf. Comput. **238**, 68–105 (2014)
11. Cardelli, L., Ghelli, G., Gordon, A.D.: Secrecy and group creation. Inf. Comput. **196**(2), 127–155 (2005)
12. Chowdhury, O., Gampe, A., Niu, J., von Ronne, J., Bennatt, J., Datta, A., Jia, L., Winsborough, W.H.: Privacy promises that can be kept: a policy analysis method with application to the HIPAA privacy rule. In: Proceedings of SACMAT 2013, pp. 3–14. ACM (2013)

13. Colombo, P., Ferrari, E.: Enforcement of purpose based access control within relational database management systems. IEEE Trans. Knowl. Data Eng. **26**(11), 2703–2716 (2014)
14. Compagnoni, A.B., Gunter, E.L., Bidinger, P.: Role-based access control for boxed ambients. Theor. Comput. Sci. **398**(1–3), 203–216 (2008)
15. Cranor, L.F.: Web privacy with P3P- The Platform for Privacy Preferences. O'Reilly, Sebastopol (2002)
16. Datta, A., Blocki, J., Christin, N., DeYoung, H., Garg, D., Jia, L., Kaynar, D., Sinha, A.: Understanding and protecting privacy: formal semantics and principled audit mechanisms. In: Jajodia, S., Mazumdar, C. (eds.) ICISS 2011. LNCS, vol. 7093, pp. 1–27. Springer, Heidelberg (2011)
17. DeYoung, H., Garg, D., Jia, L., Kaynar, D.K., Datta, A.: Experiences in the logical specification of the HIPAA and GLBA privacy laws. In: Proceedings of WPES 2010, pp. 73–82. ACM (2010)
18. Dezani-Ciancaglini, M., Ghilezan, S., Jakšić, S., Pantović, J.: Types for Role-based access control of dynamic web data. In: Mariño, J. (ed.) WFLP 2010. LNCS, vol. 6559, pp. 1–29. Springer, Heidelberg (2011)
19. Garg, D., Jia, L., Datta, A.: Policy auditing over incomplete logs: theory, implementation and applications. In: Proceedings of CCS 2011, pp. 151–162. ACM (2011)
20. Hennessy, M., Rathke, J., Yoshida, N.: Safedpi: a language for controlling mobile code. Acta Informatica **42**(4–5), 227–290 (2005)
21. Hennessy, M., Riely, J.: Resource access control in systems of mobile agents. Inf. Comput. **173**(1), 82–120 (2002)
22. Koleini, M., Ritter, E., Ryan, M.: Model checking agent knowledge in dynamic access control policies. In: Piterman, N., Smolka, S.A. (eds.) TACAS 2013 (ETAPS 2013). LNCS, vol. 7795, pp. 448–462. Springer, Heidelberg (2013)
23. Kouzapas, D., Philippou, A.: Type checking privacy policies in the π-calculus. In: Graf, S., Viswanathan, M. (eds.) Formal Techniques for Distributed Objects, Components, and Systems. LNCS, vol. 9039, pp. 181–195. Springer, Heidelberg (2015)
24. Lapadula, A., Pugliese, R., Tiezzi, F.: Regulating data exchange in service oriented applications. In: Arbab, F., Sirjani, M. (eds.) FSEN 2007. LNCS, vol. 4767, pp. 223–239. Springer, Heidelberg (2007)
25. Liu, Y., Müller, S., Xu, K.: A static compliance-checking framework for business process models. IBM Syst. J. **46**(2), 335–362 (2007)
26. May, M.J., Gunter, C.A., Lee, I.: Privacy APIs: Access control techniques to analyze and verify legal privacy policies. In: Proceedings of CSFW 2006, pp. 85–97 (2006)
27. Ni, Q., Bertino, E., Lobo, J.: An obligation model bridging access control policies and privacy policies. In: Proceedings of SACMAT 2008, pp. 133–142. ACM (2008)
28. Nissenbaum, H.: Privacy in Context: Technology, Policy and the Integrity of Social Life. Stanford University Press, Palo Alto (2010)
29. Sokolsky, O., Sammapun, U., Lee, I., Kim, J.: Run-time checking of dynamic properties. Electron. Notes Theor. Comput. Sci. **144**(4), 91–108 (2006)
30. Tschantz, M.C., Datta, A., Wing, J.M.: Formalizing and enforcing purpose restrictions in privacy policies. In: Proceedings of SP 2012, pp. 176–190. IEEE Computer Society (2012)
31. Tschantz, M.C., Wing, J.M.: Formal Methods for Privacy. In: Cavalcanti, A., Dams, D.R. (eds.) FM 2009. LNCS, vol. 5850, pp. 1–15. Springer, Heidelberg (2009)
32. Yang, N., Barringer, H., Zhang, N.: A purpose-based access control model. In: Proceedings of IAS 2007, pp. 143–148. IEEE Computer Society (2007)

On the Decidability of Honesty
and of Its Variants

Massimo Bartoletti[1]([✉]) and Roberto Zunino[2]

[1] Università degli Studi di Cagliari, Cagliari, Italy
bart@unica.it
[2] Università degli Studi di Trento, Trento, Italy
roberto.zunino@unitn.it

Abstract. We address the problem of designing distributed applications which require the interaction of loosely-coupled and mutually distrusting services. In this setting, services can use *contracts* to protect themselves from unsafe interactions with the environment: when their partner in an interaction does not respect its contract, it can be blamed (and punished) by the service infrastructure. We extend a core calculus for services, by using a semantic model of contracts which subsumes various kinds of behavioural types. In this formal framework, we study some notions of *honesty* for services, which measure their ability to respect contracts, under different assumptions about the environment. In particular, we find conditions under which these notions are (un)decidable.

1 Introduction

Service-Oriented Computing (SOC) fosters a programming paradigm where distributed applications can be constructed by discovering, integrating and using basic services [18]. These services may be provided by different organisations, possibly in competition (when not in conflict) among each other. Further, services can appear and disappear from the network, and they can dynamically discover and invoke other services in order to exploit their functionality, or to adapt to changing needs and conditions. Therefore, programmers of distributed applications have to cope with such security, dynamicity and openness issues in order to make their applications trustworthy.

A possible way to address these issues is to use *contracts*. When a service needs to use some external (possibly untrusted) service, it advertises to a SOC middleware a contract which specifies the offered/required interaction protocol. The middleware establishes sessions between services with compliant contracts, and it monitors the communication along these sessions to detect contract violations. These violations may happen either unintentionally, because of errors in the service specification, or because of malicious behaviour.

When the SOC middleware detects contract violations, it sanctions the responsible services. For instance, the middleware in [3] decreases the *reputation* of the culprit, in order to marginalise services with low reputation during the selection phase. Therefore, a new form of attacks arises: malicious users can

© Springer International Publishing Switzerland 2016
T. Hildebrandt et al. (Eds.): WS-FM 2014/WS-FM 2015, LNCS 9421, pp. 143–166, 2016.
DOI: 10.1007/978-3-319-33612-1_9

try to make some service sanctioned by exploiting possible discrepancies between the promised and the actual behaviour of that service. A crucial problem is then how to avoid such attacks when deploying a service.

However, designing an *honest* service which always respects its contracts requires one to fulfil its obligations also in adversarial contexts which play against. We illustrate below that, even for a fairly simple application composed by only three services, this is not an easy task.

An Example. Consider an online store taking orders from buyers. The store sells two items: item A, which is always available and costs €1, and item B, which costs €1 when in stock, and €3 otherwise. In the latter case, the store orders item B from an external distributor, which makes the store pay €2 per item.

The store advertises the following contract to potential buyers:

1. let the buyer choose between item A and item B;
2. if the buyer chooses item A, then receive €1, and then ship the item to him;
3. if the buyer chooses item B, offer a quotation to the buyer (€1 or €3);
4. if the quotation is €1, then receive the payment and ship;
5. if the quotation is €3, ask the buyer to pay or cancel the order;
6. if the buyer pays €3, then either ship the item to him, or refund €3.

We can formalise such contract in several process algebras. For instance, we can use the following session type [20] (without channel passing):

$$T_B = \texttt{buyA.pay1E.}\overline{\texttt{shipA}} \ \&$$
$$\texttt{buyB.}(\overline{\texttt{quote1E}}.\texttt{pay1E.}\overline{\texttt{shipB}} \ \oplus \ \overline{\texttt{quote3E}}.T_B' \ \oplus \ \overline{\texttt{abort}})$$
$$T_B' = \texttt{pay3E.}(\overline{\texttt{shipB}} \oplus \overline{\texttt{refund}}) \ \& \ \texttt{quit}$$

where e.g., $\texttt{buyA}$ represents a label in a *branching* construct (i.e., receiving an order for item A from the buyer), while $\overline{\texttt{quote1E}}$ represents a label in a *selection* construct (i.e., sending an €1 quotation to the buyer). The operator $\oplus$ separates branches in an *internal choice*, while $\&$ separates branches in an *external choice*.

The protocol between the store and the distributor is the following:

$$T_D = \overline{\texttt{buyB}}.(\overline{\texttt{pay2E}}.\texttt{shipB} \oplus \overline{\texttt{quit}})$$

Note that the contracts above do not specify the *actual* behaviour of the store, but only the behaviour it promises towards the buyer and the distributor. A possible informal description of the actual behaviour of the store is the following:

1. advertise the contract T_B;
2. when T_B is stipulated, let the buyer choose item A (buyA) or B (buyB);
3. if the buyer chooses A, get the payment (pay1E), and ship the item (shipA);
4. otherwise, if the buyer chooses B, check if the item is in stock;
5. if item B is in stock, provide the buyer the quotation of €1 (quote1E), receive the payment (pay1E), and ship the item (shipB);
6. otherwise, if item B is not in stock, advertise the contract T_D;

7. when T_D is stipulated, pre-order item B from the distributor (buyB);
8. send a €3 quotation to the buyer (quote3E) and wait for the buyer's reply;
9. if the buyer pays €3 (pay3E), then pay the distributor (pay2E), receive the item from the distributor (shipB), and ship it to the buyer (shipB).

The store service terminates correctly whenever two conditions hold: the buyer is honest, and at step 7 the middleware selects an honest distributor. Such assumptions are necessary. For instance, in their absence we have that:

(a) if the buyer is dishonest, and he does not send €3 at step 9, then the store does not fulfil its obligation with the distributor, who is expecting a payment or a cancellation;
(b) if the middleware finds no distributor with a contract compliant with T_D, then the store is stuck at line 7, so it does not fulfil its obligation with the buyer, who is expecting a quotation or an abort;
(c) if the distributor is dishonest, and it does not ship the item at line 9, then the store does not fulfil its obligation with the buyer, who is expecting to receive the item or a refund;
(d) if the buyer chooses quit at line 8, the store forgets to handle it; so, it will not fulfil the contract with the distributor, who is expecting pay2E or quit.

Therefore, we would classify the store process above as *dishonest*. In practice, this implies that a concrete implementation of such store could be easily attacked. For instance, an attacker could simply order item B (when not in stock), but always cancel the transaction. The middleware will detect that the store is violating the contract with the distributor, and consequently it will sanction the store. Concretely, in the middleware of [3] the attacker will manage to never be sanctioned, and to arbitrarily decrease the store reputation, so preventing the store from being able to establish new sessions with buyers.

The example above shows that writing honest processes is an error-prone task: this is because one has to foresee all the possible points of failure of each partner. We handle all such points in Example 6, where we show a provably honest store process.

Specifying Contract-Oriented Services. To formalise and study honesty, we first fix the formal setting, which consists of two basic ingredients:

– a model of *contracts*, which specify the *promised* behaviour of a service.
– a model of *processes*, which specify the *actual* behaviour. Such behaviour involves e.g. checking compliance between contracts, making a contract evolve upon actions, *etc.*, and so it also depends on the contract model.

Ideally, a general theory of honesty should abstract as much as possible from the actual choices for the two models. However, different instances of the models may give rise to different notions of honesty — in the same way as different process calculi may require different notions of observational equivalences. Continuing the parallel with process calculi, where a process calculus may have several different behavioural equivalences/preorders, it is also reasonable that, even in a specific contract/process model, many relevant notions of honesty exist.

In this paper we focus on a quite general model of contracts: arbitrary LTSs. In particular, states denote contracts, and labels represent internal actions and synchronisations between two services at the endpoints of a session (Sect. 2). We interpret compliance between two contracts as the absence of deadlock in their parallel execution, similarly to [1,2,13]. This model allows for a syntax-independent treatment of contracts (like e.g. session types, see Sect. 2.2).

To formalise processes, we build upon CO_2 [10]: this is a minimalistic calculus with primitives for advertising contracts, opening sessions, and doing contractual actions. In Sect. 3 we extend the calculus of [10] by modifying the synchronisation primitive to use arbitrary LTSs as contracts, and the advertisement primitive to increase its expressiveness.

Contributions. The main contribution of the paper is the study of some notions of honesty, their properties, and their decidability. In particular:

1. We show that two different notions of honesty coincide (Theorem 1). The first one (originally introduced in [8]) says that a process is honest when, in *all* possible contexts, whenever it has some contractual obligations, it can interact with the context and eventually fulfil said obligations. The second notion is a variant (introduced here), which requires a process to be able (in all possible contexts) to fulfil its obligations on its own, *without* interacting with the context. This result simplifies the design of static analyses for honesty, since it allows for abstracting the moves of the context when one has to decide whether a process is fulfilling its obligations.

2. We prove that systems of honest processes are deadlock-free (Theorem 6).

3. We introduce a weaker notion of honesty, where a process is required to behave honestly only when its partners are honest (Definition 15). For instance, weak honesty ensures the absence of attacks such as items b and d in the store example, but it does not rule out attacks such as items a and c. Unlike systems of honest processes, systems of *weakly* honest processes may get stuck, because of circular dependencies between sessions (see Example 8).

4. We show that if a process using session types as contracts is honest in all contexts *which use session types as contracts*, then it is honest in all *arbitrary* contexts (Theorem 5). This property has a practical impact: if some static analyses tailored on session types (like e.g., that in [7]) determines that a process is honest, then we can safely use such process in any context — also in those which use a different contract model.

5. We study decidability of honesty and weak honesty. First, for any given Turing Machine, we show in Theorem 7 how to craft a CO_2 process which simulates it. We then prove that this process is honest (according to *any* of the notions presented above) if and only if said Turing Machine is not halting. From this we establish the undecidability of all the above-mentioned notions of honesty, in all possible models of contracts which include session types. Overall, this generalises a result in [10], which establishes the undecidability of (strong) honesty in an instance of CO_2 using τ-less CCS contracts [13].

6. We find a syntactic restriction of CO_2 and a constraint on contracts under which honesty is decidable (Theorem 8).

7. We find a class of contracts for which *dis*honesty of (unrestricted) CO_2 processes is recursively enumerable (Theorem 9).

2   Contracts

We now provide a semantic setting for contracts. In Sect. 2.1 we model contracts as states of a Labelled Transition System (LTS) with two kinds of labels: *internal actions*, which represent actions performed by one participant, and *synchronisation actions*, which model interactions between participants. As an example, in Sect. 2.2 we show that session types can be interpreted in this setting. In Sect. 2.3 we provide contracts with a notion of *compliance*, which formalises correct interactions between services which respect their contracts.

2.1   A Model of Contracts

Assume a set of *participants* (ranged over by $A, B, \ldots$), a recursive set L (ranged over by $a, b, \ldots$) with an involution $\bar{\cdot}$, and a recursive set Λ^τ (ranged over by $\tau, \tau_a, \tau_i, \ldots$). We call $\Lambda^a = L \cup \bar{L}$ the set of *synchronisation actions*, and Λ^τ the set of *internal actions*. We then define the set Λ of *actions* as the disjoint union of Λ^a and Λ^τ, and we let $\alpha, \beta, \ldots$ range over Λ.

We develop our theory within the LTS $(\mathbb{U}, \Lambda, \rightarrow)$, where:

- $\mathbb{U}$ is a set (ranged over by $c, d, \ldots$), called the universe of *contracts*;
- $\rightarrow \,\subseteq \mathbb{U} \times \Lambda \times \mathbb{U}$ is a transition relation between contracts, with labels in Λ.

We denote with $\mathbb{U}_{fin}$ the set of *finite-state* contracts, i.e. for all $c \in \mathbb{U}_{fin}$, the contracts reachable from c with any finite sequence of transitions is finite. We denote with $\mathbf{0}$ a contract with no outgoing transitions, and we interpret it as a *success* state. We write: $\mathcal{R}^*$ for the reflexive and transitive closure of a relation $\mathcal{R}$, and $c \xrightarrow{\alpha} c'$ when $(c, \alpha, c') \in \,\rightarrow$. Furthermore, sometimes we express contracts through the usual CCS operators [24]: for instance, we can write the contract c_1 in Fig. 1 as the term $\tau_{\bar{a}}.\bar{a} + \tau_{\bar{b}}.\bar{b}$.

While a contract describes the intended behaviour of *one* of the two participants involved in a session, the behaviour of two interacting participants A and B is modelled by the composition of two contracts, denoted by $A : c \parallel B : d$. We specify in Definition 1 an operational semantics of these *contract configurations*: internal actions can always be fired, while synchronisation actions require both participants to enable two complementary actions. Note that the label of a synchronisation is *not* an internal action (unlike e.g., in CCS [24]); this is because in the semantics of CO_2 we need to inspect such label in order to make two processes synchronise (see rule [DoCom] in Fig. 3).

Definition 1 (Semantics of contract configurations). *We define the transition relation $\twoheadrightarrow$ between contract configurations (ranged over by $\gamma, \gamma', \ldots$) as the least relation closed under the following rules:*

$$\frac{c \xrightarrow{\tau} c'}{\mathsf{A} : c \parallel \mathsf{B} : d \xrightarrow{\{\mathsf{A}\}:\tau} \mathsf{A} : c' \parallel \mathsf{B} : d} \qquad \frac{d \xrightarrow{\tau} d'}{\mathsf{A} : c \parallel \mathsf{B} : d \xrightarrow{\{\mathsf{B}\}:\tau} \mathsf{A} : c \parallel \mathsf{B} : d'}$$

$$\frac{c \xrightarrow{\mathsf{a}} c' \qquad d \xrightarrow{\overline{\mathsf{a}}} d'}{\mathsf{A} : c \parallel \mathsf{B} : d \xrightarrow{\{\mathsf{A},\mathsf{B}\}:\mathsf{a}} \mathsf{A} : c' \parallel \mathsf{B} : d'}$$

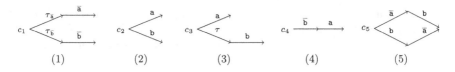

(1)   (2)   (3)   (4)   (5)

Fig. 1. Some simple contracts.

2.2   Session Types as Contracts

Session types [19,20] are formal specifications of communication protocols between the participants at the endpoints of a session. We give in Definition 2 a version of session types without channel passing, similarly to [1].

Definition 2 (Session types). *Session types are terms of the grammar:*

$$T \quad ::= \quad \&_{i \in I} \mathsf{a}_i.T_i \mid \bigoplus_{i \in I} \overline{\mathsf{a}_i}.T_i \mid \mathrm{rec}_X T \mid X$$

where (i) the set I is finite, (ii) all the actions in external (resp. internal) choices are pairwise distinct and in L (resp. in $\overline{\mathsf{L}}$), and (iii) recursion is prefix-guarded.

A session type is a term of a process algebra featuring a *selection* construct (i.e., an internal choice among a set of branches, each one performing some output), and a *branching* construct (i.e., an external choice among a set of inputs offered to the environment). We write **0** for the empty (internal/external) choice, and we omit trailing occurrences of **0**. We adopt the equi-recursive approach, by considering terms up-to unfolding of recursion.

We can interpret session types as contracts, by giving them a semantics in terms of the LTS defined in Sect. 2.1.

Definition 3. *We denote with* ST *the set of contracts of the form T or $[\overline{\mathsf{a}}] T$, with T closed, and transitions relation given by the following rules:*

$$\&_{i \in I} \mathsf{a}_i.T_i \xrightarrow{\mathsf{a}_k} T_k \;\; (k \in I) \qquad \bigoplus_{i \in I} \overline{\mathsf{a}_i}.T_i \xrightarrow{\tau_i} [\overline{\mathsf{a}_k}] T_k \;\; (k \in I) \qquad [\overline{\mathsf{a}}] T \xrightarrow{\overline{\mathsf{a}}} T$$

An external choice can always fire one of its prefixes. An internal choice $\bigoplus_{i \in I} \overline{\mathsf{a}_i}.T_i$ must first commit to one of the branches $\overline{\mathsf{a}_k}.T_k$, and this produces a *committed choice* $[\overline{\mathsf{a}_k}] T_k$, which can only fire $\overline{\mathsf{a}_k}$. As a consequence, a session type may have several outgoing transitions, but internal transitions cannot be mixed with synchronisation ones. There cannot be two internal transitions in a row, and after an internal transition, the target state will have exactly one reduct. Note that ST $\subsetneq \mathsf{U}_{fin}$.

Example 1. The contract c_1 in Fig. 1 represents the session type $\bar{a} \oplus \bar{b}$: since it is an internal choice, according to Definition 3 there is a commit on the chosen branch before actually firing the synchronisation action. The contract c_2 is in ST as well, as it represents an external choice $a \& b$. Instead, the last three contracts do *not* belong to ST: indeed, in c_3 an internal transition is mixed with an input one; in c_4 there is no internal transition before $\bar{b}$; finally, in c_5 input and output transitions are mixed (note that c_5 represents an *asynchronous* output of $\bar{a}$ followed by an input of b, as in the asynchronous session types of [9]).   □

2.3 Compliance

Among the various notions of compliance appeared in the literature [4], here we adopt *progress* (i.e. the absence of deadlock). In Definition 4 we say that c and d are compliant (in symbols, $c \bowtie d$) iff, when a reduct of $A : c \parallel B : d$ cannot take transitions, then both participants have reached success. A similar notion has been used in [13] (for τ-less CCS contracts) and in [1,2] (for session types).

Definition 4 (Compliance). *We write $c \bowtie d$ iff:*

$$A : c \parallel B : d \twoheadrightarrow^* A : c' \parallel B : d' \not\twoheadrightarrow \quad implies \quad c' = \mathbf{0} \ and \ d' = \mathbf{0}$$

Example 2. Consider contracts in Fig. 1. We have that $c_1 \bowtie c_2$ and $c_4 \bowtie c_5$, while all the other pairs of contracts are not compliant.   □

3 Contract-Oriented Services

We now extend the process calculus CO_2 of [10], by parameterising it over an arbitrary set $\mathbb{C}$ of contracts. As a further extension, while in [10] one can advertise a single contract at a time, here we allow processes to advertise *sets* of contracts, which will be stipulated atomically (see Definition 6). This will allow us to enlarge the set of honest processes, with respect to those considered in [10].

3.1 Syntax

Let $\mathcal{V}$ and $\mathcal{N}$ be disjoint sets of, respectively, *session variables* (ranged over by $x, y, \ldots$) and *session names* (ranged over by $s, t, \ldots$); let $u, v, \ldots$ range over $\mathcal{V} \cup \mathcal{N}$, and $\boldsymbol{u}, \boldsymbol{v}, \ldots$ over $2^{\mathcal{V} \cup \mathcal{N}}$. A *latent contract* $\{\downarrow_x c\}$ represents a contract c which has not been stipulated yet; the variable x will be instantiated to a fresh session name upon stipulation. We also allow for *sets* of latent contracts $\{\downarrow_{u_1} c_1, \ldots, \downarrow_{u_k} c_k\}$, to be stipulated atomically. We let $C, C', \ldots$ range over sets of latent contracts, and we write C_A when the contracts are signed by A.

Definition 5 (CO_2 syntax). *The syntax of CO_2 is defined as follows:*

$$
\begin{array}{llll}
\pi & ::= & \tau \mid \mathtt{tell}\, C \mid \mathtt{do}_u\, \alpha & \textit{(Prefixes)} \\
P & ::= & \sum_i \pi_i.P_i \mid P \mid P \mid (u)P \mid X(\boldsymbol{u}) & \textit{(Processes)} \\
S & ::= & \mathbf{0} \mid A[P] \mid C_A \mid s[\gamma] \mid S \mid S \mid (u)S & \textit{(Systems)}
\end{array}
$$

We also assume the following syntactic constraints on processes and systems:

1. *each occurrence of* $X(\boldsymbol{u})$ *within a process is prefix-guarded;*
2. *each* X *has a unique defining equation* $X(\boldsymbol{u}) \triangleq P$, *with* $fv(P) \subseteq \{\boldsymbol{u}\} \subseteq \mathcal{V}$;
3. *in* $(\boldsymbol{u})(A[P] \mid B[Q] \mid \cdots)$, *it must be* $A \neq B$;
4. *in* $(\boldsymbol{u})(s[\gamma] \mid t[\gamma'] \mid \cdots)$, *it must be* $s \neq t$;

We denote with $\boldsymbol{\mathcal{P}}_{\mathbb{C}}$ *the set of all processes with contracts in* $\mathbb{C}$.

$$(u)A[P] \equiv A[(u)P] \qquad Z \mid \mathbf{0} \equiv Z \qquad Z \mid Z' \equiv Z' \mid Z \qquad (Z \mid Z') \mid Z'' \equiv Z \mid (Z' \mid Z'')$$

$$Z \mid (u)Z' \equiv (u)(Z \mid Z') \ \text{ if } u \notin fv(Z) \cup fn(Z)$$

$$(u)(v)Z \equiv (v)(u)Z \qquad (u)Z \equiv Z \ \text{ if } u \notin fv(Z) \cup fn(Z)$$

Fig. 2. Structural congruence (Z ranges over processes, systems, latent contracts)

Processes specify the actual behaviour of participants. A process can be a prefix-guarded finite sum $\sum_i \pi_i.P_i$, a parallel composition $P \mid Q$, a delimited process $(u)P$, or a constant $X(\boldsymbol{u})$. We write $\mathbf{0}$ for $\sum_\emptyset P$, and $\pi_1.Q_1 + P$ for $\sum_{i \in I \cup \{1\}} \pi_i.Q_i$, provided that $P = \sum_{i \in I} \pi_i.Q_i$ and $1 \notin I$. If $\boldsymbol{u} = \{u_1, \ldots, u_k\}$, we write $(\boldsymbol{u})P$ for $(u_1) \cdots (u_k)P$. We omit trailing occurrences of $\mathbf{0}$.

Prefixes include the silent action τ, contract advertisement $\mathtt{tell}\, C$, and action execution $\mathtt{do}_u\, \alpha$, where the identifier u refers to the target session.

A system is composed of *agents* (i.e., named processes) $A[P]$, *sessions* $s[\gamma]$, signed sets of latent contracts C_A, and delimited systems $(u)S$. Delimitation (u) binds session variables and names, both in processes and systems. Free variables and names are defined as usual, and their union is denoted by $fnv(\_)$. A system/process is *closed* when it has no free variables. We denote with K a special participant name (playing the role of broker) not occurring in any system.

3.2   Semantics

We define the semantics of CO_2 as a reduction relation on systems (Fig. 3). This uses a structural congruence, which is the smallest relation satisfying the equations in Fig. 2. Such equations are mostly standard — we just note that $(u)A[(v)P] \equiv (u)(v)A[P]$ allows to move delimitations between CO_2 systems and processes. In order to define honesty in Sect. 4, we decorate transitions with labels, by writing $\xrightarrow{A\, :\, \pi}$ for a reduction where participants A fire π.

Rule [TAU] fires a τ prefix. Rule [TELL] advertises a set of latent contracts C. Rule [FUSE] inspects latent contracts, which are stipulated when compliant pairs are found through the $\triangleright$ relation (see Definition 6 below). Upon stipulation, one or more new sessions among the stipulating parties are created. Rule [DoTAU] allows a participant A to perform an internal action in the session s with contract configuration γ (which, accordingly, evolves to γ'). Rule [DoCom] allows two participants to synchronise in a session s. The last three rules are standard.

Definition 6. *The relation* $C^1_{A_1} | \cdots | C^k_{A_k} \rhd^\sigma s_1[\gamma_1] | \cdots | s_n[\gamma_n]$ *holds iff:*

1. *for all* $i \in 1..k$, $C^i = \{\downarrow_{x_{i,1}} c_{i,1}, \ldots, \downarrow_{x_{i,m_i}} c_{i,m_i}\}$, *and the variables* $x_{i,j}$ *are pairwise distinct;*
2. *for all* $i \in 1..k$, *let* $D_i = \{(A_i, x_{i,h}, c_{i,h}) \,|\, h \in 1..m_i\}$. *The set* $\bigcup_i D_i$ *is partitioned into a set of* n *subsets* $\mathcal{M}_j = \{(A_j, x_j, c_j), (B_j, y_j, d_j)\}$ *such that, for all* $j \in 1..n$, $A_j \neq B_j$, $c_j \bowtie d_j$, *and* $\gamma_j = A_j : c_j \,\|\, B_j : d_j$;
3. $\sigma = \{s_1/x_1,y_1, \cdots, s_n/x_n,y_n\}$ *maps session variables to pairwise distinct session names* $s_1, \ldots, s_n$.

$$A[\tau.\,P + P' \,|\, Q] \xrightarrow{\{A\}\,:\,\tau} A[P \,|\, Q] \quad \text{[Tau]}$$

$$A[\text{tell}\,C.\,P + P' \,|\, Q] \xrightarrow{\{A\}\,:\,\tau} A[P \,|\, Q] \,|\, C_A \quad \text{[Tell]}$$

$$\frac{C^1_{A_1} | \cdots | C^k_{A_k} \rhd^\sigma S' \quad \text{ran }\sigma \cap \text{fn}(S) = \emptyset}{(\text{dom }\sigma)(C^1_{A_1} | \cdots | C^k_{A_k} \,|\, S) \xrightarrow{\{K\}\,:\,\tau} (\text{ran }\sigma)(S' \,|\, S\sigma)} \quad \text{[Fuse]}$$

$$\frac{\gamma \xrightarrow{\{A\}:\tau_a} \gamma'}{A[\text{do}_s\,\tau_a.\,P + P' \,|\, Q] \,|\, s[\gamma] \xrightarrow{\{A\}\,:\,\text{do}_s\,\tau_a} A[P \,|\, Q] \,|\, s[\gamma']} \quad \text{[DoTau]}$$

$$\frac{\gamma \xrightarrow{\{A,B\}:a} \gamma'}{\begin{array}{lll} A[\text{do}_s\,a.\,P + P' \,|\, P''] & | \; B[\text{do}_s\,\bar{a}.\,Q + Q' \,|\, Q''] & | \; s[\gamma] \\ A[P \,|\, P''] & | \; B[Q \,|\, Q''] & | \; s[\gamma'] \end{array} \xrightarrow{\{A,B\}\,:\,\text{do}_s\,a}} \quad \text{[DoCom]}$$

$$\frac{X(u) \triangleq P \quad A[P\{v/u\} \,|\, Q] \,|\, S \xrightarrow{A\,:\,\pi} S'}{A[X(v) \,|\, Q] \,|\, S \xrightarrow{A\,:\,\pi} S'} \quad \text{[Def]}$$

$$\frac{S \xrightarrow{A\,:\,\pi} S'}{(u)S \xrightarrow{A\,:\,\text{del}_u(\pi)} (u)S'} \quad \text{[Del]} \qquad \text{where } \text{del}_u(\pi) = \begin{cases} \tau & \text{if } u \in \text{fnv}(\pi) \\ \pi & \text{otherwise} \end{cases}$$

$$\frac{S \xrightarrow{A\,:\,\pi} S'}{S \,|\, S'' \xrightarrow{A\,:\,\pi} S' \,|\, S''} \quad \text{[Par]}$$

Fig. 3. Reduction semantics of CO_2.

Example 3. Let $S = (x, y, z, w)\,(C_A \,|\, C'_B \,|\, C''_C \,|\, S_0)$, with S_0 immaterial, and:

$$C = \{\downarrow_x \bar{a}, \downarrow_y \bar{b}\} \qquad C' = \{\downarrow_z a\} \qquad C'' = \{\downarrow_w b\}$$

Further, let $\sigma = \{s/x,z, \, t/y,w\}$, $\gamma_{AB} = A : \bar{a} \,|\, B : a$ and $\gamma_{AC} = A : \bar{b} \,|\, C : b$. According to Definition 6 we have that $C_A \,|\, C'_B \,|\, C''_C \rhd^\sigma s[\gamma_{AB}] \,|\, t[\gamma_{AC}]$. In fact:

1. C, C' and C'' contain pairwise distinct variables;
2. letting $D_A = \{(A, x, \bar{a}), (A, y, \bar{b})\}$, $D_B = \{(B, z, a)\}$ and $D_C = \{(C, w, b)\}$, we can partition $D_A \cup D_B \cup D_C$ into the subsets $\mathcal{M}_{AB} = \{(A, x, \bar{a}), (B, z, a)\}$ and $\mathcal{M}_{AC} = \{(A, y, \bar{b}), (C, w, b)\}$, where $\bar{a} \bowtie a$ and $\bar{b} \bowtie b$.
3. σ maps session variables x, z, y, w to pairwise distinct session names s, t.

Therefore, by rule [FUSE], we have: $S \xrightarrow{\{K\}:\tau} (s,t)\,(s[\gamma_{AB}] \mid t[\gamma_{AC}] \mid S_0\sigma).$ □

Example 4. Let $S = A[(x)\,X(x)] \mid B[(y)\,Y(y)]$, where:

$$X(x) \triangleq \mathtt{tell}\,\{\downarrow_x \bar{a}\}.\,\mathtt{do}_x\,\bar{a} \qquad Y(y) \triangleq \mathtt{tell}\,\{\downarrow_y a\}.\,\mathtt{do}_y\,a$$

A maximal computation of S is the following:

$$S \xrightarrow{\{B\}:\tau} \qquad A[(x)\,X(x)] \mid (y)\,(B[\mathtt{do}_y\,a] \mid \{\downarrow_y a\}_B) \qquad\qquad\quad [\text{TELL}]$$
$$\xrightarrow{\{A\}:\tau} \qquad (x,y)\,(A[\mathtt{do}_x\,\bar{a}] \mid B[\mathtt{do}_y\,a] \mid \{\downarrow_x \bar{a}\}_A \mid \{\downarrow_y a\}_B) \; [\text{TELL}]$$
$$\xrightarrow{\{K\}:\tau} \qquad (s)\,(A[\mathtt{do}_s\,\bar{a}] \mid B[\mathtt{do}_s\,a] \mid s[A:\bar{a} \parallel B:a]) \qquad\qquad [\text{FUSE}]$$
$$\xrightarrow{\{A,B\}:\mathtt{do}_s\,a} \quad (s)\,(A[0] \mid B[0] \mid s[A:0 \parallel B:0]) \qquad\qquad\qquad [\text{DOCOM}]$$

4   Honesty: Properties and Variants

CO_2 allows for writing *dishonest* processes which do not fulfil their contracts, in some contexts. Below we formalise some notions of honesty, which vary according to the assumptions on the context. We start by introducing some auxiliary notions. The *obligations* $O_s^A(S)$ of a participant A at a session s in S are those actions of A enabled in the contract configuration within s in S.

Definition 7 (Obligations). *We define the set of actions* $O_s^A(S)$ *as:*

$$O_s^A(S) = \begin{cases} O^A(\gamma) & \text{if } \exists S'.\ S \equiv s[\gamma] \mid S' \\ \emptyset & \text{otherwise} \end{cases} \text{ where } O^A(\gamma) = \{\alpha \mid \exists \mathcal{A}.\gamma \xrightarrow{\{A\}\cup\mathcal{A}:\alpha} \}$$

The set $S \downarrow_u^A$ (called ready-do set) collects all the actions α such that the process of A in S has some unguarded prefixes $\mathtt{do}_u\,\alpha$.

Definition 8 (Ready-do). *We define the set of actions* $S \downarrow_u^A$ *as:*

$$S \downarrow_u^A = \{\alpha \mid \exists v,P,P',Q,S'.\ S \equiv (v)\,(A[\mathtt{do}_u\,\alpha.\,P + P' \mid Q] \mid S') \ \wedge\ u \notin v\}$$

4.1   Honesty

A participant is *ready* in a system if she can fulfil some of her obligations there (Definition 10). To check if A is ready in S, we consider all the sessions s in S involving A. For each of them, we check that some obligations of A at s are exposed after some steps (of A or of the context), *not* preceded by other $\mathtt{do}_s$ of A. These actions are collected in the set $S \Downarrow_s^A$.

Definition 9 (Weak ready-do). *We define the set of actions* $S \Downarrow_u^A$ *as:*

$$S \Downarrow_u^A = \left\{\alpha \mid \exists S':S \xrightarrow{\neq(A:\,\mathtt{do}_u)}{}^* S' \text{ and } \alpha \in S' \downarrow_u^A \right\}$$

where $S \xrightarrow{\neq(A:\,\mathtt{do}_u)} S'$ *iff* $\exists \mathcal{A},\pi.\ S \xrightarrow{\mathcal{A}:\pi} S' \wedge (A \notin \mathcal{A} \vee \forall\alpha.\ \pi \neq \mathtt{do}_u\,\alpha).$

The set Rdy_s^A collects all the systems where A is ready at session s. This happens in three cases: either A has no obligations, or A may perform *some* internal action which is also an obligation, or A may perform *all* the synchronisation actions which are obligations.

Definition 10 (Readiness). Rdy_s^A *is the set of systems S such that:*

$$O_s^A(S) = \emptyset \quad \vee \quad O_s^A(S) \cap \Lambda^\tau \cap S\Downarrow_s^A \neq \emptyset \quad \vee \quad \emptyset \neq (O_s^A(S) \cap \Lambda^a) \subseteq S\Downarrow_s^A$$

We say that A is ready *in S iff $\forall S', u, s . S \equiv (u)S'$ implies $S' \in \mathrm{Rdy}_s^A$.*

We can now formalise when a participant is *honest*. Roughly, $A[P]$ is honest in a *fixed* system S when A is ready in all reducts of $A[P] \mid S$. Then, we say that $A[P]$ is honest when she is honest in *all* systems S.

Definition 11 (Honesty). *Given a set of contracts $\mathbb{C} \subseteq \mathbb{U}$ and a set of processes $\mathcal{P} \subseteq \mathcal{P}_\mathbb{C}$, we say that:*

1. *S is A-free   iff it has no latent/stipulated contracts of A, nor processes of A*
2. *P is honest in $\mathcal{P}$ iff, for all S made of agents with processes in $\mathcal{P}$:*

$$\forall A : \left(S \text{ is A-free} \wedge A[P] \mid S \to^* S'\right) \implies A \text{ is ready in } S'$$

3. *P is honest   iff $P \in \mathcal{H}_\mathbb{C}$, where:*

$$\mathcal{H}_\mathbb{C} = \{P \in \mathcal{P}_\mathbb{U} \mid P \text{ is honest in } \mathcal{P}_\mathbb{C}\}$$

Note that in item 2 we quantify over all A: this is needed to associate P to a participant name, with the only constraint that such name must not be present in the context S used to test P. In the absence of the A-freeness constraint, honesty would be impractically strict: indeed, were S already carrying stipulated or latent contracts of A, e.g. with $S = s[A : \overline{\mathtt{pay100Keu}} \parallel B : \mathtt{pay100Keu}]$, it would be unreasonable to ask participant A to fulfil them. Note however that S can contain latent contracts and sessions involving *any* other participant different from A: in a sense, the honesty of $A[P]$ ensures a good behaviour even in the (quite realistic) case where $A[P]$ is inserted in a system which has already started.

Example 5. Consider the following processes:

1. $P_1 = (x) \, \mathtt{tell} \{\downarrow_x \mathtt{a} + \tau.\mathtt{b}\}. \, \mathtt{do}_x \tau . \, \mathtt{do}_x \mathtt{b}$
2. $P_2 = (x) \, \mathtt{tell} \{\downarrow_x \mathtt{a}\}. \, (\tau.\mathtt{do}_x \mathtt{a} + \tau.\mathtt{do}_x \mathtt{b})$
3. $P_3 = (x) \, \mathtt{tell} \{\downarrow_x \mathtt{a} + \mathtt{b}\}. \, \mathtt{do}_x \mathtt{a}$
4. $P_4 = (x) \, \mathtt{tell} \{\downarrow_x \mathtt{a}\}. \, X(x) \qquad X(x) \triangleq \tau . \, \mathtt{do}_x \mathtt{a} + \tau . \, X(x)$
5. $P_5 = (x \, y) \, \mathtt{tell} \{\downarrow_x \mathtt{a}\}. \, \mathtt{tell} \{\downarrow_y \mathtt{b}\}. \, \mathtt{do}_x \mathtt{a} . \, \mathtt{do}_y \mathtt{b}$

Processes P_1 and P_4 are honest, while the others are not. In P_2, if the rightmost τ is fired, then the process cannot do the promised a. In P_3, if the contract of other participant at x is $\overline{\mathtt{b}}$, then P_3 cannot do the corresponding b. There are two different reasons for which P_5 is not honest. First, in contexts where y is fused and x is not, the $\mathtt{do}_y \mathtt{b}$ can not be reached (and so the contract at y is not respected). Second, also in those contexts where both sessions are fused, if the other participant at x never does $\overline{\mathtt{a}}$, then $\mathtt{do}_y \mathtt{b}$ cannot be reached.   □

Example 6. We now model in CO_2 the store process outlined in Sect. 1. Rather than giving a faithful formalisation of the pseudo-code in Sect. 1, which we observed to be dishonest, we present an alternative version. The process P below is honest, and it can be proved such by the honesty model checker in [7]. Within this example, we use $\mathsf{do}_x^\tau\,\bar{\mathsf{a}}$ as an abbreviation for $\mathsf{do}_x\,\tau_{\mathsf{a}}.\,\mathsf{do}_x\,\bar{\mathsf{a}}$.

$$P = (x)\,\mathtt{tell}\,\{\downarrow_x T_{\mathrm{B}}\}_{\mathrm{A}}.\,(\mathsf{do}_x\,\mathsf{buyA}.\,P_A(x) + \mathsf{do}_x\,\mathsf{buyB}.\,P_B(x))$$

$$P_A(x) \triangleq \mathsf{do}_x\,\mathsf{pay1E}.\,\mathsf{do}_x^\tau\,\overline{\mathsf{shipA}}$$

$$P_B(x) \triangleq (y)\,\big(\tau.\,\mathsf{do}_x^\tau\,\overline{\mathsf{quote1E}}.\mathsf{do}_x\,\mathsf{pay1E}.\,\mathsf{do}_x^\tau\,\overline{\mathsf{shipB}} +$$
$$\tau.\,\mathtt{tell}\,\{\downarrow_x T_{\mathrm{D}}\}_{\mathrm{A}}.\mathsf{do}_y^\tau\,\overline{\mathsf{buyB}}.\mathsf{do}_x^\tau\,\overline{\mathsf{quote3E}}.\,P_{B2}(x,y) +$$
$$\tau.\,P_{abort}(x,y)\big)$$

$$P_{abort}(x,y) \triangleq \mathsf{do}_x^\tau\,\overline{\mathsf{abort}}\,\mid\,\mathsf{do}_y^\tau\,\overline{\mathsf{buyB}}\,\mid\,\mathsf{do}_y^\tau\,\overline{\mathsf{quit}}$$

$$P_{B2}(x,y) \triangleq \mathsf{do}_x\,\mathsf{pay3E}.\,P_{B3}(x,y) + \mathsf{do}_x\,\mathsf{quit}.\,\mathsf{do}_y^\tau\,\overline{\mathsf{quit}} + \tau.\,P_{abort2}(x,y)$$

$$P_{abort2}(x,y) \triangleq (\mathsf{do}_x\,\mathsf{pay3E}.\,\mathsf{do}_x^\tau\,\overline{\mathsf{refund}} + \mathsf{do}_x\,\mathsf{quit})\,\mid\,\mathsf{do}_y^\tau\,\overline{\mathsf{quit}}$$

$$P_{B3}(x,y) \triangleq \mathsf{do}_y^\tau\,\overline{\mathsf{pay2E}}.\,P_{B4}(x,y) + \tau.\,P_{abort3}(x,y)$$

$$P_{abort3}(x,y) \triangleq \mathsf{do}_x^\tau\,\overline{\mathsf{refund}}\,\mid\,\mathsf{do}_y^\tau\,\overline{\mathsf{quit}}$$

$$P_{B4}(x,y) \triangleq \mathsf{do}_y\,\mathsf{shipB}.\,\mathsf{do}_x^\tau\,\overline{\mathsf{shipB}} + \tau.\,P_{abort4}(x,y)$$

$$P_{abort4}(x,y) \triangleq \mathsf{do}_x^\tau\,\overline{\mathsf{refund}}\,\mid\,\mathsf{do}_y\,\mathsf{shipB}$$

4.2   Solo-Honesty

The notion of honesty studied so far requires that, in all contexts, whenever A has some obligations, *the system* must be able to evolve to a state in which A exposes some do (the *ready-do*) to fulfil her obligations. In other words, A is allowed to interact with the context, from which she can receive some help.

A natural variant of honesty would require A to be able to fulfil her obligations without any help from the context. To define this (intuitively stricter) variant of honesty, we modify the definition of *weak ready-do* to forbid the rest of the system to move. The actions reachable in such way are then named *solo weak ready-do*, and form a smaller set than the previous notion. The definitions of *solo-ready* and *solo-honest* consequently follow — *mutatis mutandis*.

Definition 12 (Solo weak ready-do). $S \Downarrow_u^{\mathrm{A}\text{-solo}}$ *is the sets of actions:*

$$S \Downarrow_u^{\mathrm{A}\text{-solo}} = \Big\{\alpha \mid \exists S'.\, S \xrightarrow{(\mathrm{A}:\,\neq\mathsf{do}_u)}{}^* S' \text{ and } \alpha \in S' \downarrow_u^{\mathrm{A}}\Big\}$$

where $S \xrightarrow{(\mathrm{A}:\,\neq\mathsf{do}_u)} S'$ *iff* $\exists \pi.\ S \xrightarrow{\{\mathrm{A}\}:\,\pi} S' \wedge (\forall \alpha.\ \pi \neq \mathsf{do}_u\,\alpha)$.

Definition 13 (Solo readiness). $\mathrm{Rdy}_s^{\mathrm{A}\text{-solo}}$ *is the set of systems S such that:*

$$O_s^{\mathrm{A}}(S) = \emptyset \ \vee\ O_s^{\mathrm{A}}(S) \cap \Lambda^\tau \cap S \Downarrow_s^{\mathrm{A}\text{-solo}} \neq \emptyset \ \vee\ \emptyset \neq (O_s^{\mathrm{A}}(S) \cap \Lambda^{\mathsf{a}}) \subseteq S \Downarrow_s^{\mathrm{A}\text{-solo}}$$

We say that A *is solo-ready in S iff* $\forall S', \boldsymbol{u}, s.\, S \equiv (\boldsymbol{u})S'$ *implies* $S' \in \mathrm{Rdy}_s^{\mathrm{A}\text{-solo}}$.

Definition 14 (Solo honesty). *We say that P is* solo-honest *in S iff*

$$\forall A : \big(S \text{ is A-free} \wedge A[P] \mid S \to^* S'\big) \implies A \text{ is solo-ready in } S'$$

We now relate solo honesty with the notion of honesty in Definition 11. As expected, when considering a fixed context S, solo honesty implies honesty, and is in general a stricter notion. However, being honest in *all* contexts is equivalent to being solo-honest in *all* contexts, as established by the following theorem.

Theorem 1. *For all processes P and systems S:*

1. *if P is solo-honest in S, then P is honest in S;*
2. *the converse of item 1 does not hold, in general;*
3. *P is solo-honest iff P is honest.*

Proof. Item 1 follows from definition of solo-readiness and $S \Downarrow_s^{\text{A-solo}} \subseteq S \Downarrow_s^{\text{A}}$.

For item 2, let:

$$P = A[(x,y) \, \texttt{tell} \, \{\downarrow_x \bar{a}\}. \, \texttt{tell} \, \{\downarrow_y \bar{b}\}. \, \texttt{do}_x \, \bar{a}. \, \texttt{do}_y \, \bar{b}]$$
$$S = B[(z) \, \texttt{tell} \, \{\downarrow_z a\}. \, \texttt{do}_z \, a] \mid C[(w) \, \texttt{tell} \, \{\downarrow_w b\}. \, \texttt{do}_w \, b]$$

We have that P is honest in S, but not solo-honest in S. Indeed, after both contracts of A get stipulated, A needs to perform $\bar{b}$ in session y, but she can only do that if B cooperates, allowing A to first perform $\bar{a}$ in session x.

For item 3, the "only if" direction immediately follows from item 1. For the "if" direction, assume by contradiction that P is honest but not solo-honest, i.e.:

$$A[P] \mid S \to^* (\boldsymbol{v}) \, (A[P'] \mid S')$$

where $A[P']$ has some obligations to perform for which she can not reach any related *ready do* on her own, but needs to interact with the context S' to do that. In such case, it is possible to craft another A-free initial system S'', which behaves exactly as S in the computation shown above, yet stops interacting at the end of such computation. Basically, given the computation above, we can construct S'' as the parallel composition of agents of the form $B[(\boldsymbol{x})\pi_1. \dots .\pi_n]$. Each prefix π_i performs a $\texttt{tell}$ or a $\texttt{do}$ in the same order as in the computation above. This makes it possible to obtain an analogous computation

$$A[P] \mid S'' \to^* (\boldsymbol{v}) \, (A[P'] \mid S''')$$

where S''' does no longer interact with A. However, since A is honest, she must be able to fulfil her obligations with the help of her context in $A[P'] \mid S'''$. Since the context does not cooperate, she must actually be able to do that with solo transitions — contradiction. $\qquad\square$

4.3   Weak Honesty

The honesty property requires a process to be ready even in those (dishonest) contexts where the other participants avoid to do the required actions. A weaker variant of honesty may require a process P to behave correctly provided that also the others behave correctly, i.e. that P is ready in *honest contexts*, only.

Definition 15. (Weak honesty). *Given a set of contracts $\mathbb{C}$, we define the set of weakly honest processes as:*

$$\mathcal{W}_{\mathbb{C}} = \{P \in \mathcal{P}_{\mathbb{U}} \mid P \text{ is honest in } \mathcal{H}_{\mathbb{C}}\}$$

Example 7. The process P_5 from Example 5 is *not* weakly honest. Let, e.g.:

$$Q_5 = (w)\,(\texttt{tell}\,\{\downarrow_w \overline{\mathsf{b}}\}.\,\texttt{do}_w\,\overline{\mathsf{b}})$$

which is clearly honest. However, by reducing $\mathsf{A}[P_5] \mid \mathsf{C}[Q_5]$ we reach the state:

$$S = (s,x)\,\big(\mathsf{A}[\texttt{do}_x\,\mathsf{a}.\,\texttt{do}_s\,\mathsf{b}] \mid \mathsf{C}[\texttt{do}_s\,\overline{\mathsf{b}}] \mid s[\mathsf{A} : \mathsf{b} \,\|\, \mathsf{C} : \overline{\mathsf{b}}]\,\big)$$

where A is not ready. The problem here is that there is no guarantee that the contract on x is always stipulated. We can fix this by making A advertise both contracts atomically. This is done as follows:

$$P_5' = (x,y)\,\texttt{tell}\,\{\downarrow_x \mathsf{a},\,\downarrow_y \mathsf{b}\}.\,\texttt{do}_x\,\mathsf{a}.\,\texttt{do}_y\,\mathsf{b}$$

The process P_5' is weakly honest, but it is *not* honest: in fact, in a context where the other participant in session x does not fire $\overline{\mathsf{a}}$, A is not ready at y.   □

The following theorem states that the set of weakly honest processes is larger (for certain classes of contracts, *strictly*) than the set of honest ones.

Theorem 2. *For all $\mathbb{C}$, $\mathcal{H}_{\mathbb{C}} \subseteq \mathcal{W}_{\mathbb{C}}$. Furthermore, $\mathcal{H}_{\mathrm{ST}} \neq \mathcal{W}_{\mathrm{ST}}$.*

Proof. The inclusion follows from Definition 15; the inequality from the process P_5' in Example 7, which belongs to $\mathcal{W}_{\mathrm{ST}}$ but not to $\mathcal{H}_{\mathrm{ST}}$.   □

The definition of $\mathcal{H}_{\mathbb{C}}$ requires honesty in *all* contexts, i.e. in all systems composed of processes in $\mathcal{P}_{\mathbb{C}}$. Instead, $\mathcal{W}_{\mathbb{C}}$ requires honesty in all $\mathcal{H}_{\mathbb{C}}$ contexts. This step can be iterated further: what if we require honesty in all $\mathcal{W}_{\mathbb{C}}$ contexts? As we establish below, we get back to $\mathcal{H}_{\mathbb{C}}$.

Theorem 3. *For all $\mathbb{C}$: $\mathcal{H}_{\mathbb{C}} = \{P \mid P \text{ is honest in } \mathcal{W}_{\mathbb{C}}\}$.*

Proof (Sketch). The $\subseteq$ inclusion trivially holds. For the $\supseteq$ inclusion, it is possible to craft a context of weakly honest processes which open sessions with P, possibly interact with P in such sessions for a while, and then stop to perform any action. This can be achieved as follows:

$$\mathsf{B}[(x,y,z)\,\texttt{tell}\,\{\downarrow_z c\}.\,\texttt{tell}\,\{\downarrow_x \mathsf{a},\,\downarrow_y \mathsf{b}\}.\,\texttt{do}_x\,\mathsf{a}\,.\,\texttt{do}_y\,\mathsf{b}.\,Q] \mid$$
$$\mathsf{C}[(v,w)\,\texttt{tell}\,\{\downarrow_v \overline{\mathsf{a}},\,\downarrow_w \overline{\mathsf{b}}\}.\,\texttt{do}_w\,\overline{\mathsf{b}}.\,\texttt{do}_v\,\overline{\mathsf{a}}]$$

where c is a contract compliant with some of the contracts P advertises, and Q is a honest implementation of c. Note that B above can also start two sessions with contracts $\{\downarrow_x \mathsf{a}, \downarrow_y \mathsf{b}\}$ with C, which however will deadlock because B and C perform the actions in a different order. This will cause Q to never be reached. Yet, both B and C are weakly honest: each of them would work fine in a honest context, since no deadlock would be possible there. The context above can also be adapted to postpone the deadlock so to effectively stop in the middle of executing Q, i.e. in the middle of session z. Because P must be honest in this weakly honest context, P must, at any time, be able to perform its obligations without relying on the context. Hence, $P \in \mathcal{H}_{\mathbb{C}}$. $\qquad\square$

4.4 Some Properties

The function $\lambda X. \mathcal{H}_X$ is anti-monotonic, as formalised by the following theorem (which follows directly from Definition 11).

Theorem 4. *If* $\mathbb{C} \subseteq \mathbb{D}$, *then* $\mathcal{H}_{\mathbb{C}} \supseteq \mathcal{H}_{\mathbb{D}}$.

The following theorem states a peculiar property of processes which use session types as contracts. If some of such processes is honest in all contexts where contracts are session types, then it is honest in *all* possible contexts.

Theorem 5. $\mathcal{P}_{\mathrm{ST}} \cap \mathcal{H}_{\mathrm{ST}} = \mathcal{P}_{\mathrm{ST}} \cap \mathcal{H}_{\mathrm{U}}$.

Proof. The inclusion $\supseteq$ follows by Theorem 4. For the inclusion $\subseteq$, assume by contradiction that $P \in \mathcal{H}_{\mathrm{ST}} \setminus \mathcal{H}_{\mathrm{U}}$, i.e. P is honest in $\mathcal{P}_{\mathrm{ST}}$, but *not* honest in $\mathcal{P}_{\mathrm{U}}$. Then, there exists some S made of agents with processes in $\mathcal{P}_{\mathrm{U}}$ such that:

$$\mathsf{A}[P] \mid S \rightarrow^* (\boldsymbol{v}) \, (\mathsf{A}[P'] \mid S' \mid s[\mathsf{A} : c \parallel \mathsf{B} : d]) \qquad (1)$$

where $\mathsf{A}[P']$ has some obligations at s, such that either:

1. c is an internal choice, and no internal transition of A is included in the weak ready-do set of A at s, or
2. c is an external (or committed) choice, and the weak ready-do set does not include all the labels enabled by $\mathsf{A} : c \parallel \mathsf{B} : d$.

We can craft an A-free system S'' (with processes in $\mathcal{P}_{\mathrm{ST}}$) which interacts with A as S in (1), after which it does nothing (except possibly firing $\mathsf{do}_s \tau$). We can construct S'' as the parallel composition of agents of the form $\mathsf{B}[(\boldsymbol{x})\pi_1 \ldots . \pi_n]$. Each prefix π_i performs a $\mathtt{tell}$ or a $\mathtt{do}$ in the same order as in (1), after removing from it the steps not involving A: e.g., a $\mathtt{tell}$ of a contract which is not stipulated with A is omitted. Instead, a $\mathtt{tell}$ of a contract $d_i \notin \mathrm{ST}$ which will be fused with some c_i of A is replaced by $\mathtt{tell}\,\overline{c_i}$, where $\overline{c_i}$ is the *syntactic dual* of c_i (which always exists and belongs to ST). We then obtain a computation:

$$\mathsf{A}[P] \mid S'' \rightarrow^* (\boldsymbol{v}) \, (\mathsf{A}[P'] \mid S''' \mid s[\mathsf{A} : c \parallel \mathsf{B} : \overline{c}])$$

where S''' does no longer interact with A, except possibly firing $\mathsf{do}_s \tau$, if enabled. In the resulting system, A is *not* ready: therefore, P is not honest in S'. $\qquad\square$

The following theorem establishes a crucial property of honest processes, i.e. that deadlock-freedom at the level of contracts is preserved when passing to the level of (honest) processes. This means that all open sessions can be carried forward until their successful termination.

Theorem 6 (Deadlock freedom). *Let S be a system of honest agents. If $S \rightarrow^* (\boldsymbol{u}) (S' \mid s[\gamma])$ with $O^A(\gamma) \neq \emptyset$, then there exist S'', A, and $\alpha \in O^A(\gamma)$ such that $S' \mid s[\gamma] \rightarrow^* S'' \xrightarrow{\{A\} \cup A \,:\, do_s \alpha}$.*

Proof. Assume first that $O^A(\gamma)$ only contains synchronisation actions, and let:

$$\gamma \xrightarrow{\{A,B\}:a} \qquad\qquad S = A[P] \mid B[Q] \mid \cdots \qquad\qquad S_0 = S' \mid s[\gamma]$$

with P and Q honest by hypothesis. By item 3 of Theorem 1, P and Q are also solo-honest. By Definition 7 it must be $a \in O_s^A(S_0)$ and $\bar{a} \in O_s^B(S_0)$, and so by Definition 14 it must be $a \in S_0 \Downarrow_s^{A\text{-solo}}$ and $\bar{a} \in S_0 \Downarrow_s^{B\text{-solo}}$. Since P is solo-honest, by Definition 13 we have that $\exists S_0' . S_0 \xrightarrow{(A\,:\,\neq do_s)}^* S_0'$ and $a \in S_0' \downarrow_s^A$. Since B has taken no transitions in this computation, and the contract configuration at s is still γ, it must be $\bar{a} \in O_s^B(S_0')$, and $\bar{a} \in S_0' \Downarrow_s^{B\text{-solo}}$. Since Q is solo-honest, by Definition 13 we have that $\exists S'' . S_0' \xrightarrow{(B\,:\,\neq do_s)}^* S''$ and $\bar{a} \in S'' \downarrow_s^B$. Since A has taken no transitions in this computation, and the contract configuration at s is still γ, at this point we have $a \in S'' \downarrow_s^A$ and $\bar{a} \in S'' \downarrow_s^B$. Then, by rule [DoCom], we obtain the thesis $S_0 = S' \mid s[\gamma] \rightarrow^* S'' \xrightarrow{\{A,B\}\,:\,do_s \alpha}$. The case where $O^A(\gamma)$ may contain internal actions is similar. □

Example 8. Note that Theorem 6 would not hold if we required weak honesty instead of honesty. For instance, consider the process P_5' in Example 7, and let:

$$Q_5' = (x,y) \, \texttt{tell} \, \{\downarrow_x \bar{a}, \downarrow_y \bar{b}\} . \, do_y \, \bar{b} . \, do_x \, \bar{a}$$

Both P_5' and Q_5' are weakly honest, but their composition $A[P_5'] \mid B[Q_5']$ gets stuck on the first do, since neither $do_x \, a$ nor $do_y \, \bar{b}$ can be fired. □

5   Decidability Results

In this section we prove that both honesty and weak honesty are undecidable.

5.1   Honesty Is Undecidable

The following theorem states that honesty is undecidable, when using contracts which are at least as expressive as session types. To prove it, we show that the complement problem, i.e. deciding if a participant is *dishonest*, is not recursive.

Theorem 7. $\mathcal{H}_{\mathbb{C}}$ *is not recursive if* $\mathbb{C} \supseteq ST$.

Proof. We reduce the halting problem on Turing machines to the problem of checking *dis*honesty of $P_0 \in \mathcal{P}_{\mathbb{C}}$. This immediately gives the thesis. Given an arbitrary Turing machine M, we represent its configurations as finite sequences $(\lambda_0, \star) (\lambda_1, \star) \cdots (\lambda_n, q) \cdots (\lambda_k, \star)$, where:

1. λ_i represents the symbol written at the i-th cell of the tape,
2. $\star$ is not a state of M (just used to represent the absence of the head);
3. the single occurrence of the pair (λ_n, q) denotes that the head of M is over the n-th cell, and M is in state q,
4. the tape implicitly contains "blank" symbols at cells after position k,
5. λ_i and q range over finite sets.

Without loss of generality, assume that M halts only when its head is over λ_0 and M is in the halting state q_{stop}.

We now devise an effective procedure to construct a process P_0 which is dishonest if and only if M halts on the empty tape. This P_0 has the form:

$$(x) \; \texttt{tell} \; \{\downarrow_x c\}. \; \texttt{do}_x \; \tau_{\bar{a}}. \; \texttt{do}_x \; \bar{a}. \; P \tag{2}$$

where $c = \texttt{rec} \; X.\bar{a}.X$, and P will be defined below. Intuitively, P_0 will interact with the context in order to simulate M; concretely, this will require P_0 to create new sessions. Note that some contexts may hinder P_0 in this simulation, e.g. by not advertising contracts or by refusing to interact properly in these sessions. Roughly, we will have that:

- in all contexts, P_0 will behave honestly in all sessions, except possibly in x;
- if the context does not cooperate, then P_0 will stop simulating M, but will still behave honestly in all sessions (including x);
- if the context cooperates, then P_0 will simulate M while being honest; only when M halts, P_0 will become dishonest, by stopping to do the required actions in session x.

The above intuition suffices for our purposes. Formally, we guarantee that:

1. if M does *not* halt, then P_0 is honest in *all* contexts (and therefore honest);
2. if M halts, then P_0 is *not* honest in *at least one* (cooperating) context (and therefore dishonest).

We represent each cell of the tape as a contract $d_{\lambda,\rho}$ in which λ is a symbol of the alphabet of M, and ρ is either a state of M or $\star$. More precisely, we specify $d_{\lambda,\rho}$ by mutual recursion as:

$$d_{\lambda,\rho} = \overline{\texttt{read}_{\lambda,\rho}}.d_{\lambda,\rho} \oplus \bigoplus_{\lambda'} \overline{\texttt{write}_{\lambda'}}.d_{\lambda',\rho} \oplus \bigoplus_{\rho'} \overline{\texttt{write}_{\rho'}}.d_{\lambda,\rho'}$$

where $\overline{\texttt{read}_{\lambda,\rho}}, \overline{\texttt{write}_{\lambda}}, \overline{\texttt{write}_{\rho}}$ are output actions. Note in passing that mutual recursion can be reduced to single recursion via the *rec* construct (up to some unfolding, as by Bekić's Theorem): therefore, $d_{\lambda,\rho} \in \text{ST}$.

We now sketch the construction of process P in (2). Intuitively, P uses the above contracts in separate sessions (one for each tape cell), and it evolves into processes of the form:

$$\text{Begin}(s_0, s_1) \mid \text{X}(s_0, s_1, s_2) \mid \text{X}(s_1, s_2, s_3) \mid \cdots \mid \text{End}(s_{n-1}, s_n)$$

where $s_0, \ldots, s_n$ are distinct session names, and the contract of P at session s_i is d_{λ_i, ρ_i}. The intuition underlying processes Begin, X, and End is the following:

- a process $\text{X}(\_, s_i, \_)$ is responsible for handling the i-th cell. It starts by reading the cell, which is obtained by performing:

$$\sum\nolimits_{\lambda, \rho} \text{do}_{s_i}\, \tau_{\text{read}_{\lambda, \rho}} \cdot \text{do}_{s_i}\, \overline{\text{read}_{\lambda, \rho}} \cdot \text{Handle}_{\lambda, \rho}$$

Note that only one branch of the above summation is enabled, i.e. the one carrying the same λ, ρ as in the contract at session s_i. We now have the following two cases:

  • if the head of M is *not* on the i-th cell (i.e., $\rho = \star$), we have that $\text{Handle}_{\lambda, \rho}$ recursively calls X. This makes the process repeatedly act on s_i, so making P behave honestly at that session.
  • if the head is on the i-th cell, $\text{Handle}_{\lambda, \rho}$ updates the cell according to the transition rules of M, and then it moves the head as needed. Assume that q' is the new state of M, λ' is the symbol written at the i-th cell, and that $j \in \{i - 1, i + 1\}$ is the new head position. In the process, the cell update is obtained by performing $\overline{\text{write}_{\lambda'}}$ in s_i, and the head update is obtained by performing $\overline{\text{write}_\star}$ in s_i and $\overline{\text{write}_{q'}}$ in s_j.

- the process $\text{Begin}(s_0, s_1)$ handles the leftmost cell of the tape. Intuitively, it behaves as $\text{X}(\_, s_0, s_1)$, but it also keeps on performing $\text{do}_x\, \tau_{\overline{a}}$ and $\text{do}_x\, \overline{a}$. In this way, $\text{Begin}(s_0, s_1)$ respects the contract c in (2). When $\text{Begin}(s_0, s_1)$ reads from s_0 that $\rho = q_{\text{stop}}$, it stops performing the required actions at session x. This happens when M halts (which, by the assumptions above, can only happen when the head of M is on the leftmost cell). In this way, P_0 behaves dishonestly at session x.

- the process $\text{End}(s_{n-1}, s_n)$ handles the rightmost cell of the tape. Intuitively, it behaves as $\text{X}(s_{n-1}, s_n, \_)$, but it also waits to read $\rho \neq \star$, meaning that the head has reached the (rightmost) n-th cell. When this happens, the process $\text{End}(s_{n-1}, s_n)$ creates a new session s_{n+1}, by advertising a contract $d_{\#, \star}$, where $\#$ is the blank tape symbol. Until the new session s_{n+1} is established, it keeps on acting on s_n, in order to behave honestly on that session. Once s_{n+1} is established, it spawns a new process $\text{X}(s_{n-1}, s_n, s_{n+1})$, and then recurse as $\text{End}(s_n, s_{n+1})$.

A crucial property is that it is possible to craft the above processes so that in no circumstances (including hostile contexts) they make P_0 dishonest at s_i. For example, $\text{X}(\_, s_i, \_)$ is built so that it never stops performing reads at s_i. This property is achieved by encoding each potentially blocking operation $\text{do}_{s_k}\, \alpha$. P' as $Q = \text{do}_{s_k}\, \alpha \cdot P' + \sum_{\lambda, \rho} \text{do}_{s_i}\, \text{read}_{\lambda, \rho} \cdot Q$. Indeed, in this way, reads on s_i are continuously ready, preserving honesty. A similar technique is used to handle those τ_α which need to be performed without blocking the other activities.

To conclude, given a Turing Machine M we have constructed a process P_0 such that (i) if M does not halt, then P_0 is honest, while (ii) if M halts, then P_0 is not honest in some (cooperating) context. Note that a context which cooperates with P_0 always exists: since all the advertised contracts are session types, a context can simply advertise the duals of all the contracts possibly advertised by A (a finite number), and then (recursively) perform all the promised actions. □

5.2 Decidability of Honesty in Fragments of CO_2

While honesty of general CO_2 processes is undecidable, we can recover decidability in fragments of CO_2. In particular, by using the model-checking technique of [7], we can verify the honesty of processes which are essentially finite state, i.e. they have no delimitation/parallel under process definitions. This technique uses an abstract semantics of CO_2 which preserves the transitions of an agent $A[P]$, while abstracting from the context wherein $A[P]$ is run. This is established by the following theorem.

Theorem 8. $P \in \mathcal{H}_\mathbb{C}$ *is decidable if (i) P has no delimitation/parallel under process definitions, and (ii) $\mathbb{C} \subseteq \mathbb{U}_{fin}$.*

Proof (Sketch). Building upon this abstract semantics of [7], we obtain an abstract notion of honesty which simulates the moves of unknown contexts, and it is sound and complete w.r.t. honesty. (i.e., P is abstractly honest iff it is honest, see [7] for further details). Since the abstract semantics is finite-state whenever P is such, then we can decide honesty of P by model-checking its state space under the abstract semantics. □

5.3 Dishonesty Is Recursively Enumerable

We show in Theorem 9 that dishonesty is recursively enumerable, under certain assumptions on the set of contracts. Together with Theorem 7, it follows that honesty is neither recursive nor recursively enumerable.

Theorem 9. $\overline{\mathcal{H}_\mathbb{C}}$ *is recursively enumerable if (i) for all $c \in \mathbb{C}$, $\{\alpha \mid c \xrightarrow{\alpha}\}$ is a finite set, and it is computable from c, and (ii) $\mathbb{C} \subseteq \mathbb{U}_{fin}$.*

Proof. We prove that "$A[P]$ dishonest" is a r.e. property. By item 3 of Theorem 1, it suffices to prove that "$A[P]$ solo-dishonest" is a r.e. property. By Definition 14, $A[P]$ is *not* solo-honest iff there exists some A-free context S such that A is not solo-honest in $A[P] \,|\, S$. This holds when A is not solo-ready in some residual of $A[P] \,|\, S$, i.e. when the following conditions hold for some $S, S', s, \boldsymbol{u}$: (1) S is A-free; (2) $A[P] \,|\, S \rightarrow^* (\boldsymbol{u})\, S'$; (3) $S' \notin \mathrm{Rdy}_s^{\text{A-solo}}$.

Recall that $p(x, y)$ r.e. implies that $q(y) = \exists x.p(x, y)$ is r.e., provided that x ranges over an effectively enumerable set (e.g., systems S, or sessions s). Thus, to prove the above existentially-quantified property r.e. it suffices to prove that

(1), (2), (3) are r.e.. Property 1 is trivially recursive. Property 2 is r.e. since one can enumerate all the possible finite traces. Property 3 is shown below to be recursive, by reducing the problem to a submarking reachability problem in Petri Nets, which is decidable [17]. We recall the definition of $S' \in \mathrm{Rdy}_s^{\text{A-solo}}$:

$$O_s^A(S') = \emptyset \ \vee \ O_s^A(S') \cap \Lambda^\tau \cap S' \Downarrow_s^{\text{A-solo}} \neq \emptyset \ \vee \ \emptyset \neq (O_s^A(S') \cap \Lambda^a) \subseteq S' \Downarrow_s^{\text{A-solo}}$$

To prove the above property recursive, we start by noting that, by hypothesis, $O_s^A(S')$ is a finite set, and it can be effectively enumerated from A, s, S'. We shall shortly prove that $\alpha \in S' \Downarrow_s^{\text{A-solo}}$ is a recursive property. Exploiting this, the above formula can be simply decided by enumerating all the elements of $O_s^A(S')$, and testing whether they belong to $S' \Downarrow_s^{\text{A-solo}}$.

We now show how to decide $\alpha \in S' \Downarrow_s^{\text{A-solo}}$. This is a reachability problem in CO_2, once restricted to solo transitions. This restriction allows us to neglect all the other participants but A in S'. Further, in the solo computations of S', A can open only as much fresh sessions as the number of latent contracts already in S', which is trivial to compute given S'. More in general, starting from S', A can only interact with a bounded number of sessions: those already open, and those which will be created later.

We now focus on the process P in $S' = (\boldsymbol{u})(A[P] \mid \cdots)$. W.l.o.g., we can assume P is a (delimited) parallel composition of $X_i(\boldsymbol{u})$, where each X_i is defined as $\sum_j \pi_j . P_j$, where (again) P_j is a delimited parallel composition of $X_i(\boldsymbol{u})$. Note that we only need a finite number of such X_i. Further, in the computations of S', the process of A can only be a parallel composition of (copies of) $X_i(\boldsymbol{u})$, where the components of $\boldsymbol{u}$ range over the finitely many session names discussed earlier, and (delimited) variables. Since only a finite number of variables can actually be instantiated with a session name, we focus on these and neglect the others in a non-deterministic way (roughly, we can follow the technique used in [5] to non-deterministically choose which variables to neglect).

Overall, the process of A is a multiset of finitely many copies of $X_i(\boldsymbol{u})$: hence, it can be represented by a Petri Net whose places correspond to each $X_i(\boldsymbol{u})$, and tokens account for their multiplicity. Further, when considering solo computations, the context of $A[P]$ in S' is finite-state: it has finitely many sessions, each of with finitely many states, by hypothesis. Hence, the whole system can be represented by a Petri Net, whose transitions simulate the CO_2 semantics.

Concluding, to decide $\alpha \in S' \Downarrow_s^{\text{A-solo}}$ it suffices to build the above Petri Net, and check whether a marking is reachable with at least one token in at least one of the places corresponding to $X_i(\ldots) = \mathrm{do}_s \, \alpha . P' + Q$. This is a submarking reachability problem, which is decidable [17]. □

5.4   Weak Honesty Is Undecidable

Theorem 10. $\mathcal{W}_{\mathbb{C}}$ *is not recursive if* $\mathbb{C} \supseteq ST$.

Proof. Easy adaptation of the proof of Theorem 7. Indeed, the process P_0 defined in that proof is honest when the Turing Machine does not halt (hence it is also weakly honest by Theorem 2), and it is dishonest when it halts. The dishonesty is caused by P_0 stopping to interact in session x, which instead requires infinitely many actions to be performed. Even in honest contexts, P_0 would still violate its contract, hence it is not weakly honest. $\qquad\square$

6   Related Work and Conclusions

We have presented a theory of honesty in session-based systems. This theory builds upon two basic notions, i.e. the classes $\mathcal{H}$ (Definition 11) and $\mathcal{W}$ (Definition 15) which represent two extremes in a hypothetical taxonomy of "good service behaviour". At the first extreme, there is the class $\mathcal{H}$ of honest processes, which always manage to respect their contracts, in any possible context. Systems of honest agents guarantee some nice properties, e.g. deadlock-freedom (Theorem 6). However, this comes at a cost, as honest processes must either realize their contracts by operating independently on the respective sessions, or by exploiting "escape options" in contracts to overcome the dependence from the context. At the other extreme, we have a larger class $\mathcal{W}$ of *weakly* honest processes, which make stronger assumptions about the context, but they do not enjoy deadlock-freedom, e.g. a system of weakly honest agents might get stuck.

Our investigation about honesty started in [10], where we first formalised this property, but in a less general setting than the one used in this paper. In particular, the contracts used in [10] are prefix-guarded τ-less CCS terms [13], provided with a semantics which forces the participants at the endpoints of a session to interact in turns. This is needed because the notion of honesty introduced in [10] is based on *culpability*: roughly, a participant is culpable in γ whenever she has enabled actions there. To be honest, one must be able to exculpate himself in each reachable state. The turn-based semantics of τ-less CCS contracts ensures that at each execution step only one participant is culpable, and that one can exculpate himself by doing the required actions. The turn-based semantics of contracts has a consequence on the process level: actions must be performed *asynchronously*. This means that a participant can fire $\mathsf{do}_s\,\alpha$ whenever α is enabled by the contract configuration at s. However, the requirement of having turn-based semantics of contracts has a downside: since many semantics of session types and other formalisms for contracts are synchronous, one has to establish the equivalence between the synchronous and the turn-based semantics. We did this in [7] for untimed session types, and in [2] for timed session types. The version of CO_2 defined in this paper overcomes these issues, by allowing for synchronous actions in contracts and in processes. This extension of CO_2 also makes it possible to use arbitrary LTSs as contracts. The other extension of CO_2 we have introduced in this paper is to allow processes to atomically advertise a set of contracts, so to have a session established only when *all* of them are matched with a compliant one. This enlarges the class of honest processes, making the calculus more expressive (see e.g. process $P_5{}'$ in Example 7).

The undecidability result presented in this paper (Theorem 7) subsumes the one in [10], where honesty was proved undecidable for processes using τ-less CCS contracts. The new result is more general, because it applies to any instance of CO_2 with a contract model as least as expressive as session types.

Safe computable approximations of honesty (with session types as contracts) were proposed in [7,8], either in the form of type systems or model checking algorithms. Since the new version of CO_2 can deal with a more general model of contracts, it would be interesting to investigate computable approximation of honesty in this extended setting. We believe that most of the techniques introduced in [7] can be reused to this purpose: indeed, their correctness only relies on the fact that contracts admit a transition relation which abstracts from the context while preserving the concrete executions (as in Theorem 4.5 in [7]).

In the top-down approach to design a distributed application, one specifies its overall communication behaviour through a *choreography*, which validates some global properties of the application (e.g. safety, deadlock-freedom, *etc.*). To ensure that the application enjoys such properties, all the components forming the application have to be verified; this can be done e.g. by projecting the choreography to end-point views, against which these components are verified [21,26]. This approach assumes that designers control the whole application, e.g., they develop all the needed components. However, in many real-world scenarios several components are developed independently, without knowing at design time which other components they will be integrated with. In these scenarios, the compositional verification pursued by the top-down approach is not immediately applicable, because the choreography is usually unknown, and even if it were known, only a subset of the needed components is available for verification. The ideas pursued in this paper depart from the top-down approach, because designers can advertise contracts to discover the needed components (and so ours can be considered a *bottom-up* approach). Coherently, the main property we are interested in is *honesty*, which is a property of components, and not of global applications. Some works mixing top-down and bottom-up composition have been proposed [6,15,23,25] in the past few years.

The problem of ensuring safe interactions in session-based systems has been addressed to a wide extent in the literature [20–22]. In many of these approaches, deadlock-freedom in the presence of interleaved sessions is not directly implied by typeability. For instance, the two (dishonest) processes P_5' and Q_5' in Examples 7 and 8. Would typically be well-typed. However, the composition $A[P_5'] \,|\, B[Q_5']$ reaches a deadlock after fusing the sessions: in fact, A remains waiting on x (while not being ready at y), and B remains waiting on y (while not being ready at x). Multiple interleaved sessions has been tackled e.g. in [11,12,14,16]. To guarantee deadlock freedom, these approaches usually require that all the interactions on a session must end before another session can be used. For instance, the system $A[P_5'] \,|\, B[Q_5']$ would *not* be typeable in [12], coherently with the fact that it is not deadlock-free. The resulting notions seem however quite different from honesty, because we do not necessarily classify as dishonest processes with interleaved sessions. For instance, the process:

$$(x, y) \, \texttt{tell} \, \{\downarrow_x \, \texttt{a}\}. \, \texttt{tell} \, \{\downarrow_y \, \overline{\texttt{b}}\}. \, \left(\texttt{do}_x \, \texttt{a}. \, \texttt{do}_y \, \overline{\texttt{b}} + \texttt{do}_y \, \overline{\texttt{b}}. \, \texttt{do}_x \, \texttt{a} \right)$$

would not be typeable according to [12], but it is honest in our theory.

Acknowledgments. This work has been partially supported by Aut. Reg. of Sardinia grants L.R.7/2007 CRP-17285 (TRICS) and P.I.A. 2010 ("Social Glue"), by MIUR PRIN 2010-11 project "Security Horizons", and by EU COST Action IC1201 "Behavioural Types for Reliable Large-Scale Software Systems" (BETTY).

References

1. Barbanera, F., de'Liguoro, U.: Two notions of sub-behaviour for session-based client/server systems. In: Proceedings of the PPDP, pp. 155–164 (2010)
2. Bartoletti, M., Cimoli, T., Murgia, M., Podda, A.S., Pompianu, L.: Compliance and subtyping in timed session types. In: Graf, S., Viswanathan, M. (eds.) FORTE 2015. LNCS, vol. 9039, pp. 161–177. Springer, Switzerland (2015)
3. Bartoletti, M., Cimoli, T., Murgia, M., Podda, A.S., Pompianu, L.: A contract-oriented middleware. In: Braga, C., Ölveczky, P.C. (eds.) FACS 2015. LNCS, vol. 9539, pp. 86–104. Springer, Heidelberg (2016). http://co2.unica.it
4. Bartoletti, M., Cimoli, T., Zunino, R.: Compliance in behavioural contracts: a brief survey. In: Bodei, C., et al. (eds.) Programming Languages with Applications to Biology and Security. LNCS, vol. 9465, pp. 103–121. Springer, Switzerland (2015). http://tcs.unica.it/software/co2-maude/co2-verifiable-abstractions.pdf
5. Bartoletti, M., Degano, P., Ferrari, G.L., Zunino, R.: Model checking usage policies. Math. Struct. Comput. Sci. **25**(3), 710–763 (2015)
6. Bartoletti, M., Lange, J., Scalas, A., Zunino, R.: Choreographies in the wild. Sci. Comput. Program. **109**(1), 36–60 (2015)
7. Bartoletti, M., Murgia, M., Scalas, A., Zunino, R.: Modelling and verifying contract-oriented systems in maude. In: Escobar, S. (ed.) WRLA 2014. LNCS, vol. 8663, pp. 130–146. Springer, Heidelberg (2014)
8. Bartoletti, M., Scalas, A., Tuosto, E., Zunino, R.: Honesty by typing. In: Beyer, D., Boreale, M. (eds.) FMOODS/FORTE 2013. LNCS, vol. 7892, pp. 305–320. Springer, Heidelberg (2013)
9. Bartoletti, M., Scalas, A., Zunino, R.: A semantic deconstruction of session types. In: Baldan, P., Gorla, D. (eds.) CONCUR 2014. LNCS, vol. 8704, pp. 402–418. Springer, Heidelberg (2014)
10. Bartoletti, M., Tuosto, E., Zunino, R.: On the realizability of contracts in dishonest systems. In: Sirjani, M. (ed.) COORDINATION 2012. LNCS, vol. 7274, pp. 245–260. Springer, Heidelberg (2012)
11. Bettini, L., Coppo, M., D'Antoni, L., De Luca, M., Dezani-Ciancaglini, M., Yoshida, N.: Global progress in dynamically interleaved multiparty sessions. In: van Breugel, F., Chechik, M. (eds.) CONCUR 2008. LNCS, vol. 5201, pp. 418–433. Springer, Heidelberg (2008)
12. Castagna, G., Dezani-Ciancaglini, M., Giachino, E., Padovani, L.: Foundations of session types. In: Proceedings of the PPDP (2009)
13. Castagna, G., Gesbert, N., Padovani, L.: A theory of contracts for web services. ACM TOPLAS **31**(5), 19:1–19:61 (2009)
14. Coppo, M., Dezani-Ciancaglini, M., Padovani, L., Yoshida, N.: Inference of global progress properties for dynamically interleaved multiparty sessions. In: De Nicola, R., Julien, C. (eds.) COORDINATION 2013. LNCS, vol. 7890, pp. 45–59. Springer, Heidelberg (2013)
15. Deniélou, P.-M., Yoshida, N.: Multiparty compatibility in communicating automata: characterisation and synthesis of global session types. In: Fre, S., et al. (eds.) ICALP 2013, Part II. LNCS, vol. 7966, pp. 174–186. Springer, Heidelberg (2013)

16. Dezani-Ciancaglini, M., de'Liguoro, U., Yoshida, N.: On progress for structured communications. In: Barthe, G., Fournet, C. (eds.) TGC 2007. LNCS, vol. 4912, pp. 257–275. Springer, Heidelberg (2008)
17. Esparza, J.: On the decidability of model checking for several μ-calculi and petri nets. In: Tison, S. (ed.) CAAP 1994. LNCS, vol. 787, pp. 115–129. Springer, Heidelberg (1994)
18. Georgakopoulos, D., Papazoglou, M.P.: Service-Oriented Computing. MIT Press, Cambridge, Massachusetts (2008)
19. Honda, K.: Types for dyadic interaction. In: Best, E. (ed.) CONCUR 1993. LNCS, vol. 715, pp. 509–523. Springer, Heidelberg (1993)
20. Honda, K., Vasconcelos, V.T., Kubo, M.: Language primitives and type disciplines for structured communication-based programming. In: Hankin, C. (ed.) ESOP 1998. LNCS, vol. 1381, pp. 122–138. Springer, Heidelberg (1998)
21. Honda, K., Yoshida, N., Carbone, M.: Multiparty asynchronous session types. In: Proceedings of the POPL, pp. 273–284 (2008)
22. Kobayashi, N.: A new type system for deadlock-free processes. In: Baier, C., Hermanns, H. (eds.) CONCUR 2006. LNCS, vol. 4137, pp. 233–247. Springer, Heidelberg (2006)
23. Lange, J., Tuosto, E.: Synthesising choreographies from local session types. In: Koutny, M., Ulidowski, I. (eds.) CONCUR 2012. LNCS, vol. 7454, pp. 225–239. Springer, Heidelberg (2012)
24. Milner, R.: Communication and Concurrency. Prentice-Hall Inc., Upper Saddle River (1989)
25. Montesi, F., Yoshida, N.: Compositional choreographies. In: D'Argenio, P.R., Melgratti, H. (eds.) CONCUR 2013. LNCS, vol. 8052, pp. 425–439. Springer, Heidelberg (2013)
26. van der Aalst, W.M.P., Lohmann, N., Massuthe, P., Stahl, C., Wolf, K.: Multiparty contracts: agreeing and implementing interorganizational processes. Comput. J. **53**(1), 90–106 (2010)

Author Index

Printed in the United States
By Bookmasters